# THE POLITICS OF ENVY

## Books by Doug Bandow

*U.S. Aid to the Developing World:*
*A Free Market Agenda* (editor, 1985)

*Unquestioned Allegiance* (1986)

*Protecting the Environment:*
*A Free Market Strategy* (editor, 1986)

*Beyond Good Intentions:*
*A Biblical View of Politics* (1988)

*Human Resources and*
*Defense Manpower* (1989)

*The Politics of Plunder:*
*Misgovernment in Washington* (1990)

*The U.S. South Korean Alliance:*
*Time for a Change* (co-editor, 1992)

*Perpetuating Poverty: The World Bank,*
*the IMF, and the Developing World*
(co-editor, 1994)

# THE POLITICS OF ENVY

## Statism as Theology

**Doug Bandow**

Transaction Publishers
New Brunswick (U.S.A.) and London (U.K.)

Library of Congress Catalog Number: 94-5551
ISBN: 1-56000-171-2 (cloth)
Printed in the United States of America

Library of Congress Cataloging-in-Publication Data
Bandow, Doug.
    The politics of envy  :  statism as theology  /  Doug Bandow.
        p.  cm.
    ISBN 1-56000-171-2  :  $34.95
    1. Government spending policy—United States.   2. Trade regulation—
United States.   3. United States—Politics and government.   4. Libertarianism—United States.   5. Political ethics—United States.   6. Christianity and
politics—United States.   I. Title.
HJ7537.B27   1994
382'.3'0973—dc20                                                              94-5551
                                                                                       CIP

For David and Deborah Wical, who will have to live in the world that we are making today.

# Contents

## VI. The Regulatory State

## VII. Redistribution without End

# Foreword

In an odd way, though we live in a secular age, the United States is a remarkably religious nation. Our god is not the God of traditional faiths, however. It is the modern state. As the subtitle of Doug Bandow's fascinating study suggests, our society's faith in the state has become a kind of theology, an organized system of social and cultural governance built around a godhead.

The scope of the statist theology is nearly without limit. Are there problems in families' and communities' internal lives? We then expect the state to take their place. We invest the state with the authority to properly manage our economies, organize our public lives, define our private morality, educate our children, tell us what we should eat and drink, and inform businesses how to conduct their affairs.

This theology of statism has grown to crowd out our belief in an immutable moral sense, which Hilaire Belloc rightly tells us is a mark of the Servile State. Whereas we once saw the state as necessarily limited in its proper interests and practical efficacy, we now willingly embrace the new religion of the state. In doing so we have lost faith in the idea of liberty as the organizing principle of public life and virtue as the goal of our private lives.

We should not be surprised that this theology of statism is so pervasive. People are naturally religious. Something tugs at the human soul to worship magnificence. Even in the most primitive people, there is an urge to glorify someone or something outside the self. The proper end to these longings is God, but without real faith, we find substitute gods. And so it is that Americans find themselves a society religiously devoted to the products of the political process. We imbue managers with tasks we could never imagine ourselves accomplishing in our private or community lives.

At one time in our history we were a fiercely independent people. The Americans Toqueville wrote about were devoted to the Christian God and to the concept of freedom. Solutions to social problems were dealt with on a local basis. Individuals, families, churches, and organic communities were independent of the national government. The federal purse was not theirs to draw from, and citizenship did not require paying heavy taxes.

We have come to accept levels of tyranny today that would have seemed unthinkable even a few generations ago. In 1913, for example, an amendment was proposed in Congress that would have capped federal income tax at 1 percent of income on high earners. It was rejected because many members of Congress felt it would encourage government to immediately increase the tax to that very level, creating a political and moral hazard.

Now the government at all levels extracts nearly $2 trillion a year from the public and over 40 percent of the national income. We rarely think about what could have been produced had it been left in the hands that had labored to earn it. How much more would the private sector have produced? How much more would have been given to charity?

This new religion did not come to us in the modern equivalent of the Great Awakening. It came slowly and subtly, but nonetheless deliberately. To tell the story we could return to Nixon's wage and price controls, Johnson's Great Society, Roosevelt's New Deal, or Wilson's Progressivism. In retrospect all these seminal periods seem to form a pattern. We thought we were doing good. But, as G.K. Chesterton wrote, "in some ways the modern world is far too good. It is full of wild and wasted virtues." We intended well, but we were pushing ourselves further into the mire of statism, giving up our individual and social autonomy for promises of virtue that were never fulfilled.

Slowly, a peculiar American version of Fabian socialism began to be accepted at all levels of our society. Every agency expected a larger budget, more power, and more employees next year than this. We began to exchange liberty for higher taxes and ever intrusive regulations and mandates, all of which diminished our freedom and changed the focus of faith from God to a new godhead centered in institutions of coercion and compulsion.

The process continues today. When an epidemic of poverty afflicted our nation, we looked to government to come up with a solution. What we got for this "solution" was another epidemic, one of out-of-wedlock births. History would have been different if we had had faith in our communities to encourage productivity and chastity. Rather, we started to believe that the state could solve all social, spiritual, medical, and economic ills, and paid little attention to the costs of the elusive "security" it promised.

As a Christian libertarian, Doug Bandow puts forth the idea that statism is a grave threat to both traditional religion and human liberty. He encourages Christians and libertarians to find common cause in the goal of staying the false god, and returning our society to one in which both virtue and freedom flourish.

Mr. Bandow carries many topics under the theme of statism, including a dangerous and radical environmentalism, a reckless foreign interventionism, an intrusive regulatory apparatus, and an unproductive income redistribution. Among his most provocative topics is the new prohibitionism. Even as public and private morality decay, each legislative session spawns new laws for us to obey.

As government bureaucrats oversee invasions of private property and individual consciences, people are increasingly being suspected for their thoughts and not their actions. New sins are created by government bureaucrats to replace the old sins of the Judeo-Christian tradition. The ministers of our modern religion condemn not fornication, but "unprotected sex." They banish smokers from the public square the way adulterers were once treated.

Similarly, in today's drug war we see an age-old tendency among government officials to ban harmful substances. Our nation should know better. Not so long ago, the country experienced a moral decline as dry laws were erected under Prohibition. In the desire to ban public choices, no one can doubt the good intentions of these who thought demon rum was bad for society. But by making alcohol illegal, government glamorized the illegal liquor trade and made the bootleggers rich. Today's drug dealers are the glitterati of our ghettoes, and they have the Drug Enforcement Agency to thank in part for their elevated status.

Such are the results of centralized and statist strategy to deal with what are essentially community problems. Mr. Bandow's opposition to the drug war, argued on both Christian and libertarian grounds, calls to mind a great figure from the 1920s and 1930s, Father James Gillis, a member of my own religious community, the Congregation of Saint Paul (the Paulist Fathers). As the editor of the monthly *The Catholic World,* Father Gillis undertook a fierce campaign against liquor. Yet his sense of moral outrage at alcohol abuse never clouded his reason.

Father Gillis saw government action as a threat to the reforms he was undertaking. "It is my own conviction," he wrote, that the prohibition was the greatest blow ever given to the temperance movement. Before prohibition, the people at large were becoming more and more sober. Total abstinence had become the practice, not of a few, but of millions.... Under the Volstead Law, drinking became a popular sport. The passage of the law was a psychological blunder, and a moral calamity.

For the most part, as Mr. Bandow makes so clear, our public policy failures are not due to a lack of good intentions. Consider the welfare state. It was built in an attempt to help the poor, but ended up punishing productive work, creating a bloated and impersonal bureaucracy, and drafting the poor into a dependent relationship with the state. Far from relieving poverty, welfare has merely entrenched a whole segment of society in it.

Welfare affects the character of all of us, not just the recipients. When welfare bureaucracies take over caring for the poor, what becomes of the personal virtues of love and compassion? Charity is supposed to represent obedience to the dictates of conscience; its character changes when it disintegrates into simple obedience to government agencies. It is no longer an act of free will.

What we need in this battle against moral decline and state dependency is not ideology, but ancient wisdom and contemporary facts. To this end, Mr. Bandow is a national treasure. From some books of political economy, you get ideological bombast. But this work offers relentless logic, hard facts, and the reasoning of an informed conscience. The cumulative effect is to give his readers a renewed understanding of how the expansion of government authority threatens both liberty and personal virtue.

One of the impediments to reform toward market-oriented societies in the ex-communist countries of Eastern Europe and the former Soviet Union has been the loss of the independence of spirit. Subjects invariably become used to the state providing for them. Life was gray under the communists, but for the most part people could depend on a government job and a government check. We are not immune from such social temptations. There is, after all, a modicum of security in slavery.

Yet we must ask ourselves—and Mr. Bandow encourages us to do so—do we value freedom from responsibility more than freedom itself? If we decide that we do not, then we must revive our own, uniquely American enterprising spirit and bring it to those who have been persuaded and pressured to abandon the ideal of the American dream. Only by rekindling a love of liberty, which is in itself a virtue, will we struggle free from the theology of statism, and strengthen ourselves and our weakened republic.

ROBERT SIRICO

# Acknowledgments

Putting together this collection was a labor of love, and not terribly hard—for me, at least. Others performed more of the work, most obviously the staff, headed by Irving Louis Horowitz, of Transaction, which also published my earlier book, *The Politics of Plunder: Misgovernment in Washington*. I owe a hearty thanks to Robert Sirico and the Acton Institute for backing this project; the Institute engages in a range of vitally important activities of which this publication is but a very small part. Andrea Rich of Laissez-Faire Books, too, was generous with encouragement and assistance in bringing *The Politics of Envy: Statism as Theology* to pass.

Also critical for my success has been the support of the Cato Institute, particularly its president, Edward H. Crane, and a bevy of interns who over the years helped satisfy my insatiable demand for articles, books, reports, and studies. Others at Cato, including David Boaz, Diana Brady, Ted Galen Carpenter, Linda Clark, Matt Johnson, Greg Taylor, and Ian Vasquez have assisted me in a variety of ways; nor should Jerry Taylor's contribution as a chess partner go unmentioned.

The John Locke Foundation, headed by Marc Rotterman, has generously backed my work on health care. Copley News Service carries my weekly syndicated column; numerous magazines and newspapers have run my work. Some editors have been particularly encouraging—Barbara Phillips at *The Wall Street Journal*, Mary Lou Forbes at *The Washington Times*, Jeff Zack at *Business and Society Review*, Mickey Maudlin at *Christianity Today*, and Sid Hurlburt at *USA Today*, among others. Thanks also to the following organizations and publications for permission to reprint the following: Citizens for a Sound Economy: "Tax Fairness, Clinton-Style"; Competitive Enterprise Institute: "The Ecopagan Temptation: Faith in Place of Fact"; Copley News Service: articles 5–7, 20–22, 26–27; *Foreign Policy:* "The Pitfalls of Collective Security"; *Freeman:* A

Coast-to-Coast Federal Dole," "Environmentalism: The Triumph of Politics," "The Pharmaceutical Industry: Problems or Solutions?"; John Locke Foundation: "Whither Health Care in the Age of Clinton?"; *Liberty:* "Libertarians and Christians in a Hostile World"; *Tabletalk:* "Should Christians Be Statists?"

Finally, I owe much to the members of my church, Christian Assembly, and the many friends and family members who've helped sustain me in my quixotic quest to save the world. Perhaps the most important lesson that I've learned from them is to be more realistic about my goals— while still doing my best to make things a bit better for my niece and nephew, and everyone else who will inherit an increasingly polarized and politicized planet. Special thanks go to my parents, Don and Donna Bandow, for their love, friendship, and spiritual support.

# Introduction: The Age of Politics, Continued

Ours is a secular age. But faith has not disappeared. Rather, the gods have changed. Today the reigning theology is statism: government has become god, charged with the people's salvation.

Not that this religious experiment has worked very well. What historian Paul Johnson calls "the age of politics" has unleashed untold death and destruction while solving few of mankind's most vexing problems, such as poverty. To the contrary, all too often it is government policy, usually inadvertently, but sometimes intentionally, that has created and/ or exacerbated social problems. Yet politicians of all ideological stripes refuse to accept that their time is drawing to a bloody, calamitous close, and therefore continue to fight to preserve their positions. The worst do it by inflaming ancient ethnic passions and demonizing traditional scapegoats—immigrants and Jews, for instance. The more subtle seek support by endorsing "change," proposing to "reinvent" their institutions, and pledging to offer "meaning" to people's lives.

It is difficult to predict whether these strategems will succeed. In the short term they have worked for men as different as Slobodan Milosevic and Bill Clinton, but the positions of these officials, and of the raft of thugs and mediocrities who run the vast majority of governments around the globe, are hardly secure. In the long term most of these people will be consigned to the ash-heap of history. The only question is whether they will be alive to see their memories execrated and their monuments desecrated.

But, as Lord Keynes said, in the long run we are all dead. Today we have to contend with an age of politics that has not yet fully wound down. And that politics, in the United States, at least, has increasingly been based on envy, the desire not to produce more for oneself, but to take as much as possible from others. Of course, all of the proponents of the politics of envy proclaim themselves animated by public-spiritedness: who in Washington would admit that the higher taxes he advocates will be used to pay off the interest group of the day, whether farmer, corporation, or union? Who would suggest that he has anything but good will toward those who he is intent on mulcting?

Indeed, the problem of envy has always been much more serious than that of greed. Those who are greedy may ruin their own lives, but those who are envious contaminate the larger community by letting their covetousness interfere with their relations with others. Moreover, one can satisfy greed in innocuous, even positive ways—by being brighter, working harder, seeing new opportunities, and meeting the demands of others, for instance. In contrast, envy today is rarely satisfied without use of the state. True, some people pull a gun and heist the nearest person's wallet or purse. But for the otherwise law-abiding, the only way to take what is someone else's is to enlist one or more public officials to seize land, impose taxes, regulate activities, conscript labor, and so on. Statism, then, is integral to the politics of envy. Statism has become the basic theology for those committed to using government to coercively create their preferred version of the virtuous society.

The impact of what might at first glance appear to be esoteric philosophizing has been dramatic. Between 1950 and 1990 those supposed evidences of greed, corporate profits, and personal incomes, rose 757 percent and 1870 percent respectively. However, government spending, one of the best measures of envy, grew 3163 percent. Virtually no human activity today is outside the jurisdiction of politics. What you ingest, where you work, how much you earn, from whom you receive medical care, how you have sex, what people in other lands do—all of these and more are now matters of grave concern to government at one and often several levels.

It is this continuing expansion of the state even as the luster of the age of politics fades at which *The Politics of Envy: Statism as Theology* is directed. Section I questions the moral basis of statism: put bluntly, virtue is hindered rather than advanced by government coercion. Section II focuses on one of the great moral challenges of our time—abortion. Section III takes up an issue, the environment, that has been increasingly distorted by the moral and quasi-theological arguments put forth by devotees of politics. Section IV considers the direction of American foreign policy in the aftermath of the end of the Cold War. Section V contests the conventional wisdom that foreign aid "aids" anyone other than corrupt elites in recipient nations. Section VI considers perhaps the most pernicious manifestation of state power today, regulation—of doctors, pharmaceutical manufacturers, students, the poor, drug users, and most everyone else. Finally, Section VII covers the classic weapon of the envious: redistribution through tax-and-spend policies, a weapon wielded by Democrat—new as well as old—and Republican alike.

There are, I believe, more important things in life than politics. That is not a widely held view in Washington and the capitals of most other nations, however; American opinion leaders spent months in 1993 debating "the politics of meaning," a philosophy, held by some people of enormous influence, that government can fill people's every need, spiritual as well as material. This epitomizes the theology of statism and is almost certainly both idolatrous and pernicious, aiding and abetting the expansion of the state into precisely the areas of people's lives through which they should find meaning. No one book, let alone this one, is likely to bring the age of politics to a close. But my hope is that *The Politics of Envy: Statism as Theology* will help generate some serious debate over fundamental issues, such as the moral basis, or lack thereof, for what amounts to legislated theft. And if the book contributes in even a small way to making a society that is both freer and more virtuous, then I will be well satisfied.

# I

# The Transcendent Questions

# 1

# Virtue versus Freedom?
# Allies or Antagonists?

Both freedom and virtue are under assault today. The attack on economic and political freedom is obvious enough. Government takes and spends roughly half of the nation's income. Regulation further extends the power of the state in virtually every area—how one can use one's property, what occupation one can enter, who one can hire, what terms one can offer to prospective employees, with which countries one can trade. Increasing numbers of important, personal decisions are ultimately up to some functionary some where, rather than the average citizen.

The problem only got worse during the 1980s, despite the election of avowedly conservative presidents. Spending and regulation rose particularly dramatically during the Bush administration. Alas, government is likely to expand even more quickly during the next four years.

Virtue, too, seems to be losing ground daily. Evidence of moral decline was evident enough in the 1992 presidential election. Bill Clinton's widely reported promiscuous adultery made a mockery of his church attendance; his evasions and lies regarding his draft avoidance suggested that his commitment to the truth was weak at best. George Bush, while apparently leading a more exemplary personal life, thought nothing of making a promise on taxes that he never intended to keep and appeared to have dissembled badly regarding his knowledge of the Iran-Contra affair. The shamelessness and viciousness of his attacks on his opponent on the campaign were also not the stuff of which virtue is made.

Things are scarcely better elsewhere in society. Promiscuity is not just a twentysomething phenomenon; even many preteens are sexually active. Illegitimacy rates continue to rise not only in the inner-city but also in middle-class America. Dishonesty and theft are the rage: the en-

3

tire political system is geared to faciliate special interest looting of the taxpayers. Employees as well as customers shop-lift—everywhere. A university band recently distinguished itself by stealing more than $30,000 worth of merchandise while visiting Japan. Business, too, suffers from a corrupt core, demonstrated by Ivan Boesky and his ilk.

## Freedom and Virtue under Attack

Some elements of our society have attacked both freedom and virtue. Much of the left, for instance, believes in "choice" if it means moral relativism and escape from responsibility, but abhores "choice" if it means private individuals making informed decisions about their children, kids' educations, jobs, and other aspects of their lives.

Alas, some advocates of liberty and virtue have compounded the problem by unnecessarily setting the two against each other. A number of members of the more "libertarian" right dismiss virtue as a matter of concern, while some more traditional conservatives want the state to circumscribe individual freedom to promote "morality." Both of these groups see freedom and virtue as frequent antagonists, if not permanent opponents. At the very least, they suggest, you cannot maximize both of them, but, instead, have to choose which to promote and which to restrict.

However, it is a mistake to assume that one must be sacrificed for the other. They are related, but are complementary. That is, liberty—the right to exercise choice, free from coercive state regulation—is a necessary precondition for virtue. And virtue is ultimately necessary for the survival of liberty.

Virtue cannot exist without freedom, without the right to make moral choices. By virtue I mean the dictionary definition: moral excellence, goodness, righteousness. Coerced acts of conformity with some moral norm, however good, do not represent virtue; rather, the compliance with that moral norm must be voluntary.

There are times, of course, when coercion is absolutely necessary— most importantly, to protect the rights of others by enforcing an *inter*-personal moral code governing the relations of one to another. The criminal law is an obvious example, as is the enforcement of contracts and property rights. But is coercion justified to promote virtue, that is, to impose a standard of *intra*-personal morality? At stake are some of the most controversial issues: drug use, pornography, homosexuality, and the like. All of these activities have some social impact and some people argue that it is precisely this impact that justifies state intervention. Usually more powerful, however, is the contrary case against intervention— that most of the ill consequences, such as drug-related crime, are primarily a product of legal prohibition rather than the activity itself. If, in fact, government regulation makes the social problems worse, then the only justification for intervention is to promote virtue.

## Nation's Moral Tone

Our nation's moral tone is not good; America does not seem to be a particularly virtuous place. And the moral environment seems to have gotten worse in recent days, though, of course, one should have no illusions that a perfect age ever existed. Still, if things have deteriorated, one has to ask: is that because we have become more free, and would becoming less free make America more virtuous? The answers to both questions, I think, are no.

The natural human condition, certainly in Christian theology, and in historical experience, too, is not one of virtue. "There is no one righteous, not even one," Paul wrote in his letter to the Roman church, citing the Psalms (Rom. 3:10). This explains the necessity of a transcendent plan of redemption.

But societies can be more or less virtuous. Did ours become less so *because* government no longer tried so hard to mold souls? Blaming moral shifts on legal changes mistakes correlation for causation. In fact, America's onetime cultural consensus eroded even during an era of strict laws against homosexuality, pornography, and even fornication. Only cracks in this consensus led to changes in the law. In short, as more people viewed sexual mores as a matter of taste rather than a question of right and wrong, the moral underpinnings of the laws collapsed, followed by the laws. Only a renewed moral consensus could allow the reestablishment of the laws.

But government is not a particularly good teacher of virtue. The state tends to be effective at simple, blunt tasks, like killing and jailing people. It has been far less successful at reshaping individual consciences. Even if one could pass the laws without changing American's current moral ethic, the result would not be a more virtuous nation. True, there might be fewer overt acts of immorality. But there would be no change in people's hearts: Forcibly preventing people from victimizing themselves does not automatically make them more virtuous, righteous, or good. As Christ instructed his listeners, "anyone who looks at a woman lustfully has already committed adultery with her in his heart" (Matthew 5: 28). A country full of people lusting in their hearts who don't consummate the lust out of fear of arrest is scarcely better than one full of people acting on their sinful whims. It is, in short, one thing to improve appearances, but quite another to improve society's moral core. And God, Jeremiah tells us, looks at the heart (Jer. 17: 10).

## Making Society Less Virtuous

Indeed, attempting to forcibly make people virtuous would make society itself less virtuous in three important ways. First, individuals would lose the opportunity to exercise virtue. They would not face the same set of temptations and be forced to choose between good and evil. This approach might thereby make their lives easier—it might also make them less vulnerable to a number of diseases. But they would not be more virtuous and society would suffer as a result. In this dilemma we see the paradox of Christianity: a God of love creates man and provides a means for his redemption, but allows him to choose to do evil. While true Christian liberty means freedom from sin, it seems to be tied to a more common form of freedom, the opportunity to choose whether to respond to God's grace.

Second, to vest government with primary responsibility for promoting virtue shortchanges other institutions, or "governments" in Puritan thought, like the family and church, sapping their vitality. Private social institutions find it easier to lean on the power of coercion than to lead by example, persuade, and solve problems. Moreover, the law is better at driving immorality underground than eliminating it. As a result, moral problems seem less acute and people may become less uncomfortable; private institutions may therefore be less likely to work as hard to promote virtue.

Third, making government a moral enforcer encourages abuse by majorities or influential minorities that gain power. If one thing is certain in life, it is that man is sinful. "There is no one righteous, not even one" states a biblical passage that bears repeating. The effect of sin is magnified by the possession and exercise of coercive power. Its possessors can, of course, do good, but history suggests that they are far more likely to do harm. Even in our democratic system majorities are as ready to enact their personal predilictions—okaying the use of such dangerous substances as alcohol and tobacco while outlawing marijuana— as uphold real morality.

And as America's traditional Judeo-Christian consensus crumbles we are more likely to see government promoting alternative moral views— teaching that gay unions are normal, and so on. This is possible only if government is given the authority to coercively mold souls in order to "promote virtue." Despite the best intentions of advocates of statecraft as soulcraft, government is more likely to end up enshrining immorality as morality. All told, an unfree society is not likely to be a virtuous one.

### First Do No Harm

The fact that government can do little to help does not mean that there is nothing it should do. We would all be better off if public officials adopted as their maxim "first, do no harm." Although the community-wide moral breakdown most evident in the inner-city has many causes, government policy has exacerbated the problem. Welfare, for instance, has made illegitimacy and family break-up financially feasible and often profitable. The ever-worsening drug war has robbed urban residents of hope and created well-funded criminal gangs that offer male role models and wealth to fatherless, ill-educated ghetto youth. Economic restrictions, such as the minimum wage and occupational licensing, have made it difficult for residents to find even ill-paid legal work. Monopoly government schools don't train inner-city residents for remunerative, satisfying employment even if it existed. Finally, housing regulations—rent control, zoning, and the like—have helped trap the poor in slums. The synergistic impact of all of these factors operating together has been devastating.

Governments also punish both marriage and thrift through their tax policies. The state has spent years attempting to expunge not only churches but also religious values from the public square; localities war against religion through everything from zoning restrictions to private school regulations. Indeed, government at all levels has proved itself to be the greatest of imperialists, constantly expanding—all the while displacing or regulating private activities.

Beyond doing no harm, public institutions can perform an educative role, but the moral discourse needs to be carried on at the broadest level of consensus possible. It is unreasonable, for instance, to expect a state government to launch a crusade against homosexuality, as Proposition 9, on the ballot in November 1992, would have directed the state of Oregon. Not only are gays taxpayers, but there seems little reason to single them out while ignoring adulterers and fornicators, for instance. The broader issue, with greater social consequences, is promiscuity. Similarly, there is general agreement from across the philosophical spectrum that teens should not be having children: therefore abstinence can be promoted in public schools for reasons other than adherence to traditional Jewish and Christian moral teachings.

However, advocates of virtue must be careful in using the state in even this modest fashion lest they abdicate their own essential roles in the educative process. Moreover, while the government may help buttress private instruction, it remains a very imperfect tool and subject to misuse by officials and influential special interest groups with their own, usually very political, agendas. Indeed, in the end, what goes around tends to come around again. Once advocates of virtue use the state to politicize the process, they lose their strongest argument, on principle, to prevent other forces from using government for immoral ends.

## Freedom Is Not Enough

Nevertheless, freedom is not enough. While liberty is the highest political goal, it is not life's highest objective. Morever, while a liberal, in the classical sense, economic and political system is the best one available, it will operate even better if nestled in a virtuous social environment.

For instance, a market system will function more effectively if people are honest and voluntarily fulfill their contracts. People who believe in working hard, exercising thrift, and observing temperance will be more productive. Economic life will function more smoothly if employers treat their workers fairly. Fewer social problems will emerge if families, churches, and communities organize to forestall them in the first place. Greater personal responsibility will reduce welfare expenditures and tort litigation. And so on. A lush lawn of a compassionate, cooperative, and virtuous society will make it harder for weeds of government encroachment to flourish.

Thus, advocates of a minimal state need to be concerned about both liberty and virtue. Freedom is important both as an end in itself and as a means of allowing people to exercise virtue. Virtue, too, is critically important in its own right. It also plays a critical role in undergirding a free society. How best can we promote them together? First, as noted earlier, government should do no harm. We need radical changes in policies that today restrict freedom and undermine morality. Second, private mediating institutions, particularly churches and community associations, need to retake their leading role in teaching virtue and meeting social problems. Third, people need to be more willing to tolerate the quirks and failings, even serious virtuous lapses, of their neighbors, so long as such actions have only limited effect on others. The punishment of most sins should be left to God.

Fourth, moral-minded citizens should turn to the state only as a last resort. The issue needs to be important enough to warrant government intervention; the activity involved also needs to have a significant impact on nonconsenting parties. And *private alternatives must be clearly inadequate*. For example, religious believers should lead their children in prayer at home rather than foisting that duty onto atheist teachers in the public schools. Opponents of pornography should organize boycotts before demanding the arrest of buyers and sellers. And, perhaps most importantly, vocal supporters of the importance of virtue need to exhibit morality in their own lives before suggesting that government send cops into other people's bedrooms.

Those of us who believe in both a free and virtuous society face serious challenges in the coming years. We need to respond by finding ways to strength both, not play them off against each other. In the end, neither is likely to survive without the other.

# 2

# God and the Economy: Is Capitalism Moral?

Collectivism is in retreat around the globe, but it retains some support in the American religious community. If recent events demonstrate that Marxism does not work in practice, many religious idealists still believe that capitalism is immoral in theory. And the criticism has long been ecumenical: Catholic liberation theologians dressed Marxist class analysis in religious clothing while left-wing evangelicals equated markets and materialism.

Some observers have seen virtually every human ill arising from capitalism, a system ultimately based on the simple principle of free exchange. For instance, Danny Collum, an editor of *Sojourners*, complained a decade ago that "the gross inequalities of wealth and poverty in the U.S. are the natural result of a social, political, and economic system that places the maximization of private profit above all other social goals. The human, social, cultural, and spiritual benefits that would result from a more just distribution of wealth and power will never show up on the all-important quarterly profit and loss statement." Britain's Andrew Kirk wouldn't even accept the claim that capitalism promotes liberty. A market economy, he wrote, "certainly increases the freedom of some, but always and inevitably at the expense of the freedom of others."

At heart, Christianity poses a radical challenge to the appropriateness of every human action and institution. "Do not love the world or anything in the world," wrote the Apostle John in his first epistle. "If anyone loves the world the love of the Father is not in him. For everything in the world—the cravings of sinful man, the lust of his eyes and the boasting of what he has and does—comes not from the Father but from the world. The world and its desires pass away, but the man who does the will of God lives forever." (I John 2: 15–17)

11

Capitalism is therefore not exempt from scrutiny. It is an imperfect institution, administered by sinful men, just like any other. But the harshest critics suggest that a market economy not just defective, but is fundamentally inconsistent with the Christian faith. For example, in the view of John Cort, author of *Christian Socialism*, "a Christian could, not to mention should, be a socialist." Further, he writes:

> The "spirit of Christian love" cannot be reduced to a political imperative, granted, but it most certainly has a political dimension. Feeding the hungry and clothing the naked are not precisely identical with a systematic redistribution of wealth, but in the present situation, of gross inequality, obscene wealth and wretched poverty, they most certainly cry to heaven for both systematic and unsystematic redistribution.

Is he right? Is capitalism fundamentally immoral?

Despite John Cort's emotional appeal to the "spirit of Christian love," the Bible does not specifically speak to the proper degree of government intervention in the economy. There is no explicit endorsement of any type of economic system, no equation of capitalism or socialism with the Kingdom of God. Old Testament Israel placed some restrictions on debts, interest, and property transfers but allowed relatively free economic exchange. The so-called Jubilee laws were tied to the Israelites' special status as God's people—secular America is therefore not a good analogue to religious Israel—and did not transfer property ownership from people to the state. The Gospels and epistles of the New Testament are remarkably free of any economic policy recommendations. Indeed, writes Paul Heyne, a professor at the University of Washington, "What we do find in the New Testament is an extraordinary disregard for almost everything in which economists are interested." In the absence of a holy ideology, one must answer a more subtle question: which system is more consistent with Biblical principles?

In discussing capitalism it is important to distinguish a competitive market economy from systems that merely involve some private property ownership. Kleptocracies and crony capitalist regimes exist around the globe; particularly obscene are many Latin American governments, where an elite has long used political power to exploit the rest of the population. Such systems are far closer to socialism than capitalism, however, since they involve pervasive government economic control.

Christ's message is clear: believers are not to place their faith in Mammon or any of the other idols of this world. But while the Bible is long on injunctions involving man's relationship to God and his neighbors, it says far less about the role of the state. The fact that people are not to trust in material goods does not mean that economic decision-making should be placed in the hands of a coercive institution such as government. The early Christians, at least in Jerusalem, shared their material goods with the needy in the community of faith. However, these voluntary followers of Christ never attempted to forcibly redistribute the assets of non-Christians or even fellow believers. Indeed, the Apostles consistently taught that giving was not mandatory as it was under the law of the old covenant. Peter stated that members of the Jerusalem church had no obligation to sell their property and turn over the proceeds; Paul refused to order the members of the Corinthian church to provide assistance for the believers in Jerusalem. Of course, both men expressed the hope that their readers would behave generously. Wrote Paul: "Each man should give what he has decided in his heart to give, not reluctantly or under compulsion, for God loves a cheerful giver." (II Cor. 9: 7)

A faith that refuses to order its adherents to give not surprisingly provides little support for using the state to make others give. And the commandment against theft should raise at least some questions as to when collective action exceeds Biblical authority. Moreover, there are other scriptural reasons to be more skeptical than supportive of proposals to concentrate economic power in the government's hands. Most importantly, the Christian faith recognizes that all human institutions are flawed, and that sinful men are likely to misuse their power. Consider the Apostle John's vision in Revelation of a hideous "Beast" state with expansive power, including over people's economic affairs (no one could buy or sell anything without the Beast's mark).

Less apocalyptic but nevertheless equally striking is the prophet Samuel's warning when the Israelites ask God for a king:

> He will take your sons and make them serve with his chariots and horses, and they will run in front of his chariots. Some he will assign to be commanders or thousands and commanders of fifties, and others to plow his ground and reap his harvest, and still others to make weapons of war and equipment for his chariots. He will take your daughters to be perfumers and cooks and bakers. He will take the best of your fields and vineyards and olive groves and give them to his attendants. He will take a tenth of your grain and of your vintage and give it to his officials and attendants. Your menservants and maidservants and the best of your cattle and donkeys he will take for his own use. He will take a tenth of your flocks, and you

yourselves will become his slaves. When that day comes, you will cry out for relief from the king you have chosen, and the Lord will not answer you in that day. (I Samuel 8: 11–18)

Most religious critics of capitalism respond that they opposed Stalinist communism and instead advocated some variant of democratic collectivism. But economic liberty is a prerequisite for other freedoms. Countries such as South Korea and Taiwan used market economies to prosper; demands for political reform then naturally grew. Capitalist reforms in China helped create a more prosperous population, which has grown increasingly restive under traditional communist political controls.

Economic freedom is important because it helps disperse power, allowing the development of private institutions—associations, corporations, think tanks, labor unions, and universities, for instance—that can counterbalance state power. Moreover, private property is necessary for the exercise of many political rights. If you can't buy a printing press or TV station, hire a hall, or sell newspapers, you have no press freedom. The Soviet Union's great conundrum in the early 1980s was the personal computer, necessary for economic progress but a potentially devastating weapon in the hands of dissidents.

Nevertheless, there is a spiritual sterility to market capitalism that bothers many religious people. While a number of former East Germans, for instance, deplore their old police state, they still dislike the gaudy, individualistic materialism of the West. Andrew Kirk contends that capitalism assumes "that the main purpose of man's life is the pursuit of happiness to be achieved by the constant expansion of goods and services" and that this is thereby "the basis of our daily political and economic life."

However, all men are fallen and sinful; greed and envy are common to man, not products of particular social systems. Capitalism allows those who have dedicated themselves to the pursuit of Mammon to live that way, but it also lets believers like Kirk decide to fulfill their lives differently. Kirk, for one, became affiliated with a religious institute, a choice he could not have made in the socialist East. Capitalist America has similarly proved receptive to communal religious sects like the Hutterites.

The hallmark of a relatively unregulated market economy is freedom of choice, and some people will undoubtedly use their liberty to go grievously wrong. But Marxism is profoundly materialistic, and political life in such societies revolves around gaining access to a relatively small pool of consumer goods—thus the avariciousness of the nomenklatura, the ruling elite, and the ubiquitous lines in the one-time communist world. The average citizen of a socialist state does not care any less about possessing shoes, washing machines, VCRs, and cars than an American; he is simply less able to satisfy his desires.

A related argument is that capitalism relies on destructive competition rather than constructive cooperation. Competition is obviously important to a market economy, but it has proved to be an extraordinarily valuable socially tool. Private monopolies usually break down quickly due to competition, unless they have government support. Competition drives down the price of consumer goods, enabling even people of even modest incomes to acquire clothing, food, and shelter. And competition has driven innovators to constantly seek to design better products for less.

Indeed, while competition is a hallmark of capitalism, so too is cooperation. For only by cooperating—with customers, suppliers, and workers—can a businessman succeed. In a system of state control firms can force their products on reluctant buyers, extract supplies from reluctant producers, and mandate work from reluctant employees. A private firm, however, can only succeed by inducing the cooperation of all of these parties. While money may seem a crass inducement, it is also effective; moreover, many firms, where people group together voluntarily, in contrast to collectivist systems, generate an esprit d'corps that reflects a variety of non-material values.

Perhaps the most fundamental criticism of capitalism is the prevalence of poverty amid plenty. The desperation of the inner-city was given added publicity after the 1992 riots in Los Angeles and some supporters of Cuba's Castro have responded to criticism of his repressive tactics by arguing that there are no homeless people in Havana. Indeed, Andrew Kirk wrote, before the collapse of the East in 1989, that "Marxism has exalted collective freedom—the freedom of everyone to enjoy a basically dignified life." Yet it is now painfully obvious that poverty was pervasive and income differentials were hideous in those nations. Acquisitive ruling elites may have cloaked their greed with humanitarian socialist rhetoric, but the reality of their systems was quite different.

Truly free market societies, in contrast to statist systems such as Brazil, have also performed well in enhancing the economic status of all their citizens. Taiwan, for instance, has enjoyed a dramatic increase in literacy, life expectancy, and equality of income distribution as it has expanded economically. Even in the U.S. those who are poor live far better than the bulk of the populations of many Third World states. In short, without production there is nothing to redistribute. Only in a capitalist economy may one meaningfully advocate extensive government transfer programs.

Yet today the state does far more to harm than help the poor. Indeed, much of the poverty in the U.S. is the result of government policy, often at the behest of powerful special interest groups. Labor unions back the minimum wage because it prices disadvantaged workers out of the marketplace. Occupational licensing makes it harder for poor people to enter a variety of trades, such as driving a cab. Trade barriers to protect selected industries push up the cost of clothing, food, shoes, and a host of other goods. Antiquated building codes that guarantee construction jobs increase housing costs. Expansive government transfer programs enrich influential voting blocs—farmers, retirees, and the like—at the expense of the poor and middle class. And so on.

In a true market economy, those with the least influence can still gain access to economic opportunity. The more expansive the government controls, the more likely are concentrated interest groups to twist policy to their own ends, to the detriment of the most disadvantaged in society. This does not mean that capitalism is enough for a just, and "Christian," society. Private mediating institutions, particularly associations, charities, and churches, play a critical role in helping those who, like the proverbial widows and orphans in the Old Testament, are unable to succeed in a market economy. Even public welfare programs are not per se inconsistent with a generally free society, though the current system is socially destructive, subsidizing illegitimacy and family break-up and discouraging work. And, in practice, it may be impossible to design a government program not to have such effects.

Respect for the virtues of capitalism is not limited to America's Religious Right. With the publication of the Papal encyclical, *Centesimus Annus*, or The Hundredth Year, in 1991, Catholic social teaching has explicitly recognized the benefits of a market system. The Pope's critique of Marxism is devastating: "The historical experience of socialist countries has sadly demonstrated that collectivism does not do away with alienation but rather increases it, adding to it a lack of basic necessities and economic inefficiency." In contrast, he praises capitalism, including its reliance of entrepreneurship and profits. "When a firm makes a profit," he wrote, "this means that productive factors have been properly employed and corresponding human needs have been duly satisfied." All told, he argues, "the free market is the most efficient instrument for utilizing resources and effectively responding to needs."

He remains vitally concerned about the poor, however, and believes that capitalism cannot be the sum of society. He criticizes "consumerism" and advocates government intervention to ensure that "fundamental human needs" are not left unsatisfied. Finally, he writes that individual freedom needs an "ethical and religious" core.

Is capitalism Christian? No. It neither advances existing human virtures nor corrects ingrained personal vices; it merely reflects them. But socialism is less consistent with several Biblical tenets for it exacerbates the worst of men's flaws. By divorcing effort from reward, stirring up covetousness and envy, and destroying the freedom that is a necessary precondition for virtue, it tears at the just social fabric that Christians should seek to establish. A Christian must still work hard to shed even a little of God's light in a capitalist society. But his task is likely to be much harder in a collectivist system.

August 1992

# 3

# Should Christians Be Statists?

One doesn't have to be a genius to realize that the nation's moral climate is not good. The majority of Americans may call themselves Christians, but a large share of them live by anything but Christian tenets.

Therefore, it probably isn't surprising that many Christians see political action, and an appeal to government, as a means to make things right. The religious left, carried away with the "social gospel," has long been a vigorous advocate of state redistributive activities. But on the right many evangelicals and fundamentalists, in particular, have resisted expansive state power. Except in the area of social policy.

While the new wave of evangelical activists has tended to back conservative Republican candidates who have articulated a political philosphy based on individual liberty, that commitment to freedom has not carried over to personal morals. Many of the strongest opponents of government economic intervention have pressed for anti-pornography prosecutions, tougher drug enforcement, prayer in public schools, and anti-sodomy laws. And they have done so without even recognizing the inherent contradiction between their positions.

The moral character of a society is important, so it is understandable that many Christians want the government to practice soulcraft as well as statecraft. Unfortunately, however, trusting the state to mold character misperceives the proper role of government. And, in practice, doing so entrusts to the state a responsibility that properly belongs with families, churches, and other community organizations.

## The Role of Government

The state has an ordained role, to "punish the wrongdoer," in Paul's words. This most obviously means to regulate conduct that violates the

19

proper standard of inter-personal morality—the use of force or fraud against another, for instance.

Quite different, however, is the question of intra-personal morality, the thoughts and actions of a person that directly affects only himself. In Old Testament Israel, of course, the state had a significant theological role that included overseeing this sort of personal behavior. But the geographic entity made up of God's chosen people is a far different creature than today's nation, where a majority of both the leadership and people are godless. There's nothing to indicate that God expects this state to execute his moral law, to ensure that we love him and our neighbors, that we place no other gods before him, that we do not covet, and so on. Indeed, the "enforcement function" that once ran to the country of Israel has since devolved on the church—meaning that the disciplinary reach is only to those who claim to be members of the body of faith. Consider when Paul wrote the Corinthian church in an effort to root out gross immorality. "I have written you in my letter not to associate with sexually immoral people—not at all meaning the people of this world who are immoral.... In that case you would have to leave this world.... What business is it of mine to judge those outside the church? Are you not to judge those inside? God will judge those outside" (I Cov. 5: 9–13).

Paul's indifference to the possibility of using the coercive power of government to promote his moral ends extended to the question of charitable giving. The religious left has tended to support expansive federal transfer programs, citing the Christians' duty to the poor. Yet Paul refused to even order the Corinthian believers to give to the Jerusalem church: "I am not commanding you" (II Cor. 8: 8). While such verses should not be used as proof-texts, they do indicate a dismissive attitude towards the potential of using state power to advance Christian morality.

And caution in asking government to lock up one's neighbor would seem to be a logical outgrowth of Christian love. Of course, tough love has a role, but envy and hatred more often animate those who would imprison others. Indeed, an equally persuasive reason to limit government's role in shaping morality is a recognition of the danger a powerful, fallen institution like the state can be in the hands of fallen individuals. God warned the Israelites through the prophet Samuel of the risks of getting a king; God's revelation to John painted a horrific picture of the Beast state. And the potential for abuse in resorting to the state is all too obvious when looking at the historical experience. Perhaps it is no surprise that one of Christ's parables very clearly warned believers not to try to judge their neighbors, pulling up the weeds along with the wheat; that process is to occur at the final judgment.

## The Practical Responsibilities of Government

Another problem of an interventionist state is that it tends not to do a good job. Governments are best at simple tasks, such as killing millions of people, and quite poor at the sort of subtle manipulation necessary to shape a host of personal moral characters as well as a national tone. Indeed, reviewing some of the issues where Christians want the government to intervene shows how difficult is the task they would give the state.

One of the most curious enthusiasms of some evangelicals is support for school prayer. Who, one wonders, is likely to do a better job of teaching children to pray: a believing parent offering up a heartfelt petition, or a nonbelieving teacher repeating a nondenominational bromide? Many Christians rightly feel that secularists have seized control of the public schools, but the answer is not to stage a counter-coup in an attempt to make the children of nonbelievers feel as uncomfortable as do believing kids today. Rather, religious activists should press most strongly to increase the choices available to parents—home-schooling and private schools, backed by tax credits and vouchers. Next, believers should ask not for special privileges but equal treatment in the public schools, an institution that has to serve Christian and non-Christian alike. Equal access for religious student organizations is clearly part of such treatment; organized prayer is not.

Anti-sodomy laws are another perennial favorite of the religious right, as well-known ministers met with (Republican) White House officials to denounce the "sodomites." (Rarely with the same vigor do these political clerics attack adulterers and fornicators, yet both are arguably more serious assaults on the family unit.) While restrictions on sexual conduct in public places, which cannot help escape the attention of the other people, are obviously appropriate, there is nothing particularly scriptural about arresting people for what they do privately in their homes. Even if the law could stamp out the act, and it has never been able to do so, it cannot eliminate the underlying sin of lust. Indeed, our experience here suggests that the law has done little to shape a public morality—

popular attitudes towards homosexuality changed before the law did. And in a pluralistic community made up of more unbelievers than believers, we are best off seeking common ground by empowering government to do what is most broadly considered to be legitimate, regulation of inter-personal conduct, rather than intra-personal morality.

Support for drug and obscenity laws shows a similar arrogance in trying to turn government into a coercive moral agent. Use of most drugs (arguably legal as well as illicit) and pornography may be sins, but that alone is no reason to make the acts criminal. Otherwise we would be arresting people who fail to act as godly stewards of their resources, love their neighbors, and honor their parents. Moreover, to demonstrate virtue requires the opportunity to sin. Someone who lusts for an obscene magazine but doesn't buy one merely because the government has suppressed it gains no points with God.

Nor is government intervention justified to save people from themselves. Drugs and pornography are probably best described as "self-victim" rather than "victimless" crimes, but they differ markedly from murder and rape because they chiefly harm voluntary participants rather than unwilling outsiders. If a desire to protect people against their will is sufficent reason for a government ban, then this would warrant prohibiting use of alcohol and tobacco (as was done earlier this century), as well as participation in any activity (skydiving, race-car driving) that a majority views as too dangerous. Yet does not this kind of draconian control over the lives of other human beings look more like the overweening state cited by Samuel and John (in Revelation) than an instrument of Christian love? In a pluralistic society where many people are wrong about many things, we will be best off limiting the government's power to enshrine any particular group's judgment into law.

The best argument for banning drugs and pornography is that they do affect other people. But, of course, so does most every activity that we engage in. The fact that I am a Christian may cause an activist atheist serious mental anquish. Unless we require that the harm be direct before the state can intervene, government will be controlling every action of every person. Yet the direct effects of drug use on other people are limited: Most of the worst effects of drugs come *from the attempt to ban them*—for instance, gang wars, which were frequent during Prohibition, arise from the fact that criminal organizations battle for control of an illicit market. As for obscenity, there is evidence that sex offenders like to view pornography, but not that viewing pornography turns them into sex offenders. Stronger evidence links depictions of violence to violence, but most porn is passive. In fact, if we are looking for one real cause of moral decay, it is probably the flood of soft porn on TV and in print that undermines traditional values but is beyond any effective regulation.

It is clear that Christians often are statists. But should they be? God calls us to be faithful, not to do anything possible, including jailing our neighbors to "win" by forcing Him down the throats of unbelievers. Ultimately, our freedom as believers will be more secure with a smaller rather than larger state, no matter how well motivated our proposals for intervention. And, equally important, while a freer society may be more untidy and, yes, obviously immoral, it will also yield greater opportunity for virtue to flourish. Christians need to be preachers rather than politicians.

September 1992

# 4

# Libertarians and Christians in a Hostile World

While there is nothing in principle to cause libertarianism, a political philosophy, and Christianity, a worldview regarding one's relation to God and one's neighbors, to conflict, in practice there has been substantial friction on both sides. Although libertarians and theologically conservative Christians have often found themselves on the same side of economic and fiscal issues, they have always been uneasy allies at best. Indeed, on social policy—abortion, drugs, pornography, "morals" legislation in general—their differences seem irreconcilable.

One reason for this lies in modern libertarianism's origins as a reaction against oppressive state structures that had been buttressed by organized religion. Another is that many seminal libertarian thinkers have not been Christians. Classical liberalism, for instance, grew out of the Enlightenment, and many of its adherents were deists or atheists. More recently, Ayn Rand and her Objectivist movement have promoted both limited government and atheism. In fact, Rand, who is still revered by many libertarians, considered religion to be wholly irrational.

Furthermore, libertarianism, unlike conservatism, has never emphasized traditional values. To the contrary, it has proved a refuge for those seeking to avoid persecution by the state, especially for "moral" offenses. Thus, libertarianism has attracted many gays and drug users—unrepentant sinners in the eyes of many Christians. Although libertarians have neither pushed legislation to prevent people from not associating with homosexuals nor endorsed drug use, their tolerance of open sin has rankled Christians who believe such actions conflict with God's transcendent moral law.

At the same time, many libertarians have been offended by the apparent readiness of many Christians to use the law to buttress faith when

25

people do not respond voluntarily. When preaching didn't stop gambling, churches supported a government ban. When homosexuality persisted despite America's formally Christian culture, believers wanted cops to arrest gays. In this way, many libertarians came to see Christians as enemies of freedom.

## Unlikely Allies

Yet the imagined battle between libertines and puritans reflects stereotypes on both sides. Although many libertarians do believe in "moral diversity," libertarianism is merely a political philosophy regarding the relationship of man and state, not man and God. Similarly, while many Christians believe the government should enforce God's moral law, there is nothing Biblical about using coercion to enforce the Ten Commandments and Christ's directives. The conflict between the two perspectives reflects not their fundamentals but their application.

Thus, some activists on both sides have come to recognize that their areas of agreement are greater than those of their disagreements. The result has been a growing dialogue between conservative Christians and secular libertarians. In fact, despite some misgivings, the Libertarian Party nominated former congressman Ron Paul, a pro-life Christian, for the presidency in 1988. We should hope that such efforts at a *rapprochement* will expand in the future. Surely the two sides can work together to build a freer *and* more virtuous society, one in which religious believers can promote their moral values and live their faiths unhindered by the state while tolerating sin amongst their neighbors, while libertarians, though not held by law to Biblical moral standards, can better understand and respect the convictions of Christians.

## Reasons for *Rapprochement*

Neither Christians nor libertarians have the luxury of treating potential allies as adversaries. The hold of Christianity on American culture is waning: although virtually everyone still proclaims a belief in God, most people's behavior reflects only limited adherence to the traditional Judeo-Christian moral code. And the state is increasingly antagonistic to Christian institutions and beliefs—requiring a Catholic university to fund gay groups, interfering with church discipline of errant members, barring the operation of Christian schools, funding sacrilegious art, and so on.

While libertarians with less traditional moral beliefs may feel somewhat more comfortable today, they, too, are losing the larger war. The government continues to expand; individual liberty continues to shrink. And state interference is actually increasing in some areas of moral regulation, such as drug use. Indeed, George Bush, a supposedly conservative Christian president, offended both libertarians and religious believers by supporting higher taxes, new spending programs, continued funding for the National Endowment for the Arts, and the drug war.

Since both groups seem to be losing what James Davison Hunter calls the "culture war"—a Christian, of course, does not believe that God will ultimately lose, but would still like to bring the world into closer conformity with godly standards—it is imperative that each search out new allies. Secular liberals, because they believe in neither transcendent moral law nor individual freedom, are unlikely to prove solid friends of Christians for libertarians. Their occasional support for one position or another will always give way to an agenda that is overwhelmingly statist and secular. Several different groups of Christians—particularly Protestant evangelicals and conservative Catholics—have frequently made common cause with conservatives, but that alliance has produced little fruit; the same is true of many alliances between mainstream conservatives and libertarians. Many conservative activists, despite their verbal support for both traditional values and individual liberty, are as secularized and authoritarian as their liberal counterparts. How else to explain the very small practical differences between Democrats and Republicans on domestic, international, and social issues?

Thus, Christians and libertarians need not only to talk to one another, but to work on together on issues of mutual interest. Their overall worldviews will remain sharply different, but they can coalesce when it comes to limiting state power.

All Christians and libertarians should agree on the need to protect religious liberty. Many Christians—at least those who consider themselves to be "conservative" today—and all libertarians can join to oppose expansion of governmental intervention in the economy. On foreign policy Christians are more fractured, with a more "liberal" minority closer to the libertarian position. The most serious differences, however, occur in questions of social policy.

If social policy becomes a debate over values, the gulf between conservative Christians and (secular) libertarians will be unbridgeable. The former believe that God has established timeless guidelines for personal behavior. Many of the latter believe morality to be a matter of personal choice, so long as it doesn't violate the rights of others.

However, there is room for cooperation if the issues are treated as questions of *policy,* that is, as the actions that should be taken by the various political institutions in response to social problems. One need not share the moral premise that homosexuality is right or wrong, for instance, to agree that cops should not be arresting people in their bedrooms for sexual activities.

Among the most important social issues in contemporary America are abortion, child care, drugs, education, pornography, sex, and welfare. In all of these areas there is room for greater understanding and cooperation among libertarians and Christians.

### Abortion

There is probably no more divisive issue today than abortion. Indeed, it is an issue that splits both Christians and libertarians. The majority of the more theologically conservative Christians, particularly evangelicals and Catholics, are "pro-life" (as am I, in the interest of full disclosure). In contrast, the majority of libertarians are "pro-choice," though there is an active Libertarians for Life organization headed by an atheist.

There is no one scripture that speaks to abortion; however, the Bible does make it clear that life is sacred, including the child resulting from conception, who is considered to be a gift from God (Genesis 4:1). As such, a compelling reason should be required to justify killing the unborn. In the view of some Christians and many libertarians, the liberty/privacy interest of the woman provides such a justification, leading to a legal, if not moral, right to abortion. Indeed, many of these abortions rights advocates would argue that abortion is morally wrong, but nevertheless should not be proscribed by the state. The pro-life counter is two-fold: first, that there is another life involved which, since it cannot assert its own right to life, must be protected by the state; second, that the parents, by voluntarily engaging in the act that leads to pregnancy, do not have a right to terminate the life. (Such consent is obviously lacking in the case of rape.)

While the conservative Christian and majority libertarian positions obviously cannot be harmonized, they can at least be understood, and they need not make an alliance between the two groups on other issues impossible. Pro-life Christians can recognize that importance of freedom even while believing that the state must intervene to protect the unborn; libertarians can acknowledge the importance of the life of the unborn even while emphasizing the liberty of the woman and the difficulties in banning abortion. Both groups can oppose public funding of the procedure. Moreover, libertarian support for voluntary action complements the efforts of churches and other Christian ministries to create counseling services and support structures for unwed mothers to allow them to keep their babies.

## Child Care

Christians hold the upbringing of children to be fundamentally a parental responsibility; for philosophical rather than theological reasons, secular libertarians believe the same thing. (Some libertarians, a decided minority, would endow kids with adult rights, allowing them to "divorce" their parents.) Thus, both groups can unite to oppose government day-care initiatives. Such programs favor secular over religious providers; subsidize working women to the detriment of mothers who choose to stay home; promote institutional day care over babysitting by friends, relatives, and neighbors; and create regulatory systems designed to emphasize government rather than family values.

Some Christians might still back public subsidies for day care if they did not discriminate against religious facilities and came without "strings." (There is no scriptural mandate for such a program, of course.) Libertarians, in contrast, would oppose any subsidy program, although some might support an expanded tax credit/deduction for day care. Nevertheless, to the extent that proposals for new programs are advanced, Christians and libertarians could work together to reduce their expense and intrusiveness.

## Drugs

The drug issue hosts another sharp clash between the perceived positions of Christians and libertarians. Christians generally believe the use of drugs to be a sin that is undermining society. Libertarians consider laws against drug use to be an intolerant interference with personal liberty, causing more harm than good. Can these positions be reconciled?

The Bible certainly warns against the abuse of drugs. One of "the acts of the sinful nature," wrote Paul, is "drunkenness" (Gal. 5:20). And

Peter directed his readers not to live as the pagans, "in debauchery, lust, drunkenness, orgies, carousing, and detestable idolatry" (1 Peter 4:3). Moreover, Paul instructed believers to "honor God with your body" (1 Cor. 6:20), which he earlier described as "God's temple," a "sacred" vessel in which the Holy Spirit lives. "If anyone destroys God's temple, God will destroy him." (1 Cor. 3:16–17).

This suggests that people are neither to use licit substances, such as alcohol, to excess, nor use other products that pose a high risk of harming their bodies. It is hard to set clear rules on this basis because not all drugs are created equal: moderate use of cigarettes, which kill 430,000 people a year, is probably more dangerous than either social drinking or occasional use of marijuana. The physiological consequences of pure heroin, in contrast to the adulterated substances sold in the illegal market, are actually minor; the drug's real danger is its addictiveness. By contrast, PCP, synthetic heroin, and a variety of other substances clearly harm the body. At the same time, most Christians probably believe they have a separate obligation not to take illegal substances, even those that may be relatively safe, because believers are to respect authority and must be concerned about preserving the purity of their witness.

But the fact that Christians believe they are not to use illegal drugs— or perhaps legal drugs, for that matter—does not settle the *policy* question at hand: Should the government prohibit drug use, as it once did alcohol consumption? Although the civil and ecclesiastical authorities were closely related in ancient Israel, they were separated well before the time of Jesus and remain so today. In fact, the model of the first-century church is a community focused on enforcing Biblical rules on its own members, not on those outside the fellowship. Thus, when Paul learned that a member of the Corinthian church was involved in serious immorality, he did not urge the group to lobby for civil legislation, but instead instructed his readers:

> I have written you in my letter not to associate with sexually immoral people—not at all meaning the people of this world who are immoral, or the greedy and swindlers, or idolaters. In that case you would have to leave this world. But now I am writing you that you must not associate with anyone who calls himself a brother but is sexually immoral or greedy, an idolater or a slanderer, a drunkard or a swindler. With such men to not even eat.

> What business is it of mine to judge those outside the Church? Are you not to judge those inside? God will judge those outside. "Expel the wicked many from among you." (1 Cor. 5:9–13)

Thus, while there is nothing to prohibit Christians from supporting anti-drug legislation, there is nothing that mandates they do so. It is more a matter of reason than revelation.

On these issues, then, Christians and libertarians can open a dialogue. Is it right for people who oppose drug use to use government to jail those who use drugs? Although the Bible sets standards for personal conduct, it does not specify when the state is empowered to intervene to "bring punishment on the wrongdoer," in Paul's words (Rom. 13:4). In my view, the best understanding of this phrase, especially in the context of his instruction to the Corinthian believers, is to punish those who commit crimes against other people, rather than those who transgress God's moral law.

Does drug use involve wrongs against other individuals? Drug use obviously has a social impact, but the impact of drug prohibition appears to be even more harmful. The full argument is obviously beyond the scope of this article, but a good case can be made that prohibition is a practical disaster, having funded violent criminal empires at home and abroad, resulted in an enormous increase in murder and property crime, sucked kids into the drug culture and criminal gangs, spread AIDS, and made drug-taking more dangerous. While a secular libertarian who believes he has an absolute right to take drugs will disagree on basic premises with a Christian who believes he has a godly responsibility to eschew drug use, they may nevertheless agree that, as a matter of social policy, legalization would be at least less costly than prohibition.

## Education

Although Christians and libertarians have tangled over tangential educational issues, such as gay teachers and school prayer, they agree on far more fundamental matters, such as the importance of parental control of education. Thus, both groups should be able to work together to promote tuition tax credits, vouchers, and school choice, in order to reduce the monopoly advantages of the public schools and increase parents' abilities to send their children to private schools.

As for the operation of the public schools, there is room for compromise. Christians can recognize that with public institutions paid for by all taxpayers, including non-Christians (and homosexuals), they will not be able to enforce Christian morality. (Which, of course, is a fundamental flaw in the public schools from their perspective.) Thus, trying to bar gays as teachers, or impose Christian prayers in a secular classroom, will naturally result in resistance from non-Christians. Libertarians, on the other hand, can recognize that the question is not *whether* values should be taught in the classroom, but *which* ones. At the very least, libertarians should support an educational process that provides for fair treatment of religion in history classes and extracurricular activities, such as the open access law. Moreover, they should be more tolerant of the use of harmless religious symbols, since Christians, whose tax money is also going to fund the schools, understandably feel disenfranchised when their values are deliberately purged.

## Pornography

For conservative Christians, the making and use of pornography is sinful. The Apostle Peter criticized those who, "by appealing to the lustful desires of sinful human nature," mislead others (2 Peter 2:18). Similarly, Paul wrote that God gave those who rejected him "over to shameful lusts" (Rom. 1:26).

Thus, Christians have a responsibility within their families and fellowships to discourage the use of pornography. They also can play a prophetic role to the surrounding community, including such activism as boycotts and protests, in an attempt to influence the purveyors of pornography. As with drugs, however, there is no Biblical mandate for civil government to ban the production or use of sexually explicit material. Paul's letter to the Corinthian church suggests that the community of faith is to be more concerned with the activities of those within than those without the fellowship.

With explicit Biblical direction on the issue absent, Christians must again rely more on reason than on revelation. They can demand not to be visually assaulted by pornographic advertising while walking in a public place, and many libertarians would go along with restrictions on the public display of sexually explicit material. Similarly, Christians and most libertarians can agree on the importance of protecting minors from being used in pornographic films and from acquiring pornographic materials. And libertarians, who oppose such government agencies as the National Endowment for the Arts altogether, have joined with Christians in opposing public funding for obscene art.

Libertarians are unalterably opposed to using government to keep pornography out of the hands of consenting adults. Christians might consider and accept the libertarian arguments. Christians should require a stronger justification for turning to the state than the revulsion they naturally feel at obscenity. And, in my view, the traditional rationales for arresting someone for looking at dirty pictures are too weak. Some people argue that pornography is accelerating the decline of society. Yet the availability of obscene materials is more a result than a cause of declining moral standards. Indeed, perhaps the most insidious pornographic phenomenon today is pervasive soft-core porn on TV, not hard-core obscenity in movies and magazines, which most Americans reject.

Some people have also contended that porn promotes sex crimes. However, it is important not to confuse correlation (those who commit sex crimes also like porn) with causation (porn *causes* them to commit sex crimes). In fact, the best evidence appears to be that the depiction of violence may encourage some people to commit violent crimes, while porn is largely passive. On this basis we seem to have more to fear from Freddy Krueger than Hugh Hefner.

### Sex

The Bible sets up a clear moral code for personal sexual behavior: sex belongs within the covenant of marriage. Based on their personal behavior, most libertarians, like most people in general, do not believe in such a code.

Nevertheless, it is possible for Christians and libertarians to work together in this area. For instance, both groups can oppose legislation that would force people to accept diverse sexual behavior, such as ordinances that require people to hire or rent to homosexuals and housing codes that order people to sell or rent to unmarried couples.

As for laws against non-marital sex, even Christians today seem reluctant to bring the bedroom into court. Libertarians might support a ban on sex in public places, but would oppose anti-sodomy laws (many of which also apply to heterosexuals) and criminal sanctions against adultery and fornication, which are still occasionally enforced in some states. Despite their belief that such activities violate Biblical norms, Christians could rightfully take the same position, since God has not appointed them to enforce his law on their unwilling neighbors. To the contrary, it is Christ who will wield the winnowing fork and separate the wheat from the chaff at the time of the final judgment (Luke 3:17, Matt. 13:24-30).

## Welfare

Libertarians oppose the government welfare system because it is little more than legislative theft, the taking of property form one group to give to another. They are also concerned about the pernicious consequences of welfare: its promotion of family breakup, illegitimacy, and dependency.

The Bible commands Christians to give, but individually, or through family and church. Government is not mentioned. Although there is no Scriptural proscription barring the creation of a public welfare system, Christians must be wary of establishing widespread transfer programs given the eighth and tenth commandments against stealing and coveting. Moreover, and such program should be consistent with other Biblical values, which in this case complement libertarianism: the importance of work, individual responsibility, and the family. In short, both Christians and libertarians would emphasize voluntary action. Some of the former might turn to welfare as a last resort, but both, again, should oppose the sort of expansive and disruptive system now in existence.

## Hope

The conservative Christian and libertarian worldviews are very different, but, despite the popular wisdom, not necessarily contradictory. Christians believe in a personal God who has revealed himself and established very clear standards by which men are to relate to him and each other. However, the circumstances under which people are to coerce other people through the power of the State are left largely undefined. And it is here where libertarians concern themselves. Although some libertarians are atheists, their religious beliefs can be separated from their political principles, which limit the right of individuals to initiate the use of force against one another.

Under these circumstances, a person can be both a Christian and a libertarian. In my case, my Christian faith is transcendent, but because, in my view, there is no explicit Christian political system, my faith only informs, rather than sets, my political positions. Even Christians who are not libertarians and libertarians who are not Christians have many opportunities to cooperate on protecting religious freedom, restricting state expansion, encouraging private education, keeping the government out of child care, opposing welfare systems that destroy families, and so on. And given both groups' need to find additional allies, it is increasingly important that Christians and libertarians not only talk with each other, but work together.

July 1992

# II

# Abortion
# The Irreconcilable Conflict

# 5

# The Real Meaning of Choice

Time passes, but abortion remains a debate between irreconcilable absolutes. So strong are the emotions of and great is the gulf between the opposing sides that some nominees for the U.S. Supreme Court have felt constrained to say that they have no opinion—indeed, have never even thought—about *Roe v. Wade*, the most contentious constitutional decision of our time. While the legal battle over abortion may be over, as a Supreme Court full of Republican nominees refused to overturn *Roe v. Wade*, the bloody political war continues in Congress and state legislatures across the nation.

Both parties are sensitive to divisions within their own ranks. Although the debate within Republican circles has received greater press attention, Pennsylvania Governor Robert Casey is one of a number of leading Democrats to question his party's stand in favor of unlimited abortions, and with many at taxpayer expense. Indeed, roughly one-third of Democratic congressmen do not support their party's formal position in favor of abortion-on-demand.

And most American voters view both sets of activists with disquiet. The public seems to say, at least to pollsters, that it believes the issue to be a lot more difficult than do, say, Randall Terry and Eleanor Smeal. Which should surprise no one. While abortion looks uncomfortably like the taking of innocent human life, regulating abortion turns an intimate personal decision over to the government. The issue *is* a tough one.

But part of the problem is also the rhetoric that dominates the debate. The issue is treated as life versus choice, forced pregnancy advocates versus baby killers. Such a simplistic lexicon naturally breeds confusion. Who, after all, can be against either life or choice? Certainly not the majority of Americans, who tell pollsters that they oppose most abortions (and are therefore "pro-life") but do not want to outlaw the procedure (and are thereby "pro-choice").

Both sides naturally realize the importance of grabbing ahold of a positive slogan. Yet whatever the appropriateness of "pro-life" as a label for the anti-abortion forces, the rallying cry of "choice" for advocates of legal abortion is suspect. Yes, to prohibit abortion is to restrict "choice." But the most important child-bearing choice is the decision whether to have sex, not whether to abort a pregnancy. After all, one is unlikely to desire an abortion unless one has had sex.

Making this point in today's world is not particularly easy, of course. Few people today seem to think of sex as a matter of "choice." Most unmarrieds—and even a not insubstantial number of religious singles, whose faiths formally teach that sex belongs within the marriage covenant—seem to believe it to be only natural for them to sleep together. What is seen as unnatural is the coming of a baby, not the extramarital sexual union.

However, in the age of AIDS people have been forced to acknowledge that a modern lifestyle is not risk-free. Although pregnancy is not equivalent to a deadly disease, it, too, is a "risk" of sex. That is, to have sex is to choose, voluntarily, to engage in the act that creates babies. For one to support "choice," then, does not necessarily mean endorsing the legal right to abort a pregnancy which has resulted from the *free choice* to have sex. Except in the case of rape, a choice was made. In such cases abortion becomes not an exercise in choice, but an attempt to avoid accepting responsibility for the earlier sexual choice.

Biology obviously makes it easier for a man to make this argument, since the burden of pregnancy is on women. And men have regularly attempted to shirk their responsibility for the life that they also helped create. Yet legitimizing the "choice" to abort has allowed men to even more purposefully avoid the consequences of their actions. After all, sex requires even less care when the unwanted human consequences of a one-night stand can be easily eliminated. A woman's desire for commitment can be dismissed with the statement: "get an abortion."

Thus, the point of restricting "the right to choose" is not to spitefully penalize those who do not accept traditional Judeo-Christian ethics, or any other moral code, but to ensure that everyone accepts responsibility for the serious consequences—a life—of their sexual choices. True, even broadly "pro-life" people are likely to disagree on the exact parameters of the putative parents' duties: in truth, the "hard" cases are hard. Nevertheless, there are easy cases too, like abortion as a form of late birth control to make up for a previous evening's mistake and as a means of sex selection, usually to ensure the birth of a boy. These "choices" surely do not have the same moral weight as a decision to abort made by a woman whose life is in danger or who has been raped.

Of course, moral surrender by refusing to hold people responsible for their sexual choices may look attractive when one assesses the difficulties in actually banning abortion. No one who generally supports individual freedom can be enthused about allowing the state to intrude so dramatically into private lives. But the fact that life is at stake requires us to make some hard decisions involving the balance between life and liberty and to consider at least some restrictions on the most abusive abortions. The very complexity of the issue means that abortion cannot be justified as a simplistic commitment to "choice," irrespective of the circumstances.

Today people are free to choose whether—and when and with whom—to have sex. People who create children as a result, even inadvertently, should be willing to accept responsibility for the consequences of their decisions. Unrestricted abortion, in contrast, allows everyone, men as well as women, to avoid dealing with the results of choices freely made. Even if they continue to oppose legal restrictions on abortion, "pro-choice" activists should recognize that abortion has become a convenient panacea for a world that would prefer not to confront a profoundly moral issue.

March 1993

# 6

# From Pro-Choice to Pro-Coercion

The abortion rights lobby likes to style itself "pro-choice," but the only people abortion activists believe should have a choice are those who desire an abortion. American taxpayers who don't want to subsidize a procedure they believe to be akin to murder, and foreign peoples who are now forced by their governments to undergo abortion, are not, in contrast, entitled to a comparable right to choose. Put bluntly, NARAL, NOW, and the other abortion lobbies believe more in dead fetuses than individual liberties.

The first issue is federal funding of abortion. President Clinton, having kept his promise (one of the few!) to remove executive branch restrictions on abortion, is now proposing to cover the procedure under Medicaid. Proponents act as if this is just another guaranteed "right," yet the constitutional freedom to speak does not include a publically-funded printing press. Government's failure to prohibit something does not mean that it must subsidize the activity.

The response of Rep. Pat Schroeder (D-Co.) is that, well, the taxpayers "pay for everything else." But financing abortion is different than, say, promoting dairy production. Numerous pro-lifers see no ethical difference between abortion and infanticide, while even many supporters of *Roe v. Wade* find abortion to be morally repugnant. To demand that these taxpayers subsidize the destruction of life is far worse than making them underwrite even the most stupid other federal program.

The abortion lobby also argues that lack of federal funding is "unfair" for the poor. Obviously those in poverty possess fewer opportunities than others, but that alone does not give them a right to seize other people's incomes, else those on welfare would have a "right" to single-family detached homes, luxury automobiles, and whatever else the average middle-class family takes for granted. That sort of a right would be ludicrous enough, yet the abortion lobby promotes a "right" that turns taxpayers into accomplices in killing babies. Even if the state does not intervene to protect developing life, politicians shouldn't force morally sensitive taxpayers to pay to end it.

At the same time administration officials indicate that they will ask Congress to make Americans contribute to the international abortion crusade. The International Planned Parenthood Federation, which lobbies worldwide to overturn laws restricting abortion, is the likely recipient of $15 million in cash and goods. In this way unwilling U.S. taxpayers will have to pay to promote abortion worldwide as well as stateside.

Even worse is the administration's plan to provide between $20 million and $40 million to the United Nations Fund for Population Activities. UNFPA views its purpose as reducing population growth and, like most other UN bodies, doesn't let principle get in the way of politics. Thus, UNFPA has long supported China's coercive abortion policy, helping train the very functionaries who pressure women into having abortions, for instance. Concluded the Agency for International Development in 1985, "the kind and quality of assistance provided by UNFPA contributed significantly to China's ability to manage and implement a population program in which coercion was pervasive."

When pressed to explain activities that seemed to offer little "choice" to helpless peasants, UNFPA Executive Director Nafis Sadik stated that her agency "firmly believes, and so does the government of the People's Republic of China, that their program is a totally voluntary program." After all, she observed on another occasion, "There is no such thing as, you know, a license to have a birth and so on."

The administration is trying to sell its proposal as an indispensable step in restraining foreign population growth that will otherwise overwhelm the earth. In fact, the threat from a "population bomb" has been grossly overestimated. For one thing, recent population growth is below the most apocalyptic predictions. Moreover, the problem is not too many people, but authoritarian economic policies that prevent people from being productive. There is simply no correlation between poverty and population or population density; there is, in contrast, a striking correlation between poverty and lack of economic liberty.

In any case, the U.S. has been providing half of the funds internationally—roughly $430 million this year (1993) alone—going to population programs. All that Washington has done is bar taxpayer subsidies for the coercive initiatives, redirecting the money to groups relying on voluntary measures.

The abortion rights lobby likes to portray itself as a defender of choice. But the Clinton administration's readiness to make American taxpayers pay for abortions at home and forced abortions abroad suggests that it cares less for choice than for paying off campaign debts. Thus, it will be up to Congress to protect the right of all Americans "to choose."

April 1993

# 7

# The Escalating Abortion Wars

Another abortion doctor has been shot and a Catholic priest has gained national attention for calling the killing of abortionists "justifiable homicide." For 20 years abortion has been the nation's most emotional issue. Now it is becoming the deadliest.

In March (1993) Dr. David Gunn was gunned down in Pensacola, Florida. On Thursday, August 19 Rachelle Shannon shot and wounded Wichita abortionist George Tiller. Shannon edits a newsletter published by an anti-abortion activist now imprisoned for the fire-bombing of a Planned Parenthood clinic in Cincinnati in 1985.

Naturally, the abortion rights lobby, unconcerned about the moral implication of killing *1.6 million* babies a year, has found its voice when it comes to attacks on abortion doctors. Jeanne Clark, a spokeswoman for the Feminist Majority Foundation, said that Dr. Tiller, who performs latter term abortions—when the fetus is fully developed and capable of surviving outside of the womb—is "an incredibly caring guy and real gutsy." President Clinton denounced the Tiller attack as "reprehensible" and reaffirmed his support for "choice." Francis Kissling of Catholics for a Free Choice suggested that Rev. David Trosch, who became a media celebrity after unsuccessfully seeking to run a newspaper ad defending the killing of abortionists, be required to seek mental health assistance.

Most pro-lifers, too, have repudiated the escalating violence. But not all of them. After Gunn's murder, Don Treshman of Rescue America said that "This shooting, while unfortunate, will result in babies' lives being saved." Earlier this month Rev. Trosch argued that "if 100 doctors need to die to save over one million babies, I see it as a fair trade." Although Rev. Trosch formally recanted his views after the Catholic Church threatened to depose him from his pastorate in Magnolia Springs,

47

Alabama, he said that he was "pleased" with the publicity he has received. Taking a similar position is Lutheran minister Michael Bray, who opined after the Tiller shooting that attacks on abortionists are "an act of defense." He added, "It is legitimate to use force to defend an innocent person from imminent danger."

Alas, the problem with such arguments is that there is no consensus that the unborn are "people" with the same legal rights as everyone else. However strongly pro-lifers believe that babies deserve to be defended, they should not attempt to unilaterally enforce that view, injuring and even killing people involved in a legally-sanctioned activity. The implications of such behavior for our diverse society, in which some people are willing to murder for animals and others for the earth, are truly frightening. Pro-life vigilantes simply cannot presume to simultaneously become police, judges, and executioners, forcibly establishing their own moral views, however persuasive, as law.

Still, it is not enough to recoil in horror at the latest shooting and denounce those who endorse violence. As a society we must begin to grapple with something that most people would prefer to ignore: the very real and awful moral implications of abortion itself. To abort even a young fetus is different from having an appendix removed; to destroy a baby that could survive outside the womb looks a lot more like infanticide than an exercise of a "choice."

Moreover, except in the case of rape, babies arise only as a result of *choice*—to have sex. Of course, mistakes happen and people sometimes change their minds. But anyone who voluntarily engages in the act that creates life should accept some responsibility for the baby that may result, however inadvertently. In short, people have no duty to procreate, but if they create children, they have an obligation to preserve and not destroy those lives. And while there are some hard cases, there are also some very easy ones: parents who decide to abort a female fetus because they want a boy, for instance.

Nor is abortion an issue of women fighting for their rights against a male establishment. In the case of Dr. Tiller, it was a man who was profiting from destroying third-trimester babies. It was a woman, Rachelle Shannon, who identified with the unborn being killed.

And life is being taken. It is admittedly a special kind of life: at least before "viability," the unborn are arguably only undeveloped, potential human beings. But *it is still life*. Thus, abortion should require a stronger justification than convenience and more thought than that necessary to walk into a clinic and sign a few papers.

Abortion is the most profound moral issue now facing our country. It may be dead as a political issue—all of the institutions of national power are firmly behind the abortion lobby and that is unlikely to change much even with the election of a pro-life president in the future. But the growing bitterness of the struggle, so vividly evidenced by the shooting of Dr. Tiller, demonstrates the need for a serious debate over the exclusion of the unborn from our shared human community.

August 1993

# III

# Earth Keeping or Earth Worship?

# 8

# Ecology as Religion: Faith in Place of Fact

## Introduction

The environment has become a political issue of enormous importance. Last year (1992) at the Rio "Earth Summit" the ecological crusaders captured, if only momentarily, almost the entire world's attention.

The issue has particular political potency in the U.S. In 1988 George Bush promised to be the "environmental president" if elected. Two years later he signed the nearly 800 page Clean Air Act—20 times the length of the original law—despite warnings that it would provide little ecological protection at enormous cost. Nevertheless, he still lost votes to a Democratic ticket that included Sen. Al Gore, the Tennessee Democrat who built his career on apocalyptic predictions of environmental doom.

Widespread public concern about conservation is understandable since no one wants to wake up to air that is unbreathable and water that is undrinkable. Yet the current debate, including proposals for ever more draconian "solutions," has taken on a tone that often seems frankly religious.

The problem is not that religion, particularly Judaism and Christianity, have nothing to say about conservation. To the contrary, the Jewish Scriptures emphasize that the earth is God's creation and man is but a steward of its resources. Nevertheless, humans hold a unique place in the created order and were explicitly given authority to use the earth, the so-called Dominion Covenant. The struggle for believers in this tradition, then, is to find the right balance between protection of the animals, plants, and lands that God called good and their use in order to benefit the people made in the image of God.

Unfortunately, the new environmental spirituality has taken a quite different direction, moving beyond the broad concern for stewardship

53

and towards a very partisan stance on specific issues—often in the name of Christian theology. In part, the new eco-spirituality reflects the latest fashion in liberal religious circles. Churches that have long emphasized the "social gospel" and liberation theology are now recycling products, substituting china for plastic dishes, composting plants, installing solar power, cleaning up creeks, surveying energy consumers, serving meatless meals, and praying for endangered animal species. They are also lobbying public officials: "Church Leaders Seize Global Warming Issue," ran a headline in the *Washington Post* last year (1992). "This is a spiritual issue, not just a technical problem. It's a matter of God's creation under assault," explained the Rev. Bruce McLeod, president of the Canadian Council of Churches. At a meeting of the CCC and the National Council of Churches, clerics endorsed the World Climate Convention regarding $CO_2$ emissions, then under negotiation for presentation at the Rio Conference. "As church leaders, we ourselves have been slow to recognize the seriousness of the global warming problem. We now clearly see it as both an issue of spirituality and justice," said a statement released by the two organizations.

It is not just the leading Protestant denominations that have lost much of their religious *raison d'etre* that have climbed on the environmental bandwagon. The Southern Baptists, one of the nation's most theologically conservative Christian churches, has published a series of "fact sheets," including one entitled "Endangered Earth," decrying the threat of global warming. Another flyer claims that we face a garbage crisis and proclaims that recyling "is one positive way to return to the God-given role of responsible stewardship of the earth."

Indeed, a variety of religious environmental organizations have been forming—the North American Coalition on Religion and Ecology (NA-CRE), Religion and Science for the Environment, and the Presbyterian Eco-Justice Task Force, for instance. In early 1992 Sen. Gore worked with agnostic scientist Carl Sagan and what Gore's office described as "leaders of every major denomination and faith group in the United States" to organize the Mission to Washington: Religion and Science in Partnership for the Environment to press Congress and the White House for "bold new action to protect the global environment, and to help ensure the success of the Earth Summit." And concern for the environment is not just opening up a new lobbying front for mainline churches that have already been delving into a host of other political controversies. It is also spilling over into program and worship, liturgy and theology.

For instance, back in 1979, in New York, the Cathedral of St. John the Divine issued a "program for environment" entitled *City & Planet*. Among the program activities was a sermon by James Lovelock explaining his Gaia Hypothesis, that the earth should be treated as a living being. The Cathedral hosted a book party for him. The Cathedral remains in the forefront of environmental activities. Paul Gorman manages Religion and Science for the Environment, an interfaith religious organization at the Cathedral, and explains that "This is not just religious people finding yet another social issue, but rather religious people experiencing a very profound challenge to faith and to what it means to be religious."

At times one wonders whether the formally Christian Cathedral retains an interest in Christian worship. When interviewed by *The Amicus Journal*, the Rev. James Parks Morton, Dean of the Cathedral, had a Buddha head on his desk; the Cathedral has included Buddhist meditations, African chants, and other non-Christian worship practices in its services. Moreover, Morton has placed a live blue crab and other animals in an Earth Shrine in the church's nave as "a symbol of ecotheology." He told the magazine that the blessing of animals "is the profoundest kind of religious experience we can have."

Other churches have also long taken an interest in environmental affairs and we are now seeing a steadily increasing greening of the churches, many spurred by the Cathedral's example. One Anglican minister says: "we are now beginning to see that Morton was a pioneer with the courage to challenge orthodoxy that was largely outdated." Methodist Minister Willard Moffat adapted the Cathedral's "Gaia Mass" to his own church. "When we did," he explained, "our congregation resonated in sync with the beautiful spirit expressed in its music, words, and singing. It was an idea whose time had clearly come." Similar trends are evident in the multi-church organizations. For instance, in 1990 NACRE held an Intercontinental Conference on Caring for Creation at which Bahai, Buddhist, Hindu, and Islamic texts were read along with Christian and Jewish ones. Native Americans presented a program on "healing the Wounded Earth" and Carl Sagan gave a major address. The organization also prepared a Liturgy for "Mother Earth."

While ecotheology appears to be primarily a Christian phenomenon, Ellen Bernstein has founded Shomrei Adamah (Keepers of the Earth), an "ecocultural" organization. Bernstein, author of *Let the Earth Teach You Torah*, endorses the Cathedral's activities but emphasizes the importance of maintaining a specifically Jewish environmental tradition: "In seeking to understand our traditions we reflect the *diversity* of all creation in which every thing has a purpose and a place. Such diversity needs to be cherished and nurtured not homogenized and universalized."

Moreover, the new eco-religion has moved beyond the traditional religious realm. Combined with the activism of established denominations is a growing quasi-paganistic movement in which environmentalism itself seems to have become a competing religion and the earth has replaced God as an object of worship. The new pantheism takes many forms: witchcraft, goddess worship, the occult, traditional pantheism, and Deep Ecology. Although these variants differ sharply in many details, all reflect a tendency to treat the earth as sacred and minimize the importance of human beings. At the fringe, some eco-pagans believe in the use of violence to both protect and worship the earth.

## The Environmental Movement

Most citizens who have indicated a concern for the environment have done so for understandable, even laudable, reasons. Few have a larger, spiritual agenda. But like most movements, environmentalism's most fervent activists and organizational leaders are more radical than their supporters. Many of the former want to slow growth not because they think it is necessary to, for instance, preserve good air quality, but because they believe it to be a moral duty. As a result, factual questions about the nature of our environmental problems and the efficacy of the proposed solutions become irrelevant, since the means—several variants of coerced asceticism—become the ends.

Consider Jeremy Rifkin, who cites a variety of supposedly looming environmental disasters in making his pitch for a new "biospheric consciousness." There is, however, a philosophical undercurrent to his work that suggests he would demand radical cuts in consumption for the purposes of "environmental stewardship and economic equity" even if it were proved that we faced no ecological problems. Further, he wants to end meat consumption not only as a means of "saving the planet," but also as "an acknowledgement of our kindred spirit with the rest of the animal kingdom and our empathetic regard for the intrinsic value of all of earth's creatures."

Nor is he alone. Physicist Brian Swimme and cultural historian Thomas Berry complain: "Humans now live amid limitless junk beyond any known capacity for creative use. This new world of hundred-story buildings, endless traffic, turbulent populations and mega-cities has become an affliction perhaps greater than the more 'natural' human condition it seeks to replace." And when asked about the possibility of cold fusion providing an inexpensive, virtually limitless energy source, Stanford biologist Paul Ehrlich, the perennially apocalyptic—and inaccurate— critic of population growth, stated that it would be "like giving a machine gun to an idiot child."

This semi-religious commitment to certain ecological outcomes drives much of environmental policy today. The Clean Air Act makes little trade-off between huge economic costs and minor health effects. Environmental groups that produce oil and natural gas on their own properties lobby against even controlled and limited drilling on federal land. Although African countries, such as Zimbabwe, which allow a market for ivory, have better protected their elephant herds than those, such as Kenya, which prohibit ivory sales, the conservation movement pressed for and won an international ban on the ivory trade. In all of these cases and more, hidden philosophical, even religious, tenets have skewed policy, causing public officials to pursue strategies that deliver less environmental protection at greater expense.

## Ecopaganism—Jewish-Christian Syncretism

A significant amount of today's religious fervor for the environment is coming from established denominations, particularly Christian ones. Much of what the churches are doing in the practical and political realm can be faulted for being based on poor information and for failing to achieve their purported ends. For instance, the statement adopted by the Canadian and National Councils of Churches in 1992 on global warming claimed that an "international scientific consensus" existed on the role of CO2 emissions and rising temperatures. Rev. Morton explains that he helped form the Joint Appeal on Religion and Science for the Environment in 1990 in an attempt to convince religious leaders that "the earth faced an historical calamity on the magnitude of the extinction of the dinosaurs or Noah's flood." In fact, there is great disagreement on what, if any, impact human-induced $CO_2$ increases have had on temperatures over the past century, what the causes and effects are of a thinning ozone layer, and the speed at which species are disappearing from the earth.

But of greater interest to serious religious believers should be the theological contamination posed by much of conservation ethic being pushed by a number of environmental activists, many of whom believe that Judaism and Christianity are responsible for the disastrous plight of the earth today. Criticisms of Christianity, and particularly Catholicism, have often been tied to specific theological doctrines, most obviously birth control and abortion. For instance, advocates of reduced population growth routinely single out the Catholic church for its opposition to contraception.

Attacks on traditional faiths run far deeper than just one teaching, however. Argues environmentalist Lynn White, "Since the roots of our [environmental] trouble are so largely religious, the remedy must also be essentially religious." White, a professor of history at the University of California, delivered a speech at the American Association for the Advancement of Science back in 1966 in which he termed Christianity "the most anthropocentric religion the world has ever seen." The impact of Christianity was particularly pernicious, in his view, since Christianity replaced paganism, destroying prior belief systems that considered nature to be embued with a sense of the sacred. "By destroying pagan animism, Christianity made it possible to exploit nature in a mood of indifference to the feelings of natural objects."

White's charges have been echoed by Donald Rowster, author of *Nature's Economy*, a history of the science of ecology. "The good shepherd, the heroic benefactor of man, has almost never been concerned with leading his flock to a broad reverence for life. His pastoral duties have been limited to ensuring the welfare of his human charges, often in the face of a nature that has been seen as corrupt and predatory." Writing in the Harvard Divinity Bulletin Timothy Weiskel, director of the Harvard Seminar on Environmental Values, complains of "the irreducible anthropocentrism of the Western religious traditions" and asks "Can we survive on this small planet with these sets of religious beliefs?" However, Weiskel generously allows that "we do not need to dispense with theology and religion" since he would have us all "believe religiously in the principle of human limits."

Although other faiths, like Confucianism, Shintoism, and the beliefs of Native Americans, are as man-centered or environmentally destructive as Christianity, White's thesis remains popular. Author Joseph Wood Krutch blamed the early Israelites for desanctifying nature. The reason, he observes, "perhaps was, not any impulse toward cruelty, but simply that the new monotheism was aware how easily deep concern with animals leads to animal gods and to polytheism." Historian Arnold Toynbee also criticizes the rise of monotheism through Judaism which, "removed the age-old restraint that was once placed on man's greed by his awe. Man's greedy impulse to exploit nature used to be held in check by his pious worship of nature."

Animal rights activist Tom Regan attacks "speciesism" as being "responsible for an incalculable amount of evil." And the culprit is clear: "It is an arrogant, unbridled anthropocentrism, often aided and abetted in our history by an arrogant, unbridled Christian theology...that has brought the earth to the brink of ecological disaster." Rupert Sheldrake criticizes "the Judeo-Christian tradition" for having "always emphasized the supremacy of the male God," in contrast to mother earth. He goes on to call for new forms of theology, "a new renaissance" in which we "acknowledge the animistic traditions of our ancestors."

Jeremy Rifkin and Ted Howard argue that "the traditional Christian approach to nature had been a major contributing factor to ecological destruction." Their criticism is two-fold: Christianity emphasizes "otherworldliness," leading to "disregard and even exploitation of the physical world" and "the concept of *dominion* has been used by people to justify the ruthless manipulation and exploitation of nature." They go on to call for "a radical reformulation of Christian theology" that incorporates aspects of Eastern religions.

Some within the Christian and Jewish tradition have advanced similar attacks. Lewis Regenstein, Director of the Interfaith Council for the Protection of Animals and Nature, argues that "there is little doubt that Christian theology is partly to blame for the churches' apathy, for some aspects of it have traditionally regarded this world as something less than a place to be desired or affirmed."

Two self-professed Christian theists, Herman Daly and John Cobb, contend that "Christian theism has done much to bring about the dangerous situation to which the world has come. In varied forms it has supported anthropocentrism, ignored or belittled the natural world, opposed efforts to stop population growth, directed attention away from the urgent needs of this life, treated as of absolute authority for today teachings that were meant to influence a very different world, aroused false hopes, given false assurances, and claimed God's authority for all of these sins."

James Nash, Executive Director of the Churches' Center for Theology and Public Policy, writes that "without doubt, Christian traditions bear some responsibility for propagating" destructive environmental perspectives. "Consequently, the ecological crisis is a challenge to Christians to eradicate the last vestiges of these ecologically ruinous myths," he adds. Indeed, "for the Christian churches," he says, "the ecological crisis is more than a biophysical challenge. It is also a theological-ethical challenge." He, too, talks of a new theological reformation, but a more moderate one than that envisioned by Rifkin and Howard:

> In a sense, the church does need "new" theological and ethical bases for sustaining ecological integrity. This need, however, does not entail abandoning or replacing Christianity's main themes. Rather, it requires extensions and reinterpretations of these main themes in ways that preserve their historic identity and that are also consistent with ecological data.

Less concerned about the main themes of Christianity, however, is Dominican priest Matthew Fox, who decries the "onslaught of anthropocentric...culture that began with the breakup of cosmology at the end of the Middle Ages." Fox, once silenced by the Vatican for what Cardinal Ratzinger called "dangerous and deviant" teachings, goes on to argue that "the dominant religious soil in which the West has planted Christianity is in great part exhausted." What is needed, then, he argues, is a new creation spirituality, which "has to do with the salvation, the healing of the planet and our peoples before it is too late."

On the Protestant side is Rev. Carl Casebolt of the National Council of Churches, who proclaims that "I'm very comfortable with a lot of the New Age thinking," especially earth/goddess worship. "When people talk about a goddess, if it's a correction of the patriarchy of traditional Christian faith, that may be a good thing."

Stranger still is Catharina Halkes' call for Christian eco-feminism. Halkes, Emeritus Professor of Feminist Theology at the Catholic University of Nijmegen, the Netherlands, agrees that traditional Christian theology bears some responsibility for our current environmental problems. She therefore advocates refashioning fundamental Christian doctrines. Writes Halkes: "the image of the world as the body of God belongs more to our time and is closer to our changing reality than that of the Kingdom of God."

Nor is it enough in the view of some for the church to be involved environmentally. Even activist churches have been criticized for the way in which they have engaged environmental issues. Writes Jay McDaniel, Director of the Steel Center for the Study of Religion and Philosophy: "There has continued to be an anthropocentric focus in the church's concern for the environment. It is the environment of human beings that is considered, and it is considered chiefly because it is indispensable for human life. Features of the environment that are not important for human beings are still neglected."

## Ecology as Religion

Equally significant is the tendency for environmentalism to become, for many, the new paganism, a competing religion in its own right, with a mixture of traditional pantheism and more modern forms of earth worship. The problem, explains Patricia Waak, an advocate of population control (of people, not birds) at the Audubon Society, is that "there is in the environmental movement a strong spiritual sense that doesn't fit in with any of the major religions." Instead, she explains, "What I see happening is this sort of coming together in a realization that our spiritual sense does come in part from a fundamental value for the earth and the things associated with it, and the fact that it's *alive*." Waak says that "If you walked into my living room, you'd see Buddhist prayer wheels, African divining bones, and the statue of a witch doctor." Author Michael Brown terms this phenomenon "ecological spirituality," which, he writes

in principle, is a good thing. Humanity's spiritual side can be extremely potent. When directed toward environmental issues, such spirituality can galvanize an otherwise apathetic public and marshal tremendous energy toward solving problems.

Of course, the rise of Christianity never ended paganism. Wiccans, the "good" witches, have a tradition running back to pre-Christian Europe. "Witchcraft," writes Starhawk, a priestess of the Old Religion of the Goddess (as well as an instructor at Matthew Fox's Institute for Culture and Creation), is "perhaps the oldest religion existent in the West." And it has a heavy ecological emphasis. Adds Starhawk, "witchcraft takes its teachings from nature, and reads inspiration in the movements of the sun, moon, and stars, the flight of birds, the slow growth of trees, and the cycles of the seasons."

Nor was pantheism unknown among environmentalists in the past. Ernst Haeckel, who coined the term ecology in 1866, was a pantheist who published through the Rationalist Press Association and had an influential readership. Though religious as a student, he ultimately attacked Christianity for placing man above other creatures, leading "to a regrettable contempt of all other organisms." Observes historian John Young, "the extraordinary influence of Haeckel and his successors can be attributed, in part, to the quasi-religious appeal, the incipient pantheism of his picture. But there is a deeper appeal; the return to a god-impregnated nature, which had been banished from the North by Christianity."

Increasing environmental consciousness has joined with New Age thinking, resulting in a vibrant Neo-Pagan movement. Neo-Paganism has been estimated to have up to 200,000 adherents, described by the *Utne Reader* as "a diverse lot: Included are spiritual feminists, radical environmentalists, ethnic and racial minority group members, gay males and lesbians, and others who have often been pushed aside by the major Eastern and Western religions." Near San Francisco neo-pagans have established the Bay Area Pagan Assemblies to battle Christians resisting New Age practices. Moreover, the Unitarian Church has established an official "Covenant of Unitarian Universalist Pagans" with more than 60 chapters in the U.S. The Rev. Lesly Phillips explains that "the growing awareness of the urgent need to honor and heal Mother Earth, have [sic] drawn many Unitarian Universalists to a contemporary Pagan approach to religion."

Indeed, we are seeing increasing numbers of people engaging in Goddess worship, literally worshiping the earth. Some groups have priestesses who pray to the earth: "Sacred Earth Power, bring healing to Planet Earth," intoned Selena Fox of the Circle Sanctuary on Earth Day 1991. Elinor Gadon argues in her book, *The Once and Future Goddess*, that "we are doomed as a species and planet unless we have a radical change of consciousness. The reemergence of the Goddess is becoming the symbol and metaphor for this transformation."

Margot Adler, a witch who serves on the Unitarian Covenant board, explains that "Most Neo-Pagans sense an aliveness and 'presence' in nature. They are usually polytheists, or animists, or panthiests, or two or three of these things at once." Starhawk summarizes the movement:

Common to all are the belief in the sacredness of the Earth and interconnected systems that sustain life; the focus on ritual, on ecstatic experience and lived ethics rather than dogma; the heritage of persecution and resistance to oppression; the stress on spirituality as communal healing rather than on personal salvation or enlightenment; [and] the rich symbolism rooted in the cycles of birth, growth, death, and regeneration in nature and human life.

Another religious strand is the so-called Gaia hypothesis, popularized by former NASA staffer James Lovelock. Lovelock contends that the earth is essentially alive, an argument previously advanced by geologist James Hutton in 1785. In Lovelock's view, because the biosphere has responded to outside changes, such as the temperature of the sun, and maintained a general equilibrium, the world has shown a capacity for adjustment beyond the mere sum of its parts. "The system seemed to exhibit the behavior of a single organism, even a living creature." Humans are not important because individual species are of little consequence to the larger earth. Exactly what Lovelock thinks this means in practice is unclear. On the one hand, he declares that "In no way do I see Gaia as a sentient being, a surrogate God. To me, Gaia is alive and part of the ineffable universe, and I am part of her." But he has gone further, asking: "What is Mary but another name for Gaia? Then her capacity for virgin birth is no miracle. She is...conceivably a part of God. On earth she is the source of life everlasting and is alive now. She gave birth to humankind and we are part of her."

Historian Young compares Lovelock's theories, which have been popularized by the Cathedral of St. John the Divine, to those of Fox. Lovelock never mentions Christ, but he does seem to see mankind in roughly the same way—as part of creation rather than a special creation of God—as does Fox. Says the latter, "Creation is all things and us. It is us in relationship with all things." Gaia language has also influenced the wider environmental community. In its report, the World Commission on Environment and Development observed that "from space, we can see and study the Earth as an organism whose health depends on the health of all its parts."

A different and radical form of spirituality is offered by Rifkin and Howard. They envision a world of permanent energy scarcity and environmental risk and the end of the industrial age, something which can be coped with only through a "radical change in world view" that "will have to be accomplished in a very short period of time. To succeed will require zealous determination—a militancy, if you will—of herculean proportions." The vision they proffer not only has roots in various religious traditions, as they argue, but is spiritual. For instance, Rifkin and Howard declare that "in a low-entropy society work becomes an essen-

tial component in our efforts to reach an enlightened state of consciousness." Further, they argue, "human labor is sanctified as any activity
that helps us 'know who we really are'." Their theology is essentially
that of asceticism. They write

> The governing ethical principle of a low-entropy world view is to minimize energy
> flow. Excessive material wealth is recognized as an irreversible diminution of the
> world's precious resources. In the low-entropy society "less is more" becomes not
> a throwaway phrase but a truth of the highest magnitude. A low-entropy society
> deemphasizes material consumption. Frugality becomes the watchword. Human
> needs are met, but whimsical, self-indulgent desires—the kind pandered to in ev-
> ery shopping center in the country—are not.

Rifkin's asceticism is joined with a Medieval communalism. For instance, he seems entranced by the lack of privacy and modesty in the
"premodern era," a time when "the well-being of the community and
the expression of the common will took precedence over the needs of
the individual." People rarely acted on their own, lived most of their
lives, including sexual relations, in front of one another, and shared not
only their homes but their beds with family, friends, and servants. Alas,
Rifkin seems to believe, all of this changed. Indeed, Rifkin doesn't even
like the development of the chair, "A constant reminder of the new separation between people" which "reinforced the idea of the autonomous
individual, secure in his private space, isolated from the responsibilities
and obligations of the larger community."

Moreover, Rifkin would have this anti-materialist ethic coexist with
a very different view of nature. "A low-entropy culture emphasizes man
and woman as a part of nature, not apart from it." Once this is understood, "an ethical base is established by which the appropriateness of all
human activity can be judged." To destroy another species, for instance,
would therefore be immoral: "Every species must be preserved simply
because it has an inherent and inalienable right to life by virtue of its
existence." Indeed, argues Rifkin, we need to "resacralize our relationship to" the planet. Elsewhere he argues: "Biospheric consciousness
embraces the entirety of the earth community. When man and woman
stand erect on the earth's surface, they become both incarnate and transcendent, their bodies reaching down to reparticipate with the flesh of
the planet, their spirits reaching up to embrace heavenly rapture."

But a religious reverence for nature is best epitomized by the deep
ecologists. Norwegian Arne Naess coined the phrase "deep ecology" in

a famous article in 1973. California philosophy professors Bill Devall and George Sessions call for the cultivation of "ecological consciousness." Among other things, they advocate "the revival of Earth-bonding rituals, celebrating specific places" and cite a Taoist ritual as an example.

Devall and Sessions urge Christians to work within their own framework to promote environmentalism and cite St. Francis of Assisi and Giodano Bruino as Christian thinkers who provide "a source for the deep ecology perspective of organic wholeness and biocentric equality." However, Devall and Sessions sound far more positive when they discuss Eastern religions and the Gaia, or earth as living organism, hypothesis. God is never mentioned, nor how the earth was created. Atheistic in one sense, deep ecology is deeply religious in another sense, operating as a world-view with a secular substitute for God.

In fact, there are a large number of well-known conservationists who moved toward Buddhism, in particular, and transcendentalism, with highly romantic attitudes toward nature. Some, like aviator Charles Lindbergh and preservationist William Brewster, dabbled in the occult. Explains Alston Chase:

> Rather than seeing human beings as at the center of the universe, these people saw humanity at best as part of an interconnected whole and at worst as the temple destroyers who desacralized nature. Nor did the Judeo-Christian view that only man partook of the sacred satisfy them. Instead they saw the sacred in even the smallest things of life.

Their names became a wilderness religion, but a religion with many names: Buddhism, Taoism, inhumanism, organicism, mysticism, transcedentalism, animism. Yet however seminal and inchoate, however eclectic a collection of offbeat non-Western and nonmodern theories, these variegated ideas did coalesce into one theme...: The view that the universe is one interconnected whole and that every atom in creation is part of the sacred being of God.

Thus, while the name, "deep ecology" is new, the concepts it represents are not. Devall's and Sessions' two main tenets of deep ecology, for instance, are self-realization and biocentric equality. Devall and Sessions write: "In keeping with the spiritual traditions of many of the world's religions, the deep ecology norm of self-realization goes beyond the modern Western *self....* Spiritual growth, or unfolding, begins when we cease to understand or see ourselves as isolated and narrow competing egos and begin to identify with other humans from our family and friends to, eventually, our species. But the deep ecology sense of self requires a further maturity and growth, an indentification which goes beyond humanity to include the nonhuman world." Indeed, they add, "the intuition of biocentric equality is that all things in the biosphere have an equal right to live and blossom and to reach their own individual forms of unfolding and self-realization within the larger Self-realization."

## Eco-paganism's Practical Threats

The growth of spiritual environmentalism is having an impact on government policy and thereby on the lives of Americans, whatever their religious views. Put bluntly, the agenda of many ecopagans, in contrast to average environmentalists, is anti-human. The basic problem is *the lack of* an anthropocentric focus, and a consequent disregard for the transcendent value of every person. Warns John Young, who otherwise seems to sympathize with the extreme environmental activists

> Deep ecology, Gaia theory and creation spirituality make an attractive but heady mixture. It may prove to be a less dangerous one than anthropocentrism mixed with advanced technology, but it is a good idea to know its political flashpoint.... The ecological idea appealed to the German Nazis because they, too, believed that the laws of nature could not be transcended by human society, and they opposed both capitalism and *laissez-faire* economics, the forerunner of today's "economic rationalism", from ecological principles.

Indeed, several leading Nazis were also committed environmentalists of various stripes: Hitler deputy Rudolph Hess, Agriculture Minister Walther Darre, and Fritz Todt of the Todt Organization. And this support had consequences. Writes Anna Bramwell: "Nazi Germany was the first country in Europe to form nature reserves.... It was the first country to insist, in 1934, that new tree plantations should include broad-leaved, deciduous trees, as well as conifers.... Anti-vivisection laws were passed.... land with trees on it was seen as sacrosanct." For all of their obvious concern for nature, however, the Nazis obviously did not exhibit a similar love for mankind.

Some modern philosphers, while certainly not Nazis, also let their ecological vision diminish the significance of human life. Argues psychologist Neil Daniels, "nature does not seem to demonstrate that human life is precious." Indeed, some deep ecologists today are willing to resort to violence. Dave Foreman, co-founder of EarthFirst! and a one-time Goldwater Republican, and convicted of charges that he conspired to down power pylons for an Arizona nuclear plant, considers the Earth to be a living organism and explains that eco-terrorism, violent and illegal acts ranging from disabling building equipment to placing spikes in roads and trees, is "a form of worship toward the earth. It's really a very spiritual thing to go out and do." He has also advocated allowing the poor in Third World countries to starve, "to just let nature seek its own balance," and can't seem to understand why people think his opinion to be "monstrous."

Others, like Naess, advocate "a long range humane reduction [in population] through mild but tenacious political and economic measures" in order to make room for "population growth for thousands of species which are now constrained by human pressures." Naess, who wants to bring the population down to about one billion, the population in 1800, does not, apparently, believe in violence, having authored studies on Ghandi. The problem, of course, would occur when Naess realized that nothing other than coercion will radically downsize the earth's population. That potential dilemma obviously posed no difficulty to one letter writer to the newsletter, *EarthFirst!*, who suggested using biological agents to reduce humankind while leaving unharmed other forms of life.

Even non-violent ecopaganism is not harmless. Treating the environment in religious terms has proved to be a particularly effective way to indoctrinate children with a highly partisan world view. In her book, *Under the Spell of Mother Earth*, Berit Kjos reviews a number of disturbing incidents where neo-paganistic practices have been brought into the classroom. The efforts are usually subtle and are never labeled for what they are. Observes Kjos, an evangelical Christian, "the ban on religion in public schools failed to block the promotion of pagan beliefs. Spiritual buzzwords like *reverence*—suggesting a response reserved for the Creator Himself, and *connectedness*—referring to pantheistic oneness rather than biological interdependence, flow through environmental teaching and songs, persuading our children to love Mother Earth instead of God our Father." What amounts to political indoctrination in the name of the earth should be no less offensive to parents who are not religious.

Moreover, eco-spirituality has, as noted earlier, deformed the policy debate over conservation. Most Americans believe in striking a balance between environmental protection and economic growth: they desire clean air and water, but want to achieve those results through the most economical and efficient means possible. Unfortunately, this is not the kind of policy that the system is delivering.

First, officials across the political spectrum, and across national boundaries, have proved disturbing susceptible to apocalyptic scaremongering from those who are either ideologically or theologically predisposed to believe that the end of the world is nigh. Although the issues are complicated, there is substantial reason to believe that the threats posed by Acid Rain, the Greenhouse Effect, and Ozone depletion are much less than commonly supposed.

Moreover, current government environmental policy, even when responding to genuine problems, is incredibly costly, grotesquely inefficient, and highly politicized. In contrast, there are many market-oriented mechanisms that could deliver better ecological protection for less. Privatization, pollution taxes, permit trading, and market pricing, for instance, are among the strategies that have been advanced by numerous analysts over the years.

Yet most lobbyists and policymakers consciously ignore the myriad opportunity to improve environmental regulation. Observes Brookings Institution scholar Robert Crandall:

> The inefficiencies in most federal environmental programs are well known as the result of decades of research. But most environmentalists and their supporters in Congress appear uninterested in redesigning these programs. The new Clean Air Act looks distressingly like the old one—with the exception of the acid-rain program. The results from years of research into market-based approaches to solving environmental problems have generally been ignored. We continue to spend far too much for the environmental results we obtain.

Why is this? One reason, presumably, is simple ignorance. But another is that for the most influential activists environmentalism reflects more theological discourse rather than policy debate. The cost of particular policies is seen as irrelevant since the course of action is *morally* required. According to this line of reasoning, it is simply obscene to put a value on elephants, even if doing so, by creating a viable market for ivory, would increase the number of elephants in the long-run. Moreover, costly policies may be seen as punishment, a "desire to purge ourselves of guilt for succeeding too well in taming nature and in generating economic well-being," in Crandall's words.

These factors help explain the widespread enthusiasm for recycling. In fact, much recycling is environmentally wasteful as well as economically inefficient. Polystyrene hamburger clamshells use less energy and generate less air and water pollution to produce. Aseptic packaging requires less energy to manufacture, fill, and transport. Recycling newspaper generates toxic sludge. And so on. Yet it is very difficult to objectively examine the desirability of recycling because so many people's commitment to the process is essentially religious.

Such a perspective is as entitled as any other to join the battle in the political arena, but the new eco-pagans have generally kept their radical agenda hidden from the public. Their all-too-effective Trojan Horse is moderate rhetoric focusing on health and safety; once they've breached Congress' walls they pour forth, pushing for policies that run far beyond their publicly professed objectives. This pattern repeated itself in the most recent debate on extending the Clean Air Act.

## Eco-paganism's Spiritual Threats

The new religious environmentalism poses a more esoteric, but still serious, problem. Those who take their religious faith seriously must recognize that neo-paganism or deep ecology—essentially spiritual environmentalism, whether or not God is officially mentioned—is a separate, hostile faith that threatens to infiltrate Jewish and Christian practice and theology. Indeed, this is a goal of some. Biochemist Rupert Sheldrake admits to once viewing "Christianity, like all religion, as essentially superstitious." Today, however, he sees as "a strength of Christianity that it is grounded in an animistic experience of nature and incorporates archaic mythic themes." He goes on to urge prayer that "a new harmony develops between humanity and the living world" and lauds the fact that "Within the Christian churches, the rediscovery of God of the living world is currently taking place in several ways. One is through a revival of the animistic traditions that prevailed until the Protestant Reformation and the growth of the mechanistic theory of nature."

Others with more of a Christian gloss would infuse Christianity with pantheism or similar views. Matthew Fox appears to promote a form of monism, which denies the separation of creator and creation, veering toward Hinduism. In *Christianity Today*, Robert Brow suggests that Fox is neither a pantheist (believing that everything is God) nor an absolute monist (believing that God is the world's ultimate reality with which one wants to merge), but a modified monist: "This world view understands God as the *soul* of the world. God is part of our world but also relates *to* the world, much as we feel our own personality is in some sense distinguishable from our body. The organs of the body may feel with and react to what the person experiences, but there is hardly a personal dialogue. It is a far cry from the Christian view of a Father who wants and allows a relationship with his children."

Then there are religious environmentalists, or environmental Christians, who would stretch but, in their view, not break traditional orthodoxy while making Christian theology and churches a bit greener. For instance, Ian Bradley, a minister in the Church of Scotland and a member of the Green Party, contends that "the Christian faith is intrinsically Green, that the good news of the Gospel promises liberation and fulfillment for the whole of creation and that Christians have a positive and distinctive contribution to make to the salvation of our threatened planet and the preservation of the natural environment." He says that he argues not for "new doctrines or new theology" but instead to simply "return with a new eye and new attention to the Scriptures." He contends that men are placed on the same level as other creatures, that "human beings are generally not singled out for special treatment." He further suggests "a highly ecological slant to" the Fall (man has brought about God's punishment on creation through his misbehavior) and sees "Jesus as the cosmic Christ, the One sent by God to redeem matter as well as man."

Similar language is used by Loren Wilkinson, professor of Philosophy and integrative studies at Regent College in Vancouver. He, too, refers to Jesus as the "Cosmic Christ." Vernon Visick, a campus minister at the University of Wisconsin-Madison, contends that "Jesus provides us with an absolutely crucial method for approaching the environmental crisis." Although Visick provides few specifics, he contends that we need "new political forms" and should "integrate the best features of contemporary movements into a larger and more powerful movement."

Herman Daly and John Cobb press for what they term a theocentric rather than anthropocentric Christianity. In advancing their "biospheric vision" they cite alternative worldviews, such as Deep Ecology, which they frankly term "a religious vision." And, in their opinion, "the rise of this vision, especially through the influence of ecological and feminist sensitivities, has been one of the great advances of this generation. Only as the vision deepens and spreads is there hope for making the changes that are required."

They are particularly fond of deep ecology, though they acknowledge that its commitment to "biocentric equality" is inconsistent with Christian theism. Daly and Cobb also like the Gaia Hypothesis, though they recognize that it, too, has limitations. They go on to "rejoice in the extension of community among those of our time who have come to reaffirm community with all peoples, with other animals, with all living things, and with the whole earth." While they distinguish themselves from environmentalists who see man as no better than any other species, they acknowledge that "the gulf separating us from some forms of Christianity is as great or greater than what differentiates our form of biospheric perspective from others."

Finally, Jay McDaniel presses for both "a biocentric way of thinking about God" and "a biocentric spirituality." As he explains:

A biocentric spirituality can recognize and value these traditional Christian sensitivities, and it can partake of the various disciplines— meditation, prayer, fasting, study, simplicity, solitude, service, and worship—that nurture them. In addition, however, it will emphasize three modes of awareness that directly pertain to our interactions with nonhuman nature. These are (1) a feeling for the organism, (2) a feeling for matrices, and (3) an awareness of what Buddhists call "Emptiness" as an enrichment of the first two feelings.

He also proposes "A postpatriarchal Christianity" and cites the work of, among others, Rosemary Ruether, whose theology is less than orthodox. In particular, he suggests "value-pluralistic thinking," instead of Christianity's past resistance to "the acceptance of a plurality of life paths, a diversity of life orientations, a variety of life-styles."

And these proposals are having an effect, as some churches acquiesce in and ultimately accept doctrines contrary to the basic tenets of their faiths. According to Berit Kjos, for instance, the School of Theology at Claremont reacted positively to a proposal to incorporate witchcraft rituals from Starhawk's book in a theology course. In the interests of ecumenicism the World Council of Churches included ceremonies that seemed frankly paganistic. Even the North American Conference on Christianity and Ecology, which split from the North American Conference on Religion and Ecology after the latter decided to include Buddhism and Hinduism, has at its conferences materials from Matthew Fox and similar thinkers. Moreover, as part of their celebrations of Earth Day a number of churches incorporated elements of earth and goddess worship. Warns Donald Bloesch of Dubuque Theological Seminary, there is a spiritual renaissance in many churches and seminaries, but one which "represents a kind of naturalistic mysticism, a reemergence of the ancient religion of the Earth Mother."

Indeed, in its fundamentals ecospirituality will inevitably conflict with orthodox Judaism and Christianity. "People have wanted an ecological religion that is evolutionary and global; the sort of religion able to replace Christmas Day with Earth Day," warns Tal Brooke of the SCP Foundation. "Now is the opportune moment for a planetary faith that divinizes the earth. Ecology becomes a sacrament, while shamanism, pantheism, and science form its foundations."

## Conclusion

Simple protection of the environment does not threaten Americans' religious beliefs or economic prosperity. Worship of the environment does. Unfortunately, however, environmentalism is increasingly taking on the trappings of a separate religion, with a consequent distortion of both traditional Jewish and Christian religious practices. Even the more orthodox religious greens are misguided if well-intentioned. Though rightly concerned about the environment, they tend to advance policies antithetical to the proper environmental balance required by Scripture. The popular command-and-control regulatory remedies, for instance, tend to only poorly protect the environment while wasting money— reducing the resources available to meet a variety of other pressing human needs—and slighting the very real human interest in responsible economic growth. Greater reliance on property rights and free markets, in contrast, would better establish institutions that incorporate both benefits and costs and hold parties accountable for their actions. As a result, this approach would more effectively force even nonbelievers to act as stewards, using rather than misusing God's creation.

Nonbelievers, too, have a stake in disentangling environmentalism from paganism. After all, they would also benefit from policies that delivered better ecological protection for less money. More fundamentally, since they are going to have to help pay the upwards of $40 billion extra annually for the new Clean Air Act on top of the $150 billion already spent annually to comply with environmental regulation, they should have a say not only on what policies they are paying for, but what spiritual theories they are in effect subsidizing. Indeed, if the First Amendment bars government assistance for traditional churches, perhaps the American people should use it to prohibit turning the new wilderness cathedrals into an established religion.

January 1993

# 9

# Environmentalism: The Triumph of Politics

President Bill Clinton's commitment to an activist environmental agenda is apparent in his appointment of Carol Browner, head of Florida's Department of Environmental Regulation, to run the Environmental Protection Agency. She is, warns one Florida businessman, in favor of "very rigorous environmental regulation."

The problem is not that Browner favors conservation, but that she, despite her pronouncments to the contrary, seems likely to promote the sort of politicized, command-and-control regulation that is responsible for today's upwards of $150 billion in annual compliance costs, as well as the $40 or so billion in added expenses likely to come from full implementation of the Clean Air Act. Unfortunately, these big bills do not translate into better protection.

But the American people can be forgiven for thinking that regulation automatically translates into protection. After all, during his 1988 race for president George Bush pledged that, if elected, he would be the "environmental president." And in 1992 he constantly cited his approval of the mind-numbingly complex, 800-page Clean Air Act reauthorization legislation as one of his chief accomplishments.

There's no doubt that the environment makes for good politics. Eight of ten Americans call themselves environmentalists. Overwhelming majorities say that gasoline should be less polluting, cars should be more efficient, trash should be recycled, and lifestyles should be changed.

This increasing sensitivity is reflected in business' growing emphasis on environmental products. Such catalogues as Real Goods, Seventh Generation, and Earth Care Paper offer recycled paper, vegetable-based dishwashing liquid, battery chargers, and fluorescent light bulbs. Even many mainstream firms are labeling their products CFC-free, biode-

75

gradable, and environmentally friendly. While the environmental benefits of these activities are unclear, they apparently help sell products.

Increasing numbers of people are taking an interest in environmental issues in part in response to their own concerns and in part in response to social pressure—including from their children. The schools have launched what would be called indoctrination programs for a less worthy goal. And the campaign seems to be working: *The New York Times* ran one story about parents who were relieved when their children went off to camp so they could again use styrofoam cups and toss out used plastic.

The law is also playing a greater role in people's lives. An unaccountable bureaucracy in Southern California, for instance, proposed banning use of lighter fluid for barbeques and prohibiting drive-in facilities. Federal agencies have essentially seized control of millions of acres of land arbitrarily designated as wetlands. And the Washington, D.C. suburb of Takoma Park employs what it euphemistically calls "recycling coordinators" to comb through people's trash and hand out tickets—with fines ranging up to $500—for not properly sorting garbage.

In the abstract, greater attention to environmental issues would seem to be a positive trend. After all, no one wants to breath polluted air. No one wants to visit an Everglades that is dying or see Yellowstone's Old Faithful replaced by condominiums. And who could not be concerned about the possibility of a warming environment, threatening ozone holes, and the spectre of "acid" rain?

The problem, however, is that the environment has become a hostage to politics. Many environmental activists want more than a clean environment. Their commitment to conservation is almost religious, and their goals are often far-reaching: to transform what they consider to be a sick, greedy, and wasteful consumer society. As a result, many otherwise well-meaning people have proved quite willing to use state power to force potentially draconian social changes irrespective of numerous important alternative values, including freedom, health, and prosperity.

The real political divide is not between right and left, conservative and liberal, or Republican and Democrat. Rather, it is between market process and central planning, market mechanism and command and control. Most politicians believe in government solutions. They may not be consistent in the specific ways they want the state to intervene. But they like government involvement. Although liberal enthusiasm for state action is best known, conservatives, too, often want government to arbitrarily rearrange environmental outcomes. There are no more fervent supporters of irrigation projects that deliver below-cost water to farmers, subsidies to promote logging on public lands, and cut-rate range fees on federal grazing land for ranchers than Republican legislators. Conservative Western Senators have fervently opposed selling off federal lands. In cases like these free market supporters and taxpayer advocates are aligned with left-leaning environmentalists versus centrist politicians of both parties.

## Where Do We Stand?

Much of today's support for new environmental restrictions comes from the perception that the sky is falling. In the view of Lester Brown of Worldwatch, for instance, we're in a "battle to save the earth's environmental support systems." He worries about global warming, growing populations, disappearing species, expanding deserts, depleting top soil, and so on. We face "the wholesale collapse of ecosystems," he claims.

Yet somehow the world seems rather less bleak than he suggests. Between 1970 and 1986, for instance, the amount of particulates spewed into the air fell by 64 percent, Carbon Monoxide emissions dropped 38 percent, and releases of volatile organic compounds fell by 29 percent. Ocean dumping of industrial wastes was reduced 94 percent. There were 80 percent fewer cities without adequate sewage treatment plants. Rivers unfit for swimming dropped 44 percent. Hazardous waste sites such as Love Canal and Times Beach now appear far less dangerous than once thought. Cars built in 1988 produced 96 percent less Carbon Monoxide and hydrocarbons than those made in the early 1980s. Population continues to grow sharply in some Third World states, but these increases reflect lower infant mortality rates and longer life expectancies. Total recoverable world oil reserves grew by 400 billion barrels between 1985 and 1990. Global warming trends have primarily been evident at night, which may lengthen growing seasons. And extensive product packaging, derided as wasteful, makes Americans among the most efficient eaters on earth.

The point is not that there are no environmental problems. But claims of imminent disaster are simply not supported by the facts. To the contrary, they reflect the politicization of the environment, because only claims of imminent disaster can galvanize popular support for the sort of draconian policy changes advocated by many people for ideological—or even religious—reasons. Some of environmental apocalyptics have admitted as much.

Politics has infected environmental policymaking in two different ways. The first is to create real environmental problems. The second is to generate unfounded hysteria.

### Poor Environmental Stewardship

For all of the enthusiasm of environmentalists for government programs, the government has proved to be a remarkably poor steward of the resources. Consider Uncle Sam's 191 million acres of forestland. The Wilderness Society estimates that losses on federal timberland amounted to $400 million annually during the 1980s, while losses on Alaska's Tsongass rain forest have hit 99 cents on the dollar. The problem is that the government both undertakes expensive investments, such as road-building in mountainous wilderness terrain, and underprices the timber that is produced. Washington's reason for doing so is to "create" a few jobs. The cost, however, is both needless environmental destruction and the squandering of taxpayers' money.

Federal water projects and management of rangeland have consistently led to similar results. The government has expended billions of dollars to subsidize such influential groups as farmers and ranchers, all the while leaving environmental despoilation in its wake. In fact, the greatest threat to wetlands across the country is not private development, but federal efforts like the $1.2 billion Garrison Diversion project, which destroyed some 70,000 acres of wetlands to benefit a few thousand farmers.

Nearly 90 percent of all federal water in the West is sold at heavily subsidized prices to heavily subsidized farmers. In California's San Joaquin Valley, for instance, irrigation projects typically cost $300–$500 an acre foot yet the water is marketed to farmers for less than a tenth that much—even when Los Angeles and other parts of the state were suffering from severe water shortages. Only the government would subsidize the production of a water-intensive crop like rice in a desert.

Washington similarly mismanages its 307 million acres of rangeland. The Bureau of Land Management has typically charged ranchers half of what it costs to administer federal land, and up to one-tenth the rental price for comparable private lands. The BLM also spent millions of dollars "chaining" land—literally ripping out trees—to create more rangeland on which it would lose more money. Not surprisingly, federal lands are generally in poor condition—and continue to generate a flood of red ink.

It is not just Uncle Sam who is to blame. Local governments have distorted the trash market, leading to pressure for a federal garbage law. Many localities have essentially socialized trash collection and disposal, barring any private competition to increase industry efficiency and innovativeness. Moreover, few cities charge citizens based upon how much garbage they generate, providing no incentive for people to either recycle or change their buying habits. (Localities that have implemented per bag or can fees have made people more environmentally conscious without a trash Gestapo.) Political restrictions on the placement of new landfills and construction of incinerators, both of which are quite safe with new technologies, have exacerbated the problem.

But the U.S. government is the most culpable party. World Bank loans, underwritten by American taxpayers, have financed the destruction of Brazilian rain forests; federally-subsidized flood insurance has encouraged uneconomic construction on the environmentally sensitive Barrier Islands. Years of energy price controls inflamed demand and discouraged conservation. And so on.

This sort of special-interest driven environmental abuse is not new, and the only solution is to eliminate the political malfeasance. Unfortunately, as Public Choice economists have so effectively pointed out, the political process tends to be biased towards taxpayer exploitation and against sound policy.

## Unnecessary Hysteria

The second form of environmental politicization is more recent. That is the manufacture of false crises and the exaggeration of more limited problems to achieve other ideological ends, like the banning of chemicals, closure of incineration plants, and elimination of CFCs. Unfortunately, examples of this sort of problem now abound.

For instance, in 1989 the Natural Resources Defense Council used a public relations agency to launch a campaign against the chemical Alar, a pesticide used on some 15 percent of apples in the U.S. The charges received wide attention and demand for apples dropped dramatically—as a result, prices fell almost in half, ruining some farmers. Yet the furor was based on one 1973 study, where mice were fed very high levels of Alar. Two recent reviews, by Great Britain's Advisory Committee on Pesticides and the California Department of Food and Agriculture, concluded that the risk of ingesting Alar was minimal. As Dr. Joseph Rosen of Rutgers explained, "There was never any legitimate scientific study to justify the Alar scare."

But skillful manipulation of the media to inflame people's fears—and the enlistment of such knowledgeable environmental experts as Hollywood's Meryl Streep—enabled one activist group to create a crisis. The NRDC's PR agent later circulated a memo to other organizations describing his efforts.

Indeed, pesticides have long been subject to counter-factual demagogic attacks. Natural pesticides, nature's way of protecting plants, may cause cancer and they occur in far higher quantities in at least 57 food varieties than do man-made pesticides. All told, a Natural Center for Policy Analysis study estimates that the risk of getting cancer from choloroform in tap water is greater than that of getting it from pesticides in food. And one is more than three times as likely to be killed by lightning than to contract cancer from pesticides. The risk of cancer from all pesticides residue in food consumed by the average person in a day is one-twentieth that from the natural carcinogens in a single cup of coffee.

Another apocalyptic vision emerged from the EPA, which in 1980 claimed that Acid Rain, caused by Sulfur Dioxide emissions, had increased the average acidity of Northeast lakes 100-fold over the last forty years and was killing fish and trees alike. A year later the National Research Council predicted that the number of acidified lakes would double by 1990. So naturally Congress included stringent provisions to cut $SO_2$ emissions (already down 50 percent from the 1970s) at a cost of billions of dollars annually when it reauthorized the Clean Air Act three years ago (1990).

Yet in 1987 EPA research raised doubts about the destructiveness of acid rain: a congressional firestorm forced the study's director to quit. Then came the most complete study of Acid Rain ever conducted, the half billion dollar National Acid Precipitation Assessment Project (NAPAP), which concluded that the allegedly horrific effects of Acid Rain were largely a myth. Among other things, the study found that lakes were on average no more acidic than before the industrial era; just 240 of 7000 Northeast lakes, most with little recreational value, were critically acidic, or "dead"; most of the acidic water was in Florida, where the rain is only one-third as acidic; there was only very limited damage to trees, far less than that evident elsewhere in the world where $SO_2$ emissions are minimal; half of the Adirondeck lakes were acidified due to natural organic acids; and crops remained undamaged at acidic levels ten times present levels. In the end, NAPAP's scientists figured that liming the few lakes that were acidic would solve the problem at a mere fraction of the cost of the Clean Air Act's Acid Rain provisions.

Perhaps the most famous form of the "sky is falling" claim today is global warming—the so-called Greenhouse Effect. The U.N.'s Rio summit focused on this issue. The fear is that pollution, particularly such "greenhouse gases" as Carbon Dioxide, will stay within the atmosphere, leading to a rise in the earth's temperature, which will create deserts, melt the polar icecaps, and flood coastal nations.

In fact, warnings of global warming are not new: the theory was first advanced in the 1890s and reemerged in the 1950s. But soon thereafter a new theory soon gained sway—that we were entering a new Ice Age. In 1974 the U.S. National Science Board stated that "during the last 20 to 30 years, world temperature has fallen, irregularly at first but more sharply over the last decade." In the same year, *Time* magazine opined that "the atmosphere has been growing gradually cooler for the past three decades. The trend shows no indication of reversing." Similarly, observed Dr. Murray Mitchell of the National Oceanic and Atmospheric Administration in 1976, "Since about 1940 there has been a distinct drop in average global temperature. It's fallen about half a degree Fahrenheit."

Five years later Fred Hoyle's *Ice: The Ultimate Human Catastrophe* appeared, warning that a new Ice Age was long overdue, and "when the ice comes, most of northern America, Britain, and northern Europe will disappear under the glaciers.... The right conditions can arise within a single decade." He advocated warming the oceans to forestall this "ultimate human catastrophe." Another two years passed and *Rolling Stone* magazine declared that

For years now, climatologists have foreseen a trend toward colder weather—long range, to be sure, but a trend as inevitable as death.... According to [one] theory, all it would take is a single cold summer to plunge the earth into a sudden apocalyse of ice.

A decade later we have passed into a new crisis. Climatologists like Stephen Schneider, who two decades ago was warning of a cooling trend that looked like "one akin to the Little Ice Age," now berates the media for covering scientists who are skeptical of claims that global warming is occurring. He is, at least, refreshingly honest, admitting that "to avert the risk we need to get some broad-based support, to capture public imagination.... So we have to offer up some scary scenarios, make some simplified dramatic statements and little mention of any doubts one might have."

And he does this precisely because the doubts about global warming are serious, so serious that publications like the *Washington Post* and *Newsweek* have run stories debunking the apocalytic predictions of everyone from Vice-President Gore to Greenpeace. Observed the *Post*: "Scientists generally agree that it has been getting warmer over the last hundred years, but the average rate of change is no greater than in centuries past, and there is no consensus that human activity is the cause. And while there is no doubt that continued emissions of 'greenhouse gases' tend to aid warming, it is not clear that cutting back on emissions could do much to stop a natural trend, if that is what is happening." Indeed, a survey by Greenpeace, one of the most radical environmental organizations, of scientists involved in the Intergovernmental Panel on Climate Change found that only 13 percent of them believed there was probably a point-of-no-return in the future leading to a runaway greenhouse effect. Just 17 percent of climatologists in a broader Gallup poll believed that human-induced warming had occurred at all, while 53 percent did not.

The problems with the theory are many. First, there is no reason to assume that any change in temperature is undesirable. In fact, peoples living in colder climates would benefit from small increases; higher temperatures at night also would likely have a positive impact.

Second, the evidence does not support the contention that human activity is raising temperatures. We have seen slight warming over the last century, but 90 percent of it occurred before 1940, when greenhouse gas emissions started rising dramatically. The models suggest that daytime temperatures should rise in the Northern Hemisphere, but most of the limited warming so far observed has occurred at night in the Southern Hemisphere. The ice caps have been growing, not shrinking. And so on. Even those predicting a much hotter future have had to lower their forecasts over the last decade. In the end, it is obvious both that mankind, which accounts for just a couple percent of the atmosphere's $CO_2$, has only a limited impact on the earth's climate, and that the globe has a dramatic ability to adjust. For instance, increased pollution may help shield the earth from sunlight, counteracting any temperature increase. Higher temperatures at the poles actually allow more precipitation. Since serious warming could cause serious damage, there is cause to monitor changes in climate, but not yet to implement the sort of draconian changes demanded by the Greenhouse crowd.

The ozone issue has been similarly politicized. The fear is that chlorofluorocarbons (CFC's) are thinning atmospheric ozone, allowing in more ultraviolet (UV) rays. In January 1992 a Harvard University chemist, James Anderson, held a press conference warning of a "hole" in the ozone in the so-called polar vortex, the upper atmosphere over New England and Canada. His claims were based on the initial findings from a scientific expedition monitoring atmospheric conditions and received wide attention. Yet four months later he was forced to admit that "the dreaded ozone hole never materialized."

A decade ago apocalyptic environmentalists were warning of a reduction of 18 percent in ozone levels. Today the predictions are down to two to four percent. Even if these forecasts are borne out, the impact may not be dramatic: it would be like moving roughly 60 miles south, from Palm Beach to Miami in Florida. And, oddly, UV radiation levels have dropped over the last decade, even as the ozone layer was supposedly thinning. Moreover, there is some question as to whether CFC's—inexpensive, safe chemicals that have no obvious replacement—are really villainous destroyers of ozone after other factors are taken into account. Such things as ocean salt spray, for instance, may help counteract increasing CFC levels. Explains Dr. Melvyn Shapiro of the National Oceanic and Atmospheric Administration, in making their claims even many atmospheric chemists "have little regard for the impact of atmospheric variability on chemical processes." In fact, the higher levels of chlorine monoxide detected in early 1992 did not create an ozone hole because temperatures were higher than expected.

Population growth has been cited as an impending disaster for nearly two centuries, starting most dramatically with Thomas Malthus' 1798 *An Essay on the Principle of Population*. His philosophical descendents today include Paul Ehrlich of Stanford, who predicted mass famine and death in the 1970s; Worldwatch's Lester Brown, who believes that entire ecosystems are collapsing; and former World Bank President Robert McNamara, who went so far as to compare the threat of population pressure to that of nuclear war.

The argument is simple: more people means the use of more resources and creates more waste. The end result is lower incomes and disaster.

This apocalyptic scenario ignores the fact that some part of the population "explosion" is short-term, since infant mortality rates have fallen more swiftly than have fertility rates. Moreover, people normally produce more than they consume—otherwise even one person would be too many. Further, fears of population growth assume a static view of the world, that economics is a zero sum game. Yet the market naturally adjusts as the number of people and demand for goods and services increase; technological innovation and behaviorial changes work together to allow better and more efficient resource use.

In practice we see no relationship between population, population density, and economic growth. Population density is very high in such places as Hong Kong, Singapore, and Taiwan, yet their economic growth has grown similarly. The Netherlands is 50 percent denser than India, Great Britain is twice as dense as Thailand, and South Korea possesses less territory but twice the population of the North. In all of these cases the more populated state has achieved much higher levels of development.

The issue of population growth, then, is really not one of population growth, but adaptation to population growth. If adaptation to growth is blocked, then growth appears to be a problem. The most important means of adaptation is through the marketplace—if governments prevent people from being entrepreneurial, freely producing goods and services, charging prices that reflect changing resource values, and responding to changing human needs, then worsening poverty will result. Third World states are impoverished not because they are populous, but because they have adopted largely *dirigiste* economic strategies.

Related to the supposed problem of too many people is that of too few resources. Such reports as the Club of Rome's 1972 *Limits to Growth* and the Carter Administration's 1980 *Global 2000* predicted that we would soon run out of key resources. Indeed, much of the Carter energy program was predicated on the assumption that we would soon run out of fossil fuels. (Almost since oil was first discovered in the U.S. last century people have been predicting that America's petroleum reserves faced near immediate depletion.)

The Club of Rome, which foresaw the imminent exhaustion of such resources as gold, lead, and zinc, has already been proved wrong. Even more significant, however, is the fact that real resource prices fell consistently throughout the 1980s. According to the Cato Institute's Stephen Moore, in a study for the Institute for Policy Innovation, "of 38 natural resources examined in this study, 34 declined in real price" between 1980 and 1990. Prices for two remained constant, while only the cost of Manganese and Zinc rose. Moore found that American and international prices of food, energy, timber, and minerals all fell.

Again, the doomsayers have ignored the powerful adjustment process that occurs through the marketplace. As goods become scarcer, prices rise, encouraging entrepreneurs to locate new supplies, manufacture synthetic equivalents, find substitutes, use products more efficiently, and reduce consumption. As long as prices can rise freely, the market will ensure that catastrophic shortages will not occur.

Apocalyptic predictions regarding a number of other issues, such as toxic wastes and desertification, have proved to be equally flawed. The point is not that there are no environmental problems, but rather, that environmental issues tend to be quite complex and that one makes long-run assumptions based on short-term risks at great risk. Unfortunately, many activists are willing to distort the facts because they have either ideological or even quasi-religious reasons for believing disaster is imminent.

The environment has become as much a spiritual as a political issue for even many people of mainstream religious faiths. Some environmentalists go far further, turning ecology into a separate religion by mixing traditional pantheism and more modern forms of earth worship. Many other environmentalists have radical philosophical rather than theological agendas. Most of these activists are implicitly anti-capitalist, anti-profit, and, frankly, anti-freedom, since it is people acting freely that leads, to what conservationists commonly view as consumerism, greed, pollution, and waste. In fact, it has been jokingly said that the only remaining socialists in the world are in the environmental movement, since they are promoting a centrally-planned system based on government command-and-control regulation.

The problem is not so much the motives of such activists, but the fact that their ideological biases lead them to ignore evidence questioning the genuineness of alleged environmental problems and refuse to make trade-offs in drafting solutions to real concerns. While a doctrinal environmentalist might be happy with the policy result for religious or philosophical reasons, it is foolish for the rest of us to waste resources on non-problems and on unnecessarily inefficient clean-up strategies.

## Conclusion

Environmental protection is important, and good people can disagree on the best policies to adopt. But today the public discussion over conservation is being distorted by politics, making the American public poorer and less free and the environment dirtier. In approaching environmental issues in the future policymakers should act on facts and balance several different values and interests. Policy results should be based more on prudence than ideology. How do we do this?

First, we need to make a nonpartisan assessment of the problem. Is the globe warming? The question should be answered before we embark on a costly crusade to slow down economic growth around the world. Imagine if the government had acted on Fred Hoyle's proposal to warm the oceans in order to forestall a new ice age. It is as irresponsible to act without sufficient cause as to refuse to act in the face of clear evidence.

Second, we need to eschew ideological or de facto theological dogmas. Recycling, for instance, is often treated as an unchallengeable good because it is essentially viewed as an "act of religious contrition," in the words of John Baden of the Foundation for Research on Economics and the Environment. Yet fervent recyclers may be hurting the environment. For instance, though polystyrene clamshells for hamburgers are not recyclable like paperboard containers, their production uses 30 percent less energy and generates 46 percent less air pollution and 42 percent less water pollution. Aseptic packages cannot be recycled, but they allow the storage of milk without refrigeration, use one-third as much energy to make, one-half as much energy to fill, and one-fifteenth as much energy to transport as glass containers.

Third, we need to be honest about the tradeoffs involved. Cost does matter, for instance, if for no other reason than the fact that a wealthier society is more capable of protecting the environment. Years ago the EPA considered setting standards around a smelter in order to protect a hypothetical asthmatic jogger. While there would be some marginal benefits in doing so, such a policy would be socially wasteful since the money expended to comply could be better used for any number of more important purposes. Personal liberty, too, is of great value and should not be reflexively sacrificed for one or another environmental goal.

Fourth, we need to be skeptical of government solutions and recognize the opportunities to rely on market forces. Political agencies have consistently proved to be poor stewards of resources. And the government's power to do harm is far more vast than that of any landowner, who has control only of his own property. At the same time, entrepreneurs and businessmen have an economic incentive to care about the residual value of their property and promote environmental amenities, such as the timber firms that develop their wildlife populations in order to offer permit hunting. There are problems, like the Los Angeles Basin, where environmental problems require some government action. But we need to rethink today's assumption that the public sector must always act first, preempting any private solutions.

Fifth, we need to look for private strategies to protect the environment. Privatizing federal timber and range land, for instance, would end subsidized development, since no private individual or company would willingly turn a dollar investment into a few cents in revenue. Establishing full private property rights in water would help conserve this precious resource in the western U.S. Creating a market for ivory, as have such nations as Botswana, Zimbabwe, and South Africa, would better preserve elephants than outlawing the ivory trade, the strategy of Kenya and other states with declining elephant herds.

Sixth, where the state must intervene, we need to develop cost-effective means of advancing conservation. Setting overall emission levels and allowing the trading of permits, or imposing pollution taxes based upon emissions, would be more effective in reducing air pollution than present policies while saving billions of dollars annually. Taxing cars based on their emissions would be a far better means of reducing auto-generated pollution than imposing ever more draconian standards on new vehicles.

In short, we need to depoliticize the environment, making the issue one of balancing competing interests rather than imposing ideological or religious dogmas. If we succeed in doing so, we will end up with not only a cleaner society, but also a wealthier and freer one.

September 1993

# IV

# Republic or Empire: The New Wilsonism

# 10

# Keep the Troops and the Money at Home

We are living in exciting times, a world of dramatic change. Who would have believed, when George Bush was elected president, that a year later the Berlin Wall would fall? That noncommunist governments would take power throughout Eastern Europe, Germany would reunite, and the U.S.S.R. would disintegrate? That the menace of aggressive Soviet communism would disappear? That the chairman of the Joint Chiefs of Staff would soon admit "I'm running out of villains. I'm down to Castro and Kill Il Sung."

In this new world we need to reconsider the interventionist stance that has dominated U.S. foreign policy for nearly five decades. The United States will be a global power irrespective of official government policy, but we must still answer the question: What kind of power is it to be? Should it continue to seek global hegemony, or should it go back to being, in Jeane Kirkpatrick's words, a "normal country"?

## The Interventionist Outlook

The American military is today spread around the globe. President Clinton says that 100,000 U.S. troops in Europe is the minimum required, despite the disappearance of any credible threat to the West and the ability of the prosperous European community—which includes two nuclear powers, Britain and France—to deter a resurgent Russia in the future. Indeed, President Bush went so far as to state that he did not foresee the arrival of the "utopian day" when all of America's soldiers might come home for perhaps another hundred years.

The Clinton administration, again following the lead of its predecessor, also seems committed to retaining at least 100,000 soldiers in East

Asia. Japan is the world's second-ranking economic power and faces no serious military threats: nevertheless, Tokyo is, apparently, to continue as an American defense dependent indefinitely. South Korea possesses 12 times the GNP and twice the population of communist North Korea, yet the president suggests that U.S. troops will remain so long as Seoul wants them, which could be forever.

And many would like to further expand America's role as global policeman. After a mercifully short war in the Persian Gulf, the United States remains entangled in Kuwait, Saudi Arabia, and the affairs of Iraq's Kurds, risking a long-term presence in one of the world's most volatile regions. Bulgaria, the Czech Republic, Hungary, and Poland all want U.S. defense guarantees, preferably through formal membership in NATO. America is enmeshed in Somalia and has threatened to intervene in the Balkans. Some also pressed for involvement in Liberia's three-sided civil war to bring peace and against Haiti's military regime to bring democracy. Others write of America's obligation to guarantee Taiwan's security, prevent North Korea, Iran, and others from building weapons of mass destruction, and wage low-intensity conflicts around the world—in Latin America, Asia, the Middle East, and Africa. And columnist Ben Wattenberg wants the United States to continue to build weapons simply to remain "Number One."

Moreover, the United States continues to provide money to virtually every Third World country through a variety of national and international bodies. The UN is one of these bodies, and the Bush and Clinton administrations successively have pressed Congress to make up past arrearages that accumulated as a result of congressional resentment over the way the United Nations was taking advantage of America's status as the body's largest funder.

Ronald Reagan, despite his conservative reputation, repeatedly pushed through funding increases for multilateral development institutions, including the International Monetary Fund (IMF), the International Development Association, the World Bank, and the African Development Bank. President Bush agreed to a 50 percent hike in the International Monetary Fund's resources, as well as the creation of the European Bank for Reconstruction and Development. The Clinton administration has pressed for expansive aid to Russia and creation of a North American Development Bank. And Washington, despite supposed budget stringency, will spend $12 billion annually on foreign aid in coming years.

This money goes to leftist dictators, socialist planners, and a host of nonpartisan, garden variety thugs, all in the name of advancing America's interests.

Obviously, some advocates of military intervention oppose much of the current foreign aid program, just as some supporters of foreign aid oppose military intervention. But most believers in an expansive American presence abroad—including the president, secretary of state, and leading legislators, analysts, and columnists—are equally avid supporters of both forms of intervention. Indeed, while military involvement has the most dramatic impact, financial assistance is the most pervasive form of Washington's foreign activity.

Given the expansiveness of the U.S. role abroad, it is time to ask: Is there anything for which the American people are not forced to pay? Is there anything for which young Americans are not expected to die?

## Justification of Foreign Policy

To answer these questions, one must first decide on the purpose of the national government. Alas, rarely is this issue even addressed. The current administration speaks of a foreign policy of "enlargement," hyper-internationalists cite the alleged need to spread democracy and enforce peace, and unreformed Cold Warriors warn of new enemies and threats requiring a military as large as that which successfully contained the Soviet Union. None consider whether their grand designs are consistent with America's organization of government, however.

What are the primary duties of the U.S. government? The first is to safeguard the country's security, in order to protect citizens' lives and property. (The federal government also has some obligation to attempt to protect American citizens traveling abroad, but ultimately those who do business outside the U.S. must voluntarily incur the risks of doing so. Thus, the formal justification for the United States's entry into World War I—to preserve the right of Americans to travel on armed belligerent merchantmen carrying munitions through declared submarine zones— was frankly absurd.) The second primary duty of the government is to preserve the constitutional system and liberties that make America so unique and worth living in. Every foreign policy action should be consistent with these two functions, and there are no higher goals for the president, legislators, and other officials.

This is not, of course, to say that there are no other important ideals in life. For instance, the Apostle John wrote in his first epistle that "This is how we know what love is: Jesus Christ laid down his life for us. And we ought to lay down our lives for our brothers." But moral duties that apply to individuals are very different from the obligations and authority of the civil institutions that govern all. The Apostle John did not suggest that we should force our neighbors—indeed, everyone in our entire country—to lay down their lives for others.

Yet many people no longer perceive any moral dimension to taxing and drafting others to implement the government's policies. Joshua Muravchik of the American Enterprise Institute, for instance, sees no problem in promoting "common purposes" so long as such actions "don't involve curtailing the rights of our own citizens, but involve only taxing them." Yet both taxation and conscription, the policy used for years to man Washington's extensive overseas commitments, certainly "involve curtailing the rights of our own citizens." An activist foreign and military policy should therefore require a justification that is important enough to warrant circumscribing, often severely, people's freedom.

## A Foreign Policy of Higher Principles?

Advocates of an interventionist foreign policy have, of course, advanced many lofty justifications for their policy: To promote democracy. To ensure stability. To protect human rights. To stop aggression. To enforce international law and order. To create a new world order. And on and on. Such appeals to higher principles and values are very seductive. Suggesting that foreign policy should be based on the promotion of the national interest sounds decidedly cold and selfish in comparison.

The moral goals articulated by many interventionists are important, but we should have no illusions about the ability of the U.S. government to promote, let alone impose, them. Furthermore, recourse to such principles is often simply a rationalization for pursuing strategic or political ends. A cursory survey of activist foreign policy decisions ostensibly taken in the name of higher moral principles reveals ample evidence of both näivete and sophistry.

For instance, in 1990 policy makers in Washington proclaimed their love of democracy and the free market, but years later there is still little sign of reform in Kuwait City, "liberated" during the Gulf War; American troops fought to make the Middle East safe for a monarchy that has largely evaded its promises of greater domestic freedom. Despite its professed ideals, the United States used its military to prop up authoritarian regimes in Korea and Vietnam. In two world wars, it cultivated grand alliances with, respectively, an authoritarian Russia (although by the time the United States officially declared war, the tsar had been overthrown) and a totalitarian U.S.S.R. It viewed its bases in and defense treaty with the Philippines as equally important during the presidencies of Marcos and Aquino.

Washington has used financial intervention in the same way, creating, for instance, the Export-Import Bank in 1934 to underwrite private exports to the U.S.S.R., then ruled by the bloodiest dictator to arise in history. More recently, this institution funded Nicolae Ceausescu of Romania, bizarre even by communist standards, and continues to subsidize virtually every authoritarian regime to come along. The United Nations Development Program has undertaken projects in North Korea; the World Bank is again lending to China. Mengistu's murderous Ethiopia was a client of the IMF as well as the Bank. The list goes on and on.

Not only has America's intervention often been motivated by factors other than disinterested selflessness, but Washington has equally often bungled the job. Financial assistance to a host of Third World autocracies has strengthened the enemies of freedom and democracy. Aid and support tied the United States to failing dictatorships in Iran and Nicaragua; their respective collapses resulted in neither democracy nor allies. America's entry into World War I to promote a utopian world order had perhaps the most disastrous consequences of any international meddling by any state ever; by allowing the allies to dictate an unequal and unstable peace, it sowed the seeds of this planet's worst conflagration, which bloomed just two decades later.

Even more important than the question of Washington's sincerity and realism in promoting higher principles in its foreign policy is the question of cost. How much money—and how many lives—are we prepared to sacrifice to bring American principles to other countries? The price of restoring Kuwait's sovereignty proved surprisingly cheap, but nothing guaranteed the paucity of U.S. and allied casualties. Although they refused to discuss specific casualty estimates in advance, U.S. commanders engaged in hostilities fully expected a casualty figure many times greater. How many American lives did policy makers think Kuwait's liberation would have been worth? Five thousand lives? Fifty thousand lives? And, even if Iraq was the aggressor, the deaths of tens or even hundreds of thousands of Iraqis, many of them either civilians or military conscripts, must also be recognized as a very real cost of U.S. intervention.

How many body bags per foreign life saved would make intervention elsewhere worthwhile? Why did Iraq's earlier brutal assaults on its Kurdish minority not warrant war? How about Syria's depredations in Lebanon? China's swallowing of Tibet? The war between India and Pakistan? Or Pol Pot's mass murder in Cambodia?

If young American males—and now females—are born to give their lives overseas to forestall aggression, protect human rights, and uphold a new world order, should not the United States have gone to war to unseat the two dictators who (unlike say, Ho Chi Minh, Saddam Hussein, and Slobodan Milosevic) truly were the moral equivalent of Hitler—Stalin and Mao? Why was protecting human rights in these instances not worth war? If the answer is that the cost would have been too great, then those who attempt to make moral distinctions between sacrificing 58,000 Americans for Vietnam but refusing to offer up some unspecified larger number to free more than one billion Chinese need to explain their methodology—unless, of course, they believe that the U.S. really should have ignited World War III in the name of some new world order.

In fact, the United States did not intervene to liberate the two largest communist states because doing so was not perceived to be in America's interest, owing to the catastrophic costs that such actions surely would have entailed. For all the idealism embodied in the moral explanations for U.S. behavior, American intervention is usually animated by a general sense of realpolitik.

In the case of the Gulf War, humanitarian concerns may have eventually come to dominate President Bush's thinking. But had the initial fighting been between, say, Ethiopia and Somalia, the United States is unlikely to have intervened, just as Washington did not act when those two countries fought more than a decade before. Concerns about the regional balance of power and Iraq's growing arsenal of weapons of mass destruction were also real, but secondary; after all, the United States was prepared to leave Saddam's military strength intact had he withdrawn from Kuwait before the inauguration of hostilities. Despite President Bush's rhetoric, Washington's real interest in the Gulf was to ensure allied access to oil. Likewise, past aid to President Mobutu of Zaire can be explained only as an attempt to buy influence with a dictator who controls important natural resources. The presence of troops in South Korea is often justified by U.S. officials as giving America an advanced outpost to be used against the Soviets in the event of war.

Washington's only military intervention for truly humanitarian purposes was Somalia. But America quickly turned from famine relief to political meddling, essentially joining an ongoing civil war between rival clans. The result was to simultaneously build Somali popular support for the forces opposing the U.S. and destroy American popular support for the more humanitarian aspects of the mission.

As unsatisfactory as an emphasis on U.S. national interest may be to some, it is the only proper basis for American policy. Such an approach reflects the purpose of the United States government—to protect the security, liberty, and property of the American people—in a sense that the international pursuit of utopian ideals does not. Reasons of national interest and security are the only legitimate justification for U.S. intervention abroad.

## Weighing Costs

However, it is not enough to decide that the United States has one or more interests at stake in some foreign matter, because interests are not of unlimited value. The benefits of such objectives have to be balanced against the costs of intervention.

Perhaps the most obvious expense is financial. NATO accounts for roughly half of the entire military budget; the defense of the Pacific runs to about $40 billion. Operation Desert Shield cost $60 billion or more (although that bill was largely covered by allied states). Foreign aid adds another $12 billion annually to the deficit. All told, roughly 70 percent of America's military outlays goes to prepare for conventional wars abroad. Observes General Wallace Nutting, former commander-in chief of the U.S. Readiness Command, "We today do not have a single soldier, airman, or sailor solely dedicated to the security mission within the United States."

Our domestic freedoms also suffer as a result. World Wars I and II resulted in massive assaults on civil liberties, including the suppression of dissent and free speech, and culminated in the incarceration of more than 100,000 Japanese-Americans. Much more modest, but still unsettling, was the anti-Arab sentiment unleashed during the short war against Iraq. Moreover, a panoply of security restrictions that grew out of the cold war continues to limit our freedom.

Both wars also vastly expanded the government's economic powers. Federal spending in 1916 was just $713 million; it shot to $18.5 billion in 1919, eventually settling back to the $3 billion level throughout the 1920s, more than quadruple its prewar level. Similarly, federal outlays in 1940 were $9.5 billion. Spending increased nearly tenfold, to $92.7 billion, fell to $29.8 billion in 1948, triple prewar levels, and then began its inexorable growth upward. Observes Burton Yale Pines of the National Center for Public Policy Research, "today's mammoth federal government is the product not so much of the New Deal but of the massive power assembled in Washington to wage World War II and the Cold War." Some of the government's new regulations were never reversed: New York City, for instance, still suffers from the destructive effects of rent control, a supposedly temporary wartime measure. All told, writes Robert Higgs of Lafayette College, after World War II:

a host of legacies remained: all the government-financed plants and equipment and the military-industrial complex to continue operating them; important postwar legislation inspired by wartime practices, including the Employment Act, the Taft-Hartley Act, and the Selective Service Act of 1948; the GI Bill and the new middle class it fostered; a voracious and effective federal income-tax system; a massive foreign aid program. More importantly the war left the constitutional structure of the country deeply altered in the direction of judicial abdication and excessive autonomy; the nation no longer possessed a "peacetime Constitution" to which it could return. Most significantly the war moved the prevailing ideology markedly toward acceptance of an enlarged governmental presence in the economy. At last even the majority of businessmen had come to accept, and often to demand, Big Government.

Similarly, America's interventionist foreign policy has malformed the domestic constitutional system. We have seen both a centralization of power in the federal government and the aggrandizement of the presidency. How far we have come is reflected by the fact that serious thinkers who purport to believe in jurisprudential interpretation based on the original intent of the framers argued that the president had the unilateral authority to move more than 500,000 men and women far from home and launch a war against another sovereign state without congressional approval. While reasonable people may disagree over the exact demarcation line between presidential and congressional war-making powers, the Constitution means nothing if it does not require congressional action in this instance. And, although U.S. participation in formal United Nations forces is rather limited, it represents an even greater abrogation of Congressional authority, since the U.N. Act dispenses with the need for a declaration of war when such troops are involved.

Further, intervention has a great human cost. Woodrow Wilson's fantasies of a new world order led him to enter the mindless European slugfest of World War I, which left 116,000 young Americans dead and led inevitably to the outbreak within one generation of an even worse war, which killed another 407,000 Americans. Since the end of the Second World War, more than 112,000 young Americans have died in undeclared conflicts. It is one thing to ask young Americans to die for the U.S. Republic. It is quite another to expect them to sacrifice their lives in the interest of power-projection politics more characteristic of an empire.

Finally, intervention could one day threaten the very national survival even of the U.S. We live in a world where biological, chemical, and nuclear weapons are spreading, along with the availability of ballistic missiles. Terrorism has become a fixture of international life. With the growing ability of even small political movements and countries to kill U.S. citizens and to threaten mass destruction, the risks of foreign entanglements increase. No longer are the high costs limited to soldiers in the field. In coming years, the U.S. could conceivably lose one or more large cities to demented or irrational retaliation for American intervention. A modest SDI program would reduce these risks, but it would never be able to provide full protection.

## Considering Alternatives

How, then, should we formulate a foreign policy? Every action taken abroad should reflect the purpose for creating the U.S. government; namely, to serve the interests of American society and the people who live there. Washington's role is not to conduct glorious utopian crusades around the globe. It is not to provide a pot of cash for the secretary of state to pass out to friendly regimes to increase U.S. influence abroad. It is not to sacrifice the lives of young Americans to minimize other peoples' sufferings. In short, the money and lives of the American people do not belong to policy makers, even the president, to expend for purposes other than defending the American community.

Of course, some analysts argue that promoting moral values, particularly democracy and human rights, advances American national interests by making conflict—or at least, war—less likely. The link is tenuous, however. Indeed, in the Middle East, North Africa, and some other states, true democracy is as likely to unleash destabilizing as stabilizing forces, particularly Islamic fundamentalism. The end of the totalitarian rule that kept simmering ethnic tensions in Eastern Europe under control has already resulted in violent conflict in the Balkans: indeed, it was "democratic" decisions after free elections by Slovenia and Croatia to secede from Yugoslavia that sparked war. The best we can say is that democracies generally do not attack their neighbors.

Further, America's ability to advance democratic values is inconsistent at best. There is little that the United States can do to make Haiti a free country, for example; sustaining in power a demagogue, even an elected one, certainly will not. And Washington's policies often throw the United States's commitment to democracy into question. Foreign aid, in particular, has more often assisted authoritarian rulers than liberal forces throughout the Third World. In the absence of any direct link between important U.S. objectives and the imperative to advance democracy in a particular country, Americans' resources should not be used in this way. This would in no way preclude private groups from undertaking such efforts, just as many organizations are now active in Eastern Europe and the former Soviet Union.

Furthermore, to decide that a specific intervention is consistent with the purpose of the U.S. government is not enough to justify it. We also need to assess whether there are alternative means of achieving the goal. A free Europe is certainly important to the United States, but the maintenance of 100,000 soldiers there is not necessary. The Soviet threat has disappeared, while Europe's ability to defend itself has expanded. A sharply reduced potential Russian threat may remain in coming years as Moscow struggles with daunting economic, ethnic, and political problems, but we are far more likely to see civil war than aggression against the West. Indeed, today, according to the International Institute for Strategic Studies, Russia spends less than *Germany alone* on the military. Thus, there is no reason why the Europeans, with thrice the economic strength of a decaying Russia (and a larger GNP than America) and a new buffer in the former Warsaw Pact states, cannot create their own security system that would deter any potential threat.

Indeed, those who should be most concerned about a Russian revival, the Germans, aren't. Earlier this year (1993) Chancellor Helmut Kohl announced that his nation was going to cut troop levels by 40 percent through 1995. If Bonn sees no need to maintain a large military for its protection, there is certainly no cause for America to maintain troops in Germany. The spectacle of Washington begging the Europeans for the right to defend them may seem ludicrous but is increasingly becoming fact.

Similarly, South Korea is vastly stronger than North Korea in every way except current military strength. Seoul's growing edge has become increasingly obvious as South Korea has stripped away all of the North's allies, particularly Russia and China. The South is fully capable of eliminating the military imbalance in the peninsula. South Korean officials do not deny their country's ability to sharply increase its defense efforts; instead, they tend to complain about having to bear the added expense. (Others privately advocate retention of America's conventional defense guarantee in order to deter Japan, not the North.) This is hardly a justification for an American presence. Seoul could gradually increase its military spending—which would be unnecessary if the North enters into meaningful arms control negotiations—as U.S. forces were phased out. The potential of North Korean acquisition of a nuclear weapon is serious, but the continued presence of American ground forces will do nothing to stop nuclear proliferation; rather, they would simply act as nuclear hostages.

There were even alternatives in the Persian Gulf. One justification for American intervention was to help restore a regional balance of power. Concern over maintaining a post-war balance of power was at least one factor in the administration's decision to end the war when it did, and allied forced commander General Norman Schwarzkopf warned in the fall of 1990 about the threat to the "long-term balance of power in this region" posed by attempting to "drive on to Baghdad and literally dig out the entire Baathist regime and destroy them." (Of course, such a balance would be of considerably less concern to the United States if an aggressive Iraq were not believed to threaten vital U.S. economic and strategic interests in the region; few Americans would advocate the use of military force to maintain a balance of power in, say, central Africa.)

However, such a balance could well have been achieved without 500,000 American troops. Iraq was surrounded by enemies and could have been constrained by a combination of Iran, Syria, Turkey, and Egypt. Although these states were unlikely to initiate war to free Kuwait, the status of which is essentially irrelevant to anyone's security, they had a real interest in deterring an Iraqi assault on Saudi Arabia. And they were fully capable of doing so, despite the popular build-up given Saddam Hussein's forces. (In retrospect, Iraq's capabilities were obviously greatly overestimated, at least in part as a matter of Pentagon policy.)

It might be difficult to fashion alternative solutions that do not involve direct U.S. intervention, and Washington might not always be fully satisfied with the outcome. But it is unrealistic to expect the United States to assume the responsibility for maintaining global order. Instead, Washington should seek to promote cost-effective policies that yield results most consistent with the U.S. government's duty to protect Americans' security and constitutional freedoms.

Indeed, even if there appear to be no alternatives to a U.S. commitment, the United States must weigh benefits against costs before it intervenes, and avoid or extricate itself from tragic but ultimately irrelevant conflicts.

For example, more people have died in 1993 in Angola than Bosnia. Yet why is there no groundswell for intervening in the former? Starvation stalks Liberia and Sudan, both victims of vicious civil wars. Why no UN relief missions there? The Transcaucasus is suffering from seven separate conflicts. All of these conflagrations are human catastrophes, but none affects a single vital American interest and warrants the sacrifice of even one U.S. soldier. The point is not that American lives are worth more, but that the primary duty of the U.S. government is to safeguard the lives of its own citizens, including servicemen, not sacrifice them for even seemingly worthy causes.

Similarly, what if U.S. policy makers concluded that South Korea would not defend itself if Washington pulled out its troops. In fact, Seoul would probably be the last American ally to give up, but what if it decided to do so? A northern takeover of the South would be a tragedy for the latter, but it would have little impact on the U.S., whose security would remain largely unchanged and whose economy would suffer only marginally from the loss of a mid-sized trading partner. Obviously, other deleterious effects are also possible; it has been argued that China, for instance, might be more likely to invade Taiwan absent an American defense guarantee for Seoul. However, like politics, aggression is primarily local, and there are many good reasons for Beijing to exercise restraint irrespective of the likelihood of an American military response. The threat to go to war should be reserved for cases involving vital American interests. Korea is a peripheral, rather than a substantial, interest of the United States, and does not warrant spending billions of dollars and risking tens of thousands of lives every year, especially if the peninsula becomes nuclearized.

A similar analysis could have been performed on the Gulf. Even if the other regional powers had not taken steps to contain Iraq, the likelihood of Saddam Hussein striking Saudi Arabia was overplayed, since it would have left him dangerously overstretched. (In fact, U.S. intelligence knew at the time that he was withdrawing his best units back to Iraq after seizing Kuwait.)

Similarly, the consequences even of a highly unlikely conquest of the entire Gulf were overstated. Iraq and Kuwait together accounted for about 7.3 percent of international oil production before the embargo; control of Saudi Arabia would have given Saddam 15.6 percent, and if the other small sheikdoms were also included, the total would have increased to 21.5 percent. Thus, in the fantastic worst-case scenario, Saddam would have controlled about one-fifth of international production; enough to nudge prices up, to be sure, but not enough to control prices or wreck the international economy. If proponents of Operation Desert Storm believed that energy prices and the consequent repercussions on the international economy warranted war, they should have been more forthcoming about how many body bags per unit increase in oil prices they believed to be acceptable. Nor did Saddam's invasion of Kuwait threaten America's ally Israel. To the contrary, Iraq only attacked Israel in a desperate attempt to split the coalition; absent the U.S. presence, Baghdad would surely not have attacked Israel, because that country was fully capable of and willing to retaliate.

## Conclusion

The U.S. enjoys many advantages that provide it with the luxury of remaining aloof from geopolitical conflicts that engulf other countries. America benefits from relative geographic isolation, for example. (This does not insulate it from nuclear attack, of course, which is why we should try to develop some form of missile defense.) The U.S. also has the world's largest single economic market, which reduces the impact of the loss of one or more trading partners. (Germany and Japan, for example, would suffer far more if the American market was denied to them.) Moreover, United States has a constitutional system and political philosophy that have endured for more than two hundred years and proven to be popular around the world.

This unique status allows America to balance the costs and benefits of intervention differently from most other states. Alliances make a lot more sense among European states threatened by the Soviet Union, for instance, or between Saudi Arabia and its neighbors when they are threatened by Iraq. Observes Patrick Buchanan, "Blessed by Providence with pacific neighbors, north and south, and vast oceans, east and west, to protect us, why seek permanent entanglements in other people's quarrels?"

For this reason, the United States is rarely open to charges of appeasement, such as are sometimes rightly leveled at other countries, for intervention is rarely require to protect its vital interests. For example, had France and Britain accurately perceived the potential threat posed by Nazi Germany, they should have blocked the remilitarization of the Rhineland, and they certainly should not have helped dismember Czechoslovakia (through active intervention, it should be noted). Washington's failure to leave its expeditionary force in Europe in 1919, or raise a new one in 1933, however, did not constitute appeasement. Similarly, it would not be appeasement for the United States to decline to defend a populous and prosperous South Korea; for Seoul to choose not to augment its forces once U.S. troops were gone, however, would be.

In fact, there is nothing wrong in principle with appeasement, if that means only diplomatic accommodation and avoidance of war. In the late nineteenth and early twentieth centuries, Austria-Hungary, Britain, France, Germany, and Russia all resolved potentially violent disagreements without conflict by making concessions to one another that could be called "appeasement." The case of Nazi Germany was different because Hitler wanted far more than could be given to him, and because the allies materially weakened themselves—for example, by eviscerating Czechoslovakia—in attempting to satisfy him.

The end of the Cold War has resulted in a new world order, whether or not the United States defines or polices it. The Russian military remains a potent force, of course, but it is far less capable than that possessed by the old U.S.S.R., and Moscow's will to use it in an aggressive fashion appears to have dissipated. Moreover, the ability of our allies—a Japan that is the second-ranking economic power in the world, a reunited Germany that dominates Europe, and so on—to contain Russia has grown. These two changes alone give the United States an opportunity to refashion its foreign policy. What should a new, noninterventionist policy look like? It should rest on the following bedrock principles:

- The security of the United States and its constitutional system should remain the U.S. government's highest goal. Individuals may decide to selflessly risk their lives to help others abroad. Policy makers, however, have no authority to risk their citizens' lives, freedom, and wealth in similar pursuits.
- Foreign intervention is usually expensive and risky, and often counterproductive. Many smaller nations may still need to forge preemptive alliances to respond to potentially aggressive regional powers. Because of America's relative geographic isolation and other advantages, however, intervention is rarely necessary to protect its security and free institutions. This is especially true today, with the disappearance of a threatening hegemonic power.
- America's most powerful assets for influencing the rest of the world are its philosophy and free institutions, the ideas of limited government and free enterprise that are now sweeping the globe, and its economic prowess as the world's most productive nation. These factors ensure the nation's influence irrespective of the size of its military and where its soldiers are stationed. The U.S. can best affect others through private means—commerce, culture, literature, travel, and the like.
- The world will continue to suffer from injustice, terror, murder, and aggression. But it is simply not Washington's role to try to right every wrong—a hopeless task in any event. The American people are entitled to enjoy their freedom and prosperity, rather than having their future held hostage to unpredictable events abroad, however laudable the goals of intervention seem to be. Their lives and treasure should not be sacrificed in quixotic crusades unrelated to their basic interests.

The world is changing faster today than it has at any time since the end of World War II. As a result, the United States has no choice but to refashion its foreign policy. While Washington should remain engaged throughout the world culturally, economically, and politically, it should bring its military home and curtail expensive foreign aid programs. After bearing the primary burden of fighting the cold war, the American people deserve to enjoy the benefits of peace through a policy of benign detachment. War may still be forced upon them, of course. But as John Quincy Adams observed shortly after the nation's founding, America should not go "abroad, in search of monsters to destroy."

January 1994

# 11

# The Pitfalls of Collective Security

The collapse of the Soviet Union and end of the Cold War have forced a long-overdue reevaluation of American security policy. Traditional containment is dead, since there is no longer an opposing, hegemonic power to contain. What new strategy, then, should replace containment?

Various unilateral approaches have been suggested, ranging from the sort of strategic independence advocated by the Cato Institute's Ted Galen Carpenter to some form of unilateral intervention long promoted by Irving Kristol, among others. Absent from both the these strategies is a reliance on other countries, either through bilateral or multilateral relations. Both stances reflect a willingness to "go it alone" on security issues.

## The Collective Security Alternative

An important alternative is collective security. At its extreme, such a system seeks to control every conflict everywhere, though in practice most advocates seek to respond to only the most serious wars and disorders. Such an approach is inherently interventionist, but it prefers that American military activity be carried out within a multilateral framework, whether regional alliance or the United Nations. In fact, a diluted form of collective security has long been an important aspect of American foreign policy. The U.S. created several geographically-oriented security organizations, such as the North Atlantic Treaty Organization (NATO), through which military action would be undertaken collectively; gained the U.N.'s imprimatur for combat in South Korea and more recently the Persian Gulf; and long supported U.N. peacekeeping efforts in various parts of the globe.

The question today, then, is whether the U.S. should "strengthen" collective security. One strategy would focus on America's Cold War alliances, particularly NATO, attempting to update them for the post-Cold War world. (The "whither NATO?" debate of recent years involves a range of justifications for maintaining NATO and is therefore broader than the question of collective security.) The other plan would grant the U.N. more authority to mount military operations to punish aggressors and perhaps even settle civil wars. Collective security is being advanced today under the rubric of President George Bush's "new world order," but its roots go back to Woodrow Wilson's self-proclaimed crusade for democracy in World War I.

That experience, however, illustrates the many potential pitfalls of collective security. President Wilson's desire to play global peacemaker led the U.S. to enter a war with only limited implications for its own security and sacrifice nearly 120,000 young men in a conflict not their own. Moreover, America's intervention allowed its allies to impose a one-sided peace that spawned a new, far worse war within a generation. With the world entering a phase when the international environment may grow more chaotic even as the threats to U.S. security decline, it is not in America's interest, nor is it even feasible, for Washington to act as the star player on a collective security team.

## Collective Security: Regional Arrangements

The United States emerged from World War II as the only power strong enough to contain what was believed to be an aggressive and dangerous Soviet Union. America's policy of containment was implemented by literally ringing the U.S.S.R. and its new ally China with a global network of alliances, bases, and forward deployments including the Rio Pact, NATO, the Australia-New Zealand-U.S. (ANZUS) agreement, Southeast Asia Treaty Organization (SEATO), Baghdad Pact (METO), Central Treaty Organization (CENTO), and mutual defense treaties with Japan, the Philippines, and South Korea. This system of worldwide commitments obviously was intended first to protect American security, but it was also viewed as complementary to the broader goal of collective security.

Unfortunately, Washington's series of alliances did not come cheap. In the early 1930s the United States fielded an armed forces numbering about 250,000; even in 1939 as Europe careened towards war, America had only 334,000 personnel in uniform. But America's participation in

World War led to a 12.8 million man military (supported by another 1.9 million civilians) and military expenditures of $83 billion in 1945 (roughly $870 billion in today's dollars).

Although American force levels fell rapidly after the war, the military averaged 1.64 million personnal and the army alone remained larger than the entire military of the 1930s. Equally significant, the Pentagon proved unable to maintain that size force at the wages it was willing to pay. As a result, after letting the Selective Service Act expire in 1947, a year later Congress reinstated the draft, beginning 25 years of conscription. Military spending, too, was high compared to that during previous peacetimes: $9.1 billion in 1948, $13.2 billion in 1949, and $13.7 billion in 1950. After the inconclusive end of the Korean War, not only had military expenditures risen dramatically again, but the United States had agreed to a "mutual defense" treaty guaranteeing the South Korea's security and never again reconsidered its strategy of global containment.

However, the collapse of the U.S.S.R. has eliminated the justification for Cold War collective security system, the cornerstone of which is NATO. Multilateral alliances like ANZUS were obsolete the day they were signed; CENTO, METO, and SEATO collapsed long ago. The Rio Pact has lost all meaning. But NATO remains in place, even as Russian troops withdraw from Europe. The Bush administration saw NATO as essentially permanent, with the President indicating that perhaps in some "utopian day" a century or so from now, it might be possible to withdraw all U.S. troops, but "that day hasn't arrived." President Clinton seems no less committed to a major, continuing military presence in Europe.

Yet the mere fact that the Europeans would like the U.S. to stay and defend them is not likely to persuade Congress or the American people that 100,000 U.S. soldiers—the number set as the minimum necessary by the Clinton administration—should remain in Europe. In short, what is the quintessential anti-Soviet alliance to do without the Soviet Union? After spending a couple of difficult years floundering around after the fall of the Berlin Wall, many pro-NATO policymakers and analysts seem to have fastened upon retaining collective security as the alliance's *raison d'etre*. They would, in short, turn NATO into a mini-U.N., responsible for maintaining order and adjudicating disputes throughout Europe, among the former Soviet republics, and possibly elsewhere in the world. (A number of other duties have also been suggested for NATO—detering a resurgent Russia, containing Germany, and carrying out such non-security tasks as promoting student exchanges, but these all go to the larger "whither NATO?" question rather than to the debate over collective security.)

Supporters of NATO argue that their attempt to broaden the organization's role is simply showing flexibility. Said Defense Secretary Richard Cheney in 1991, NATO's efforts to recast itself "are clear proof of its ability to adapt creatively to the new security environment." But these efforts more likely reflect the bureaucratic interest of an influential constituency in preserving an outmoded institution than an attempt to further American interests. In fact, the interest in turning NATO into a mini-U.N. demonstrates a phenomenon studied by Public Choice economists—the tendency of those in government as well as in the private sector to seek to protect their own interests, which, in this case means preserving one's organization.

Proposals to reconfigure NATO concentrate on extending security guarantees to Eastern Europe against a resurgent Russia, seeking to manage the ethnic and nationalist instability now rippling through the Balkans and the former Soviet Union, and creating a rapid deployment force for use in crises inside and outside of Europe.

*Security Guarantees to Eastern Europe*

In March 1992 Bulgaria requested formal security guarantees from NATO. Poland previously requested a defense treaty with the U.S. to protect it from a resurgent Russia, while Hungary has asked NATO to dispatch troops if requested by an Eastern European government facing aggression. These latter two countries, along with Czechoslovakia and, most recently, Russia, have indicated an interest in joining what formally remains the *North Atlantic* Treaty Organization. Former Alexander Haig has proposed explicitly expanding NATO to encompass all of the former Warsaw Pact members, while NATO itself declared in June 1991 that the alliance would treat any "coercion or intimidation" of the Central or Eastern European states as a matter of "direct and material concern."

Moreover, in November 1991 the NATO members created a North Atlantic Cooperation Council to expand collaboration with Russia, Eastern Europe, and the Baltic states. While the organization does not formally guarantee the security of any country, it opens the way for expanded military ties. Defense coordination and planning is likely to lead to greater Western entanglement in Central European military affairs and demands for an explicit security commitment of one sort or another. In fact, in March 1992 the Council discussed a possible military role for NATO in Azerbaijan, a region about as far from the North Atlantic as is possible. While NATO officials rejected any immediate intervention, they indicated they were pleased with the idea of backing up the alliance's peacekeeping efforts with force.

*Seeking to Manage Ethnic and Nationalist Instability*

Proposals to intervene in Azerbaijan exemplify another potential collective security duty of a new NATO—"managing" change in areas now free of their one-time Soviet overlords. Civil war in former Yugoslavia, conflicts between the former Soviet republics, tension between Hungary and Romania, and revanchist sentiments fueled by displaced ethnic and nationalist groups throughout the East have combined to worry Western Europeans. "We need NATO to protect us against ourselves," one Dutch official told *The Wall Street Journal*.

How far NATO will go in an attempt to enforce stability is not clear. The NATO-created North Atlantic Cooperation Council envisions discussions; at least one observer, Karen Elliot House, has suggested "a massive distribution of Western food aid by NATO military forces." However, NATO is preeminently a military alliance and its relative "competitive advantage" compared to other organizations is its ability to intervene with force. Indeed, military action is the only way that the alliance can ensure "both security and stability," the benefits cited by then British Prime Minister Margaret Thatcher when asked why NATO was needed in the aftermath of 1989.

Indeed, many NATO officials seem to favor military intervention for these reasons. Early in 1992, for instance, before the bitterest fighting in Bosnia and Herzegovina, Gen. John Galvin, then the commander of U.S. troops in Europe, identified Yugoslavia as an example of "regional tensions" threatening U.S. interests. He was later joined by numerous other analysts and officials advocating NATO's intervention in that conflict. Moreover, Turkey, worried about the possible spread of combat in Azerbaijan, urged NATO involvement to curb that civil war. Potentially even more far-reaching was the proposal of Dutch Foreign Minister Hans van den Broeck that NATO troops enforce ceasefires arranged through the 48-member Conference on Security and Cooperation. Then Secretary of State Baker lauded the idea and NATO Secretary General Manfred Woerner stated that "NATO may well lend material support or even troops to the CSCE if needed and if agreed by our member states."

*Rapid Deployment Force for Use in Various Crises*

Gen. Galvin long advocated creation of a "fire brigade" to respond to emergencies. In late 1990 he stated that "there is pretty good military agreement" among NATO officers to move in this direction and cited the Persian Gulf war as a model for future NATO actions. Although NATO officials argue that such a force might be needed within Europe to meet threats from states other than Russia, the only other nation presumably capable of dominating Europe is Germany. Despite some largely-suppressed disquiet about the potential economic and political influence of a united Germany, however, few expect any military aggression from the wealthiest country in Europe.

Thus, to most advocates of NATO the real issue of responding to unnamed crises is conflicts outside of Europe. For instance, the British magazine *The Economist* pointed to "the explosive Gulf" even before Saddam Hussein's invasion of Kuwait as a reason to preserve NATO. After the Gulf war editorialists at *The New York Times* viewed the Persian Gulf as a region where NATO forces "could usefully be dispatched." And *The San Diego Union* has urged formally "amending the NATO treaty to give NATO the flexibility to intervene militarily outside Europe," which, the paper argued, "could provide the United Nations a valuable adjunct in its efforts to maintain global stability." (In fact, NATO's Woerner argues that NATO has already effectively done so, providing important assistance to the U.N. during the Persian Gulf war.)

NATO has traditionally avoided so-called out-of-area activities, but, despite French reluctance, in particular, the alliance seems to be slowly moving toward a broader view of its authority. In 1990, for instance, the NATO members issued a declaration indicating their intent to restructure the alliance's forces, making them more mobile and versatile "so that Allied leaders will have maximum flexibility in deciding how to respond to a crisis." In May 1991 NATO initiated the creation of a rapid reaction force of up to 70,000 men. The following November the member governments announced a new "strategic concept" that focuses on instability in Eastern Europe and the Mediterranean rather than a conventional assault from Russia.

So far the European members of NATO have not been ready to formally extend the alliance's reach to other territory, but at the Atlantic Treaty Association meeting in Washington in October 1991 Gen. Galvin suggested that "in the future, NATO may address out-of-area threats." And the following month the U.S. pressed its case that without broader responsibilities NATO was likely to suffer reduced political, and hence, financial, support in the U.S. In part to satisfy the U.S., the NATO declaration explained that "We reaffirm the continuing importance of consulting together on events outside the treaty area which may have implications for our security." By the summer of 1992 NATO governments were dancing around the Yugoslavian imbroglio, with Manfred Worner announcing NATO's readiness to provide some 6,000 troops for use by the U.N. to protect humanitarian shipments to Sarajevo.

Moreover, cooperation with Eastern Europe and Russia appears to be further pushing open the door for out-of-area intervention. A mechanism to enforce CSCE cease-fires would also subtly expand NATO's military jurisdiction to other regions.

## Collective Security: The United Nations

The second major variant of the strategy of collective security is reliance on the U.N. Although both NATO and the U.N. could simultaneously enforce such a security regime, one or the other is likely to end up with a paramount role should both attempt to perform essentially the same function. Given the fact that NATO commands real troops, it is likely to "win" any competition with the U.N. (unless the alliance effectively put its forces at the disposal of the U.N. Security Council). Only in out-of-area activities far from Europe—which could, however, account for the bulk of the conflicts in the post-Cold War world—does the U.N. arguably have a comparative advantage over NATO. Moreover, NATO may not survive, given the U.S.S.R.'s collapse, which would leave the U.N. as the major forum for a collective security approach.

This was, in fact, the original vision for the U.N. The allied success in World War II led to a widespread desire for an international regime to achieve what Woodrow Wilson expected his ill-fated League of Nations to deliver: international order policed by the world's countries collectively. At the peace talks in Versailles Wilson stated that "armed force is in the background" of his proposal and that "if the moral force of the world will not suffice, the physical force of the world shall." A generation later America enthusiastically joined the global organization that it had helped establish, and agreed to a charter that explicitly vests the U.N. Security Council with "primary responsibility for the maintenance of international peace and security." The Charter goes on to establish procedures for dispute resolution, enforcement activity, and use of armed forces provided by member states. Most of these provisions have never been used, largely because the Cold War disrupted what was expected to be continued allied cooperation, with the Soviet Union using its veto to deadlock the Security Council.

In theory the U.N. has enormous authority. Article 42 empowers the Security Council to "take such action by air, sea, or land forces as may be necessary to maintain or restore international peace and security." Article 45 orders member states to "hold immediately available national air-force contingents for combined international enforcement action" so that the U.N. can "take urgent military measures." Plans for military action are to be drafted by a Military Staff Committee. Of particular interest is Article 43, which specifies how the U.N. can raise a military:

> All Members of the United Nations, in order to contribute to the maintenance of international peace and security, undertake to make available to the Security Council, on its call and in accordance with a special agreement or agreements, armed forces, assistance, and facilities, including rights of passage, necessary for the purpose of maintaining international peace and security.

With the end of the Cold War and Moscow's subsequent cooperation in the Persian Gulf war, an increasing number of people wish to embrace the U.N.'s original promise. Secretary General Boutros Boutros-Ghali, for one, has issued a report, "Agenda for Peace," advocating fulfillment of Article 43. In September, the Security Council established a working group to review his proposals. Similar ideas were advanced at a Stanley Foundation conference, when a number of participants urged that the Security Council seek agreements with member states under Article 43. One proposal was to create a small standing force, to be deployed to areas where bloodshed seemed imminent. Some conferees wanted to revive the Military Staff Committee (MSC); another suggested periodic meetings between U.N. and military officials to discuss world hot spots.

Similarly, in early 1991 French President Francois Mitterand proposed revitalizing the MSC, after which his nation would put 1,000 soldiers at the disposal of the U.N. on 40 hours notice and another 1,000 troops within a week. Other people, including former U.N. Under Secretary General for Special Political Affairs Brian Urquhart, have promoted the idea of using Article 43 to provide the U.N. with sufficient forces to intervene in such civil wars as Yugoslavia and Somalia, as well as in other nations where "sovereignty is also dissolving into anarchy." Urquhart envisions these forces as performing a role in between peacekeeping and large-scale intervention as in the Persian Gulf, what he calls essentially "armed police actions."

Seizing upon Mitterand's proposal, *New York Times* columnist Flora Lewis urged the U.N. to acquire "a permanent force in readiness, loyal to its flag and to no state," perhaps made up of Nepal's Gurkhas, which could be supplemented by national contributions. Harvard University's Joseph Nye proposed creating a U.N. "rapid-deployment force" of 60,000 soldiers, with a core of 5,000 troops who would train regularly. In the case of large-scale aggression, as in Kuwait, or a major civil war, as in Yugoslavia, he called for "an American-led coalition."

The *Washington Post's* Jim Hoagland envisions a UN operation backed, but not led, by the U.S. to suppress the Yugoslavian conflict. He would give the UN "peacekeeping power," exercised through the Security Council, in order "to turn the UN into an effective agent to restrain regional conflict." Similar seems to be the sentiments of Sen. Joseph Biden (D-Del.), who wants to "regularize the kind of multilateral response we assembled for the Gulf War" through the Security Council. And, since the U.N. lacks its own forces, this approach is implicitly what the Council had in mind in June 1992 when it demanded that Bosnia's Serbs put their heavy weapons under U.N. control or face unspecified consequences. Superficially, at least, there appears to be popular support in the U.S. for such a U.N. role. Some 55 percent of Americans now say that they are willing to rely on U.N. forces even in conflicts involving U.S. interests.

## Models for U.N.-Organized Collective Security

Two different models have been offered for expanding the U.N.'s collective security responsibilities. The first is the organization's traditional peacekeeping activities. The second is the U.N.'s formal major wars: Korea and Iraq.

## Peacekeeping

The U.N. has currently undertaken eleven different peacekeeping operations encompassing 50,220 soldiers, all volunteered by their respective nations. The enterprises vary dramatically in scope, ranging from 40 observers in Kashmir to 22,000 participants planned for Cambodia. Other forces are stationed in Angola, Croatia, Cyprus, El Salvador, the Mideast (Arab states/Israel, Kuwait/Iraq, and Lebanon), and the Western Sahara. (In its first 40 years the U.N. instituted 13 peace-keeping missions. Between 1988 and 1991 it undertook eight.) Proposals have also been made to establish U.N. peacekeeping forces elsewhere— to ensure freedom of transit in the Persian Gulf during the Iran-Iraq war, for instance, and more recently to establish order in Somalia. The major controversy surrounding U.N. peacekeeping today is cost. Under antiquated rules the U.S. is to provide 30 percent of total funding, and the rapid expansion of U.N. activities over the past year has caused expenses to dramatically outstrip contributions, leaving the U.S. deep in arrears on its peacekeeping assessments.

## Major wars

Quite different from the U.N. peacekeeping operations are the two large-scale conflicts undertaken under the authority of the Security Council. In 1950, with the Soviet delegate boycotting the Security Council to protest the failure to seat China's new revolutionary government, the Security Council authorized, under Chapter VII of the U.N. Charter, creation of a multinational force to repel North Korean aggression against the Republic of Korea. U.S. General Douglas MacArthur was designated the commander of the U.N. forces, but he never reported to the Security Council and Washington unilaterally made all of the war's major decisions—to cross the 38th parallel, for instance, and refuse forced repatriation of prisoners.

The U.N. troops were predominantly American (joining Seoul's numerically strong but qualitatively weak forces). After one year of war, in June 1951, the U.S. provided 253,250, or more than 93 percent, of the

271,311 non-South Korean troops. The largest other contingents came from Britain, Canada, and Turkey. By June 1953, the American forces had risen to 302,483, roughly 89 percent of the 341,628 non-ROK soldiers. Casualties showed a similar distribution: 36,823 non-Korean servicemen died, of whom 33,629, or 91 percent, were Americans.

In the Persian Gulf war the Security Council didn't create a U.N. joint command. The U.S. formally observed the conditions of the Council's resolutions, but had some latitude in deciding how to implement them. America provided the bulk of the U.N. forces, as in the Korean War. (The major difference is that the victim of aggression, Kuwait, provided virtually no troops since it had been occupied.) The U.N. effort amassed roughly 652,600 combat troops, 510,000 of whom—78 percent—were American. The U.S. death toll, a mercifully few 148, also comprised the bulk of the allied casualties.

### Is Collective Security Desirable?

Attempting to achieve collective security through regional alliances has quite different practical ramifications than using the U.N. But both methods assume it is in America's interest to work to eliminate international disorder and instability, both preventing aggression and squelching civil conflicts. Indeed, the cornerstone of a policy of collective security is stability. Whatever the formal rhetoric of policymakers about human rights and democracy, the primary goal of collective security is to prevent unauthorized border crossings and ensure popular submission to the relevant national government, irrespective of the "justness" of the cause at stake.

Instability in the post-Cold War world should not come as a surprise. For decades the two superpowers were largely successful in suppressing often severe cultural, ethnic, linguistic, nationalistic, and religious differences within allied states. Many of the disputes now surfacing around the world are entirely legitimate and long-overdue.

Of course, it would be best if previous political settlements, however artificial, were not challenged violently. But the fundamental issue of U.S. policy should be how to best advance America's security. (Respect for human rights in other nations is obviously an important moral value, but the foremost duty of the U.S. government is to protect the American people's lives, freedom, property, and constitutional system.)

The question, then, is: does maintaining the international status quo make America more secure? It should be obvious that global disorder per se does not threaten the U.S. A variety of African states, for instance, have suffered grievously for years without any impact on America. Even during the Cold War that status of many small nations was at best a peripheral concern to the U.S.

Moreover, whatever the value of international stability, Washington paid a high price for intervening. It made many a bargain with the Devil, or his surrogates, like Iran's Shah, Nicaragua's Somoza, and Zaire's Mobuto, that ultimately left the U.S. less secure. For example, Islamic fundamentalists, now considered the greatest threat in the Persian Gulf (and the reason the West backed Saddam Hussein in his aggression against Tehran) if not the rest of the world, might never have gained power in Iran had not the U.S. meddled in that nation for years.

In any case, the end of the Cold War has terminated the potentially zero-sum nature of international relations and thereby reduced the value to the U.S. of stability in distant lands. The disintegration of Somalia, an American ally, is tragic but has few security implications. Even the Yugoslavian civil war, occuring in the ever-unstable Balkans, can be viewed with detachment from Washington. Some people have, of course, advanced lurid scenarios involving the conflict spreading to Albania, Greece, Turkey, and beyond, but years have passed without the bloodshed expanding. Absent the interlocking alliances, worsening tensions, and widespread popular support for war that characterized all of the major powers before World War I, conflict in the Balkans in 1914 would never have spread to the rest of Europe, let alone America. It is difficult to construct an even slightly plausible chain of events leading to a similar global conflict today. If the risk is still thought to be serious enough to warrant action, then the Europeans, with the most at stake, should take action. If they judge the costs of intervening to outweigh the benefits, there is certainly no reason for Washington to act.

What about the Persian Gulf, however? Many advocates of collective security view it as the exception that proves the rule, the distant conflict between third rate powers that threatened American security. In fact, reliance on the Persian Gulf as an example of the need for collective security demonstrates the weakness rather than strength of the case. It is impossible to point to another regional conflict with as potentially far-reaching implications for the U.S. Thus, at most Iraq's invasion of Kuwait called for a unique, one-time response.

Moreover, in retrospect it looks increasingly likely that Iraq's aggression could have been treated as a limited threat best met by other regional powers. First, Saddam Hussein was never in a position to gain a "stranglehold" over the West's oil supply and thus its economy. Even had Iraq conquered the entire Gulf it would have controlled little more than one-fifth of the international petroleum market. Such a share would have allowed Iraq to increase oil prices, but only modestly. Second, the protection of Saudi Arabia, not the liberation of Kuwait, was of primary U.S. interest. And that required at most a thin military tripwire, not offensive action. Third, Iraq's neighbors, particularly a revenge-minded Iran, were capable of containing Hussein, especially if the objective was limited to guaranteeing Saudi Arabia's security. (Iraq's nuclear program posed a particular challenge to efforts at regional containment, but it did not motivate Washington's intervention. Nor is the very difficult and continuing problem of nuclear proliferation a matter of collective security per se.)

Indeed, regional arrangements are a possible solution to many disputes. Four nations, Gambia, Ghana, Guinea, Nigeria, and Sierre Leone dispatched 7,000 soldiers under the aegis of the Economic Community of West African States to police a cease-fire between three competing factions in a devastating civil war. In 1991 Australia, Canada, New Zealand, the Soloman Islands, and Vanuatu created a multinational supervisory team to break a blockade of the Pacific island of Bougainville by Papua New Guinea. Russia joined Georgia in attempting to establish a buffer zone in the territory of South Ossetia in Georgia. And for a time the European Community considered taking military action in Yugoslavia, in an attempt to enforce several EC-sponsored ceasefires. Although the EC eventually encouraged the U.N. to send peacekeepers, the Europeans have been slowly rejuvenating, over fierce American resistance, the heretofore moribund Western European Union, which could organize European military action in the future. While all of these efforts are small relative to the Gulf war, they illustrate the possibility of relying upon cooperative efforts among the parties most concerned about potential conflict in a region.

But one's judgment as to the necessity of America's intervention in the Gulf is less important than a recognition that Iraq's aggression posed a worst-case scenario for the rest of the world. However compelling the case for action against Hussein, his aggression does not prove the need for some international mechanism, backed by the U.S., to maintain "order" everywhere else. In most cases instability poses little danger to America and can be contained by other states, met by more modest steps such as sanctions, or simply ignored.

What if, in the future, an international incident sufficiently serious to warrant intervention arises? Then the U.S. should help organize an ad hoc force, whether through the U.N. or amongst its alliance partners, to meet the specific contingency. The standard for American participation should be the same for unilateral military action: the threat impinges a vital rather than peripheral interest (and therefore warrants the sacrifice of life, potentially huge expense, and other risks inherent to foreign intervention), there are no other powers that can meet the challenge, and no peaceful alternatives exist to resolve the issue.

## Is Collective Security Feasible?

The objection to collective security is not purely theoretical. There are also a number of practical pitfalls as well. Although the strategies of regional alliances and U.N. are afflicted by different problems, neither is an attractive vehicle for policing the world.

### Regional Alliances

Limited arrangements and organizations can be quite effective in achieving security goals in specific regions. But they are likely to be far less able to promote the broader goal of international stability. In particular, transforming NATO, an alliance constructed to constrain the U.S.S.R., into a regional constabulary to keep the peace not only in Europe but elsewhere is no easy task. The most serious difficulty is reaching a consensus on new, out-of-area duties. What long unified the fractious European states was fear of Soviet aggression. Questions of Croation and Slovenian independence, the boundaries between Hungary and Romania, and Islamic fundamentalism in Iran are likely to generate no similar unanimity of opinion.

Indeed, the NATO members long had difficulty in agreeing on policies involving Europe. Persistent unfilled promises by the European members to hike defense spending, for example, demonstrated their tendency to free ride on the U.S. European support for natural gas pipeline to the Soviet Union, over strident American objections showed that the

Europeans assessed Moscow's threat very differently. And when it came to out-of-area issues, cooperation was often nil. There was no higher priority for the Reagan administration than ousting Nicaragua's Sandinista government, yet several European countries provided aid to Managua. Some European states were equally uncooperative when it came to bombing Libya.

Disagreements between just the Europeans on pressing international issues are evident today. Early on Germany recognized the independence of Croation and Slovenia over the objections of its neighbors. Germany was also criticized for suspending arms sales to Turkey, a member of NATO, because of bloody fighting between Turkish soldiers and Kurdish guerrillas. These sort of differences will only grow in number in the future, calling into question the ability of NATO to act as a peacekeeping organization even if its European members agree to amend its charter to so expand its responsibilities.

The potential gulf between American and European geopolitical interests is likely to be even greater. Some issues that understandably worry the Europeans, like the Balkans imbroglio, have no discernible impact on the U.S. Other matters, such as Turkey's Kurdish problem, may may be viewed from a broader perspective by Washington, given its ties to Israel. The likelihood of a transatlantic consensus on many international issues in the absence of the Soviet threat is, frankly, nil. Even the specter of an aggressive Iraq led to only general agreement with such nations as France, which appeared to judge the risks differently than the U.S. In short, NATO, or any other regional alliance, is too flawed to become the new vehicle for collective security.

*The United Nations*

The other strategy is the U.N., and particularly the Security Council. Given the low esteem in which most Americans held the U.N. throughout the 1970s and 1980s, the notion of using the U.N. to police the world would probably be considered a joke were it not for the Persian Gulf war, which President Bush declared had rejuvenated "the peacekeeping function of the United Nations." But now serious commentators want to give the international body its own military.

Is such an approach feasible? To work, collective security requires the cooperation of most major states and a generally impartial application of agreed-upon principles. Unfortunately, however, the U.N. has never demonstrated a capacity to impartially settle international disputes. Moscow's new willingness to cooperate should not obscure the fact that for 45 years the U.N. was merely another Cold War battleground. In fact, the failure of the U.N. collective security system fueled the expansion of regional alliances in order to avoid Security Council vetoes.

Today U.N. policymaking in the Security Council remains at the mercy of the communist rulers in Beijing who, despite a demonstrated willingness to shoot down unarmed students and workers, possess a veto in the Security Council. And while more states are moving toward democracy, a majority of the U.N.'s members are still dictatorships. Thus, even if the growing number of free states survive, collective security is likely to be ineffective so long as the aggressor is a permanent member of the Security Council, a client state of a permanent member, or a country able to amass eight votes from the Security Council's 15 members, many of which will be ruled by venal autocrats. Indeed, it is conceivable that even Western democracies might act to shield friendly states from U.N. censure and enforcement action. Consider Washington's likely attitude should Israel or South Korea launch a preemptive attack against Syria or North Korea, respectively.

The flip-side risk is that increased "peacekeeping" authority might cause the U.N. to shift towards a broader enforcement role not necessarily related to peacekeeping. That is, it might become a coercive tool in the hands of shifting international majorities that happen to control the Security Council from time to time. This would be a particular concern if the U.N. possessed its own military. Although the U.S. could always veto what it viewed to be inappropriate intervention, it would pay a political price for doing so. Moreover, a recalcitrant Washington could then hardly count on Security Council backing for instances where it wanted U.N. support for military action.

In any case, in practice the U.N. seems unsuited to the task of maintaining global order. Neither of the supposed models for U.N. enforcement of collective security offers much hope. True, traditional U.N. peacekeeping does have some value. First, peacekeeping forces probably help prevent small incidents that could spread and thereby threaten a fragile peace accord. Second, the presence of "world" representatives may give responsible officials an excuse to resist domestic political pressure to provoke a conflict. In the end, however, U.N. peacekeeping can only prevent fighting where both parties desire peace for other reasons. For instance, it is ultimately Israel's military superiority, not the presence of U.N. troops, that prevents Syria from attempting to reclaim the Golan Heights. U.N. peacekeepers arrived in Croatia only after the costs of war turned Serbian opinion against continuing Slobodan Milosevic's campaign for a greater Serbia in that direction. And the patrons of the different combatants in Cambodia, not the U.N., brought an end to fighting in that tragic nation; moreover, a continuing refusal of Khmer Rouge guerrillas to disarm threatens to destroy the peace settlement. In short, the U.N. cannot stop war by determined participants.

And the major conflicts fought under the U.N. flag were U.N. conflicts in name only. An American commitment to intervene, even without allied support, was the most important factor in both Korea and the Gulf. While U.N. authority was a convenient and politically popular patina, it was not necessary to prosecute the war.

Nevertheless, the U.S. had to pay a price for the U.N.'s imprimatur. Washington's desire for Soviet support forced the administration to ignore the U.S.S.R.'s crackdown in the Baltic states. China's abstention in the critical Security Council vote authorizing the use of force appears to have been purchased by new World Bank loans, which were approved shortly thereafter, possibly supplemented by reduced pressure on human rights issues. And consider the ten non-permanent members who had a voice in shaping Persian Gulf policy: Austria, Belgium, Cuba, Ecuador, India, Ivory Coast, Romania, Yemen, Zaire, and Zimbabwe. Many of those nations were interested in gaining additional Western financial assistance, if nothing else, for their votes, something the U.S. was not above providing. Secretary of State Baker responded to Yemen's opposition to the resolution authorizing force with a note to Yemen's ambassador stating "That is the most expensive vote you have ever cast." While such log-rolling might seem unexceptional in a political forum like the U.N., it hardly augurs well for the creation of an effective system of collective security.

In the future other nations might expect not only bribes but also real influence. France's Mitterand, for instance, apparently advanced his proposal for rejuvenating the Military Staff Committee because it would break America's military monopoly in U.N. actions. His foreign minister later argued that Europe and the U.N. should help counteract U.S. power: "American might reigns without balancing weight," he complained. (After the June 1991 NATO conference French officials also grumbled about Washington arrogance in the wake of its victory in the Gulf war.) Increasingly wealthy and influential Germany and Japan both want permanent seats on the Security Council and may eventually also request a say in military operations. Similarly, India, which possesses a potent military, may not be so quiescent in the future. Among the new non-permanent members of the Security Council are Cape Verde, Hungary, Morocco, and Venezuela, all of which will bring their own perspectives into Security Council deliberations.

There is nothing intrinsically wrong with the French desire to turn what has been a Potemkin collaborative security enterprise into a real one. But it is not clear that a system subject to the usual vagaries of any international organization, especially the U.N., is going to either achieve its purpose or advance American interests. Not only might the U.N. be unduly restrictive where Washington felt intervention was necessary, but more important, a truly effective collective security system could drag the U.S. into conflicts with no connection to American interests and which could be solved without Washington's assistance. What if, for instance, Germany, France, Italy, and Greece demand Security Council military action in the Balkans? Or if Turkey, Russia, and Armenia propose U.N. intervention in Azerbaijan? Should America again become the major combatant, perhaps consigning thousands of citizens to their deaths in a potentially bloody, interminable conflict with no impact on U.S. security?

Moreover, Washington would have to accept the theoretical possibility of U.N. action *against* the U.S. Granted, America has the veto power, but to exercise it in the face of a "world" demand for action would be embarrassing. Put bluntly, to vest the U.N. with significant peacekeeping power requires that one trust a council of fifteen foreign states more than one's elected domestic government. Sadly, past experience does not warrant placing that kind of confidence in the Security Council.

The proposal to give the U.N. an independent combat force to be used at the Secretary General's discretion is even less attractive. Whatever the international body's value as a debating chamber within which to let off steam, it has never demonstrated principled leadership unhampered by multitudinous and arcane political pressures. Today, of course, the U.N.'s potential for abuse is tempered by the role of the Security Council, but if the U.N. gained the sort of influence that would come with an independent armed forces, a coalition of smaller states might attempt to move security power back to the General Assembly. Indeed, the U.S. itself looked at ways of circumventing the Soviets during the U.N.'s intervention in the Congo in 1960 and 1961. So long as the U.N. is governed by a majority of nation states, ruled by some of the worst people on earth, the U.N. should not be trusted with even one soldier.

## Conclusion: Regional Peacekeeping Without the U.S.

The dramatic international changes of recent years have truly yielded a "new world order," one providing America with a unique opportunity to reassess its global role. For nearly five decades the U.S. has acted more like empire than republic, creating an international network of client states, establishing hundreds of military installations around the world, conscripting young men to staff these advanced outposts and fight in distant wars, and spending hundreds of billions of dollars annually on the military. Indeed, this globalist foreign policy badly distorted the domestic political system, encouraging the growth of a large, expensive, repressive, secretive, and often uncontrolled state. The American republic gave way to empire.

The justification for this interventionist military strategy, so alien to the original American design, was the threat of totalitarian communism. With that threat gone, the U.S. should return to its roots, rather than look for another convenient enemy. And that requires a much more limited foreign policy with much more limited ends.

Nevertheless, while the threat of war involving vital U.S. interests seems to be the smallest in six decades, that does not mean that globe is destined to enjoy a golden era of peace. The end of the Cold War has released long-standing ethnic and nationalist conflicts in Eastern Europe; the collapse of the U.S.S.R. has loosed similar conflicts throughout Eurasia; the Third World remains riven with warfare between tribes, religions, and nations. To combat these threats many people now advocate reliance on collective security, whether through existing military alliances or the U.N.

But most fundamental is the question of American interests. Put bluntly, what policy will best protect the lives, liberty, property, and constitutional system of the people of this nation? Entangling Washington in a potentially unending series of international conflicts and civil wars? Or remaining aloof from struggles that do not affect the U.S.? If one's chief concern is preserving American lives and treasure, the latter position is clearly preferable.

To advance a unilateral policy of strategic independence, benign detachment, "America First," or even isolationism, as some derisely term this strategy, is not in fact to advocate economic autarchy and political isolation. To the contrary, the U.S. would be actively involved, as the world's most important trading nation, in the global economy. American culture and political ideals would continue shaping nations around the globe. And Washington would still cooperate internationally where collective action was required.

But most foreign security concerns would be handled locally and regionally, rather than globally. Without the existence of a central communist puppeteer orchestrating probes by its surrogates, each future act of aggression is likely to be unique, dictated by the specific circumstances and histories of a particular region. Thus, conflict, and the potential for conflict, will be best met by the surrounding nations that more fully understand the issues and have the most at stake. In fact, peacekeeping is not a new activity. Over the years there have been numerous successful efforts to prevent conflict, particularly in Europe and Latin America. And as the acceptance of war as a weapon of statecraft continues to decline, regional peacemaking efforts are likely to meet with increasing success.

Such regional arrangements may include a capacity to take military action. The Europeans, either through the Western European Union or the European Community, have sufficient vehicles for taking intervening if they believe their interests to be threatened. For instance, in 1991 France and Germany discussed expanding their joint forces from 5,000 to 50,000 men and invited other European states to contribute troops. French President Mitterand and German Chancellor Helmut Kohl simultaneously proposed breathing new life into the WEU, to which nine of the 12 EC countries belong, in order to develop a stronger European voice on defense. Unfortunately, their efforts ran into stiff resistance from the U.S., backed by Britain, lest a meaningful WEU weaken America's ties to the continent through NATO. (The spectacle of Washington demanding to be allowed to defend Europe seems rather odd.) Nevertheless, at the EC summit in Maastricht in December 1991 the Europeans agreed to begin channeling additional defense resources through the WEU.

Even if there is cause for the U.S. to maintain a residual protective role in Europe—a dubious position, given the fact that the latter possesses a larger population (328 million compared to 251 million) and GNP ($6.0 trillion compared to $5.4 trillion in 1990) than the U.S.— there is no need for NATO to become a collective security organization. Rather, a separate European force would allow the EC to deal with nearby instability if it wished. NATO's Woerner, for instance, argues that the WEU will be complementary to NATO, and will "act where NATO does not act." In such instances NATO "could lend NATO-assigned forces" to the WEU. Former Yugoslavia is an example where the WEU is far better suited to action than is NATO. Indeed, many if not most of Europe's interests in the Balkans and Eurasia will not be shared by the U.S., if for no other reason than the simple fact of geography.

Today there is no Soviet Union to contain and local and regional quarrels are no longer of vital concern as a result of their being part of the overall Cold War. Moreover, those states that were once possible victims of aggression—underdeveloped Korea, defeated Germany and Japan, war-torn France and Britain, and smaller nations like Australia and New Zealand—have developed potent militaries and are capable of meeting any likely threats to themselves or their neighbors. Collective security was never desirable nor practical. It has even less appeal as a strategy today.

December 1992

# V

# International Debt or Development?

# 12

# The Misdeeds of International Aid

The G-7 countries have focused their foreign aid attention on Russia, but the real tragedy of economic and social chaos is occurring in Africa. Consider the disasters in Liberia, Somalia, and the Sudan, with untold tens of thousands dying from starvation and war. The problems in the Sudan, which led to unprecedented U.S. and U.N. intervention, demonstrate particularly dramatically the horrendous consequences of the disintegration of a nation. The country's collapse also illustrates the failure of foreign aid, for Somalia was long a favored recipient of international transfers, collecting more than $900 million in concessional aid during the 1980s, along with another $623 million in nonconcessional public and private loans. As of 1990 Somalia's accumulated debt was $2.4 billion. Most other African nations have also received substantial foreign assistance, particularly from the OECD countries. Total concessional loans to Africa amounted to some $58 billion during the 1980s, supplemented by $160 billion in nonconcessional public and private lending. Financial flows have been even greater to other developing states, like the major Latin American borrowers. All told, by 1992 Third World nations amassed a debt of some $1.7 trillion.

Yet the continuous flow of foreign funds appears to have done little to achieve its formal objective of promoting economic development. Somalia's situation is unusually bad, but many other African nations face serious economic, health, and social crises. For instance, between 1965 and 1990 per capita GNP fell in Benin, Central African Republic, Ethiopia, Ghana, Guinea-Bissau, Liberia, Madagascar, Mauritania, Niger, Sao Tome & Principe, Senegal, Tanzania, Uganda, Zaire, and Zambia. Life expectancies remain appallingly low—in the 40's for almost 20 African states. Agricultural production has dropped in a number of

131

African nations—Angola, Ethiopia, Botswana, Lesotho, Namibia, and Rwanda—over the last decade. Manufacturing output has slid in a number of others. And so on.

This record suggests that foreign aid is not much of an aid. While not all African states have moved backward, there is no correlation between economic growth and foreign receipts. Tanzania, a heavy aid recipient, has the world's second lowest per capita GNP. Botswana, in contrast, has received far less assistance but has nevertheless achieved significant levels of economic growth.

Not only do most foreign transfers seem useless, however. There is substantial evidence that foreign aid has often proved to be a hindrance rather than a help. The problem is not mere waste, though much foreign assistance has been misspent. More fundamentally, "aid" has subsidized both uneconomic investment projects and counterproductive economic policies. In the end, African states cannot look to foreign transfers to energize their economies, but rather must assert control over their own destinies.

## What Causes Development?

Unfortunately, development economics has long looked at the problem of international poverty from the wrong perspective—studying the causes of poverty rather than prosperity. Indeed, advocates of foreign aid often do not get even this far, acting as if the absence of money itself is a, if not the, cause of poverty. But as economist P.T. Bauer observes, "lack of money is not the *cause* of poverty: it *is* poverty." This misunderstanding may be why foreign aid has been so frequently thought of as the answer to poverty. After all, if incomes are thought to be too low, then providing funds should solve the problem.

The result has been a long fascination with statist development strategies, propagated particularly by the "structuralist" economic school represented by Gunnar Myrdal and others. Unfortunately, this approach incorporates the "fatal conceit" spoken of by the late Friedrich Hayek, the belief that human behavior and progress can be carefully planned and guided. Mixed with such hubris, so recently brought down in stunning fashion in the former Soviet Union and Eastern Europe, is a patronizing attitude to Third World peoples. Observes Indian economist Deepak Lal, "at its bluntest, behind at least part of the [statist development strategy] is a paternalistic attitude born of a distrust of, if not contempt for, the ordinary, poor, uneducated masses of the Third World."

But it should be obvious by now that the attempt to impose development from outside and above has failed. Long missed in the search for government-led development strategies was the lesson of the West's dramatic escape from poverty and East Asia's astonishing successes over the last four decades. That is, the way to solve the problem of underdevelopment is not so much to figure out why people are poor but to understand why others are wealthy. Adam Smith long ago knew why, but his work was largely ignored in a century that historian Paul Johnson has dubbed the "age of politics," a time when the "mountebanks, charismatics, *exaltes*, secular saints, mass murderers, united by their belief that politics was the cure for human ills," offered plans and more plans.

Centuries of practical experience demonstrate that economic growth generally occurs where markets operate, the rule of law is respected, private property is protected, and competition is permitted. What was true of Great Britain, the U.S., Japan, and South Korea is also true of today's poor developing states. One detailed study, by economists E. Dwight Phaup and Bradley Lewis, concludes: "It would appear that whether LDCs are winners or losers is determined mainly by their domestic economic policies. Resource endowment, lucky circumstances, former colonial status, and other similar factors make little difference in the speed with which countries grow economically. The results of domestic policy choices pervade every economic area."

The World Bank, too, has recognized the importance of market-oriented policies even while providing credit for statist development programs. A 1983 survey found that developing nations that introduced fewer "distortions" into their economies—particularly price controls, import restrictions, interest rate limits, and similar policies—did better, while "those countries with the worst distortions experienced significantly lower domestic saving and lower output per unit of investment, thus leading to slower growth." Subsequent research has reached similar conclusions. Today even many one-time socialists realize the importance of economic freedom. Once we thus understand why development occurs, and only after we do so, can we evaluate the real effects of foreign aid.

## On Which Road?

Unfortunately, for decades most developing states have generally followed a *dirigiste* rather than a market model. Thus, their economic failure should come as no surprise. This problem has proved to be particularly
acute for Africa. As the continent moved towards independence theo-
rists like Leopold Sedar Senghor lauded the virtues of an unique African
socialist path. Abdul Babu, a native of Zanzibar and later Tanzanian
Minister of Economic Development, went so far as to declare that: "Socialism is not only a social science with a future in terms of efficient
utilization of labor and other resources for rapid economic development;
it is *the* social system of the future. If African capitalism is a practical
impossibility, and if mixed economies lead to economic impasse, the
only course open to us is socialism." These ideas were implemented by
virtually every newly independent nation. In the 1960s, writes economist Andrew Karmarck, "the highest rate of economic growth may well
have been reached in the production of plans—increasly more 'comprehensive' and sophisticated plans. *The Plan* had become a symbol of
independence, and a great deal of public attention was devoted to, and
praises sung over, the plan document."

African states implemented their invariably *dirigiste* plans with the
active support of Western aid agencies. Tanzania's leader, Julius Nyerere,
for instance, was widely toasted and showered with aid as he traveled
the world promoting "African socialism." The World Bank subsidized
his "Ujamaa movement," or forced collectivization program. Similar
Western support was offered to countries across the continent.

Alas, the result of Africa's fixation on "The Plan" has been disastrous. The world's four poorest states are in Africa; 16 of the 20 most
impoverished lie in Africa. Tanzania's per capita income lags behind
that of every other nation except Mozambique, the victim of a lengthy
and particularly bitter civil war. Although the causes of Africa's veri-
table implosion are many and complex, the most important is the fact
that virtually every nation has followed the path of statism. Only radical
policy reform, then, can yield self-sustaining growth. Even the World
Bank, busy making billions of dollars in loans annually to authoritarian,
socialist governments, argued nearly a decade ago that for SubSaharan
Africa: "better use of investment—both domestic and foreign—is the
key issue. Making the most of investment requires not only appropriate

pricing policies, but also adequate management capacity in the government, supplemented by technical assistance. In addition, it requires a more active role for nongovernmental institutions and for the private sector."

Although there has been some recent movement away from collectivist economic strategies, many nations on the continent remain trapped by their *dirigiste* past. The problem, indeed, is more than socialism, for economic and political freedom tend to go together. What we see, argues Dr. George Ayittey, an economist from Ghana, is "black neocolonialism" in which elites left Africa to be educated and "assumed the trappings of foreign cultures and ideologies" before returning "with a vengence to denigrate, to enslave, to destroy, and to colonize by imposing alien ideological systems upon the African people." Africans across the continent are now desperately struggling for freedom—economic as well as political—but dictators like Zaire's Mobutu Sese Seko continue to desperately hold on. And as long as such autocratic, venal ruling establishments remain in place, self-sustaining development will remain but a distant dream.

## The Role of Foreign Aid

Foreign assistance has long been a sacred cow, with studies of program effectiveness usually paid for by aid agencies themselves. Critical thinking has not been thought to be necessary because, notes Graham Hancock, formerly of Britain's *Economist* magazine, "The notion that increased aid from the North will result in improved conditions in the South is...treated as though it were a self-evident truth." Alas, the charade can continue no longer. Far too many examples of failure, many of them relentlessly exposed by Hancock, exist to ignore the misdeeds of foreign aid any longer. Indeed, in this sad way Hancock notes that "Africa contains many lessons for the aid lobby"—almost all bad.

In evaluating foreign aid, we need to answer two questions. The first is, What contribution has foreign assistance so far played in determining the course of African development? The second is, Can we make aid work any better in the future than it has in the past?

*What contribution has foreign assistance played in determining the course of African development?* Not all foreign aid is created equal. A relatively small amount of international assistance, both bilateral as well as multilateral, has been largely humanitarian—disaster relief and food shipments, for instance. Individual nations have also regularly provided security aid, largely intended to promote military and political interests. Although these programs are not directly intended to affect the development of recipients, they inevitably have an economic impact.

Humanitarian assistance largely takes three forms. First, Western aid agencies have provided pre-disaster planning, technical, and managerial assistance to poorer nations to help reduce the impacts of floods, cyclones, droughts, fires, landslides, and epidemics. Second, assistance has taken the form of goods and services in direct response to emergencies. Both of these forms of assistance have proved to be largely beneficial. The third type of "humanitarian" aid, however—subsidized food, especially that from the United States—has a less positive record.

Food for Peace, or P.L. 480, as the American program is known, was created more to dump surplus U.S. crops in foreign markets than to alleviate starvation; just 14 percent of food shipments go to disaster-stricken areas. Even in the latter case poorly timed assistance can have perverse effects—wheat shipments to Guatemala following the 1976 earthquake devastated local farmers, whose crops remained intact, by undercutting the demand for domestically produced wheat. Moreover, the potential availability of even temporary aid may exacerbate the irresponsibity of callous governments, like the communist Mengistu regime in Ethiopia. The latter squandered upwards of $200 million on its tenth anniversary celebration in 1984 with the knowledge that the West would probably help meet any food needs that might result from its consequent lack of resources to purchase needed food.

Of course, in some cases, like Somalia today, temporary food assistance might not have such negative effects. However, the bulk of Food for Peace aid is distributed on a continuing basis over the long-term in normal peacetime, not temporarily during dire crises. The almost inevitable result is to harm indigenous farmers. Large, ongoing shipments of food to India bankrupted native farmers throughout the 1950s and 1960s. Farmers in Haiti learned not to bring their produce to market during periods when P.L. 480 food was distributed. Even an internal Agency for International Development audit found that "the long-term feeding programs in the same areas for ten years or more have great potential for food production...disincentives." Such permanent doles have appeared in Tanzania and other African countries as well. Complained one Tanzanian priest, "residents of this area could grow all the food they wanted, but had chosen no to" do so because of U.S. food aid.

Long term crop aid programs have a second deleterious effect, and that is to effectively subsidize perverse recipient policies that discourage indigenous agricultural production. The effect is indirect but powerful: ongoing food assistance ameliorates and disguises the fall in production that always accompanies government price controls, monopoly marketing boards, crop seizures and the like. In this way governments are insulated from the folly of their policies and face none of the reform pressures that would otherwise build. In Egypt, for instance, generous Western crop aid has allowed the government to maintain food price controls that make it worthwhile for farmers to feed bread to their animals and poultry. Without foreign assistance this policy would be quickly seen as ruinous.

Since money is fungible, some forms of military assistance can have as much economic effect as official development aid. As such, it can have some of the same disincentive effects discussed later. More narrowly targeted security aid—particularly weapons shipments and military training—pose different problems for recipient nations. The first is to encourage countries to divert larger shares of their resources to military purposes. Foreign funding that enhances security establishments also probably helps militarize what are often fragile and unstable political systems. The second problem, again, is more indirect and harder to measure, but remains serious nonetheless. And that is, military aid helps strengthen regimes that are socialist if nevertheless perceived as "pro-West." The negative impacts of security aid on economic development are evident in the nearby Mideast, particularly Egypt and Israel. These nations receive the largest shares of U.S. assistance—both in direct military aid and in economic aid provided for security purposes—and both have highly collectivized economies. The free market advice routinely dispensed by the Agency for International Development and private analysts and organizations has been just as regularly ignored because these two nations can count on extremely high levels of assistance irrespective of the quality of their policies.

Still, supporters of humanitarian and especially military assistance can at least argue that their programs yield alternative benefits that compensate for any unintended development disincentives. What of economic assistance, which exists solely to promote growth in recipient nations? By and large these programs have failed to fulfill their objectives, without rendering any countervailing advantages.

This is not, of course, to say that no good has been achieved from the hundreds of billions of dollars provided by the OECD and OPEC countries, the World Bank and regional lending institutions, the International Monetary Fund, and the United Nations Development Fund. It would, in fact, be hard to spend so much without achieving something. But the results are surprisingly meager, and in many cases aid appears to have retarded rather than promoted development.

This should come as no surprise. Much concessional aid is merely cheap loans. Compared to the GNP of most countries, then, this contribution, the interest rate savings, is quite small—less than one-half of a percent for India, for instance. Concludes economist P.T. Bauer, foreign aid can do little more than "reduce somewhat the cost of a resource which is not a major independent factor in economic development." In any case, poorer countries have not demonstrated a lack of access to capital. Rather, the problem is that these loans have not been well-used, which is why so many poorer nations have had difficulty servicing their debts.

*Foreign Aid by Its Very Nature Discourages Efficient Use*

A fundamental problem with foreign assistance is that donors and recipients are both using other people's money. Borrowers are likely to value less, and thus use less well, cheap foreign funds, especially where aid seems likely to continue year after year, than resources garnered at real cost. Moreover, size of foreign transfers, rather than the use to which they are put, becomes the most obvious sign of success within ruling circles.

Similarly, aid agencies usually reward staffers who give prodigiously, not those who give wisely. The Agency for International Development's Inspector General concluded in one report that "considerable pressure existed to program and spend project funds, with a lesser concern for effective use of the monies." Similarly, observed one official at the World Bank during the busy McNamara years, "We're like a Soviet factory. The push is to maximize lending. The...pressures to lend are enormous and a lot of people spend sleepless nights wondering how they can unload projects. Our ability to influence projects in a way that makes sense is completely undermined." One would like to believe that this problem was only in the past, but more recent studies of Bank programs have found that loan officers continue to be overly desirous of making loans, often more so than recipients to receive them. In 1987, for instance, one internal Operations Evaluation Department audit conceded that "the Bank's drive to reach lending targets" had resulted in "poor project performance." The so-called Wapenhans report, issued in late 1992, reached a similar conclusion.

The results are often comic-tragic. Blaine Harden reports on the utter fiasco resulting from Western-subsidized projects involving Nigeria's nomadic Turkana people in which so-called experts worked hard to destroy traditional social structures while ignoring climatological, political, and scientific realities. In a scorching critique of Western aid policies in Africa scientists Karl Borgin and Kathleen Corbett argue that aid money is routinely spread over small, transitory projects; wasted on programs the Africans could undertake themselves; used to subsidize small-scale ventures that contribute little to development; and promote inappropriate agriculture, "either primitive small-scale farming or huge state-owned enterprises."

The bureaucratic imperatives of foreign assistance manifest themselves in another way: a bias, on the part of recipients as well as donors, towards new projects rather than upkeep on old ones. Of aid to Africa, concludes the World Bank, "African governments and donors continue to prefer new projects, especially new schools and hospitals, when the greatest urgency is to provide more resources to operate and maintain (and, increasingly, rehabilitate) existing projects." This problem bedevils agricultural programs as well. Blaine Harden writes that most "donor-funded African development schemes" fail the sustainability test: "irrigation often flunks even before donors leave." It should come as no surprise, then, that a 1987 Operations Evaluation Department study of two decades of rural development programs found a failure rate of 37 percent.

## Foreign Aid Encourages Borrowers to
## Put Resources into Fiscal Black Holes

It is bad enough when assistance from abroad must be repaid. Developing states are thus left with painful debts even after the projects for which the money was lent are in ruins: collapsed warehouses, impassable roads, contaminated wells, unfinished mills, unlit runways. Yet far more serious are the projects that result in continuing red ink. Most pronounced in Latin America and India but still a serious problem in Africa has been the rise of aid-funded parastatals, or government enterprises. Countries have borrowed lavishly to create heavy industries, like steel and petrochemicals, and prestige concerns, like universities, glittering capital cities, and state airlines. In India, for instance, economist Shyam Kamath writes that U.S. assistance "was used to finance government fertilizer and industrial plants, large-scale irrigation projects, state-owned power and rural electrification projects, dairy development, highway construction, locomotives and rolling stock for the government-owned railway system, airplanes for the state-owned international airline, agricultural extension and the establishment of agricultural universities, and technical assistance and equipment for large state-owned institutions of higher education." Much of this spending would have been impossible without foreign funds from organizations like the IMF and World Bank, as well as the OECD nations.

Yet although foreign loans often help offset the initial investment in such projects, the borrower must not only repay the loan but also absorb often enormous operating losses. The public sector's red ink in the big Latin debtors, Argentina, Brazil, and Mexico, has been particularly staggering. But the burden has also proved overwhelming for many smaller, poorer African states. Of Tanzania, for instance, economist Thomas Sowell observed that after receiving more foreign aid per capita than any nation, "nearly half of the more than 300 companies expropriated by the government ('nationalized') were bankrupt by 1975, with many of the remainder operating at a loss."

*Foreign Aid Has Accelerated the Disastrous
Politicization of Third World Societies*

Despite their rhetoric, recipient governments may not be genuinely committed to development, "not simply because of the obvious fact that the process of development is intrinsically destabilizing—resisting development may also be destabilizing—but also because the gains from development may go to the wrong groups," observes Robert Rothstein. The tendency of ruling elites, then, particularly in societies where political power is so important, is to use aid, or domestic funds released by foreign assistance, to strengthen their own position, reward their supporters, and buy off or crush opposition movements. Dictators around the world disagree about many things, but all recognize the importance of preserving their own power.

However, the problem is not just that foreign assistance is used in normal political battles. Alas, aid exacerbates and intensifies such struggles. Politics already dominates life in many developing states because control of the government and the political apparatus is control of virtually everything worth controlling. In the main, there are fewer alternative power structures—independent business, labor unions, media organizations, and the like—in poorer countries. Thus, funneling more resources, including those from abroad, through the state enhances both state power and the rewards for seizing power.

## Foreign Aid Reinforces Poor Nations' Psychological Dependence on Outside Actors to Solve Their Problems

Many Third World leaders have long blamed their economic difficulties on foreign governments and international economic forces. Colonialism and imperialism, for instance, as well as an allegedly unfair international economic system, have been favorite targets. The answer, then, is obviously not only to right the alleged wrong, but also to win reparations as redress. Tanzania's Julius Nyerere was one of the Third World leaders most effective at making Westerners feel guilty. He told one audience that "in one world, as in one state, when I am rich because you are poor, and I am poor because you are rich, the transfer of wealth from the rich to the poor is a matter of right; it is not an appropriate matter for charity."

Yet the premise that some countries are poor *because* others are rich is simply false. Most poor countries cannot blame other nations for their problems. Colonialism was a grotesque violation of personal liberty and affront to human dignity, but many former colonies have had higher incomes than many independent states. Indeed, Third World states have been most harmed by *interferences with* the international marketplace, particularly protectionism. Yet the pursuit of "aid" from abroad has diverted innumerable personnel and significant resources from private development efforts.

*Foreign Aid Effectively Subsidizes Growth Inhibiting Policies*

As noted earlier, there is no longer any doubt as to why many Third World economies have performed so poorly. Again and again, developing states have mismanaged their economies by trying to manage them. Ill-considered state intervention in the economies of developing nations has taken four general forms. The first involves the size of the public sector and the number of goods and services directly produced by it. Many countries have a host of state enterprises that, either on a competitive or monopoly basis, are involved in nearly every aspect of business activity, including electrical utilities, steel manufacturing, pharmaceutical distribution, and textile milling. The vast majority of these entities lose money, draining valuable capital and personnel from more productive activities.

Restrictions on prices and production, which skew the incentives of suppliers and the demand of consumers, are a second type of self-inflicted economic wound. Some Third World countries prop up their exchange rates, overvaluing their exports and making imports artificially inexpensive. High tariffs and import licensing prorams are used by others to protect selected domestic industries, raising costs to other indigenous enterprises, including those that export abroad. Many countries favor their urban populations by subsidizing the cost of food, utilities, and other goods and services; some use state marketing boards to hold down the prices paid to farmers. Such policies discourage private production and innovation, inflate demand, and exacerbate national budget deficits.

Third, many governments have adopted perverse monetary, fiscal, and credit policies. Expansionary monetary growth, exceptionally high marginal income tax rates and heavy overall tax burdens, large budget deficits, strict interest rate limits, and other disruptive credit controls have all contributed to widespread economic instability and stagnation.

Finally, foreign investment is actively discouraged by many developing countries. A host of burdensome rules have been imposed on multinational corporations, including: limits on repatriation of profits and ownership of shares in local operations; hiring preferences and quotas for local labor; business disclosure requirements; patent and trademark abridgments; detailed business regulations, including producer and supplier controls; and technology transfer requirements. These many investment disincentives are compounded by the difficulty of dealing with often grossly inefficient and corrupt bureaucracies, the risk of nationalization, and a prohibition of outside investment in certain economic sectors.

In short, Dr. Ayittey's conclusion that the basic cause of African underdevelopment is faulty policies promulgated by authoritarian elites is correct. Perhaps the most important measure of the value of foreign aid, then, is whether or not it encourages governments to improve those policies. Unfortunately, the answer is usually no.

At times donors have advanced bad policies that recipient governments have only too happily executed. The IMF, for instance, is responsible for tax increases and currency devaluations throughout the Third World. For decades the World Bank has promoted state-run development programs. In 1983 Bank staffer Stanley Please reflected on his two decades at the institution:

> As a committed socialist...I was surprised and shocked by the emphasis which the Bank at the time gave to the public sector in general and to the government in particular. Here was an institution which had the reputation of being ultra free-enterprise and market-oriented, yet had more confidence in the rationality, morality and competence of governments than I ever had.

Indeed, observed one Reagan administration official, "it's hard to expect a government-owned multilateral body not to be primarily responsive to other governments and take the view that government-sponsored, government-owned, government-guaranteed projects are the best thing going." Even where donors officially and publicly deplore recipient policies, however, foreign aid has proved to be an impediment to growth because it has subsidized the very policies being criticized. In the case of foreign assistance, money speaks louder than words.

Project lending by the World Bank, which accounts for the bulk of that institution's credit, has had a similar effect. The Bank talks about conducting a "policy dialogue" with borrowers, yet it has admitted that "the link with lending was still not as close as desirable." And how could it be, since the Bank has regularly underwritten millions, even billions, of dollars worth of projects in nations irrespective of their policy environments? And aid officials know what they are doing. In 1981, for example, the Bank reported that the collapse of agricultural production and exports in Ghana and Tanzania was due to heavy taxes on farmers.

Yet the previous year the Bank approved a $29.5 million loan to Ghana to help train farmers and a $77 million loan to Tanzania for four agricultural projects. In 1984 the Bank's annual World Development Report repeatedly scored investment policies in developing countries, singling out Brazil, the Ivory Coast, Nigeria, Peru, and Turkey for having "over-ambitious or inefficient investment programs." Yet that same year Brazil borrowed $1.6 billion for ten different projects, while the other four countries together collected an equivalent amount. In the end, lending institutions and governments rarely ever try to get tough with recipients.

The IMF has a fearsome reputation for "conditionality," yet positive results from its efforts are hard to see. Even friends of the organization have found few success stories to praise. Richard Feinberg and Catherine Gwin, for instance, concluded in 1989 that "the record of IMF-assisted adjustment efforts in Sub-Saharan Africa is discouraging. Many IMF-assisted programs, adopted in response to steep economic decline, have broken down." Harvard economist Jeffrey Sachs admits that most agreements "are now honored in the breach." Raymond Mikesell of the University of Oregon reports that "most oil-importing LDCs are not pursuing policies associated with successful adjustment and growth" despite the IMF's efforts.

In fact, the Fund has been subsidizing the world's economic basket cases for years, without apparent effect. Countries like Egypt, India, Sudan, Turkey, and Yugoslavia first started relying on the IMF more than 30 years ago. Dozens more began using credit between 20 and 30 years ago. While the IMF has not necessarily caused nations to become permanently dependent on foreign aid, its efforts do not appear to have helped any nation achieve independence through self-sustaining growth.

The same lack of result has been evident even with World Bank loans that require policy reform, since the organization often fails to enforce its conditions. Observed one internal Bank audit: "Where failure to comply with covenants has occurred, the Bank has generally been complaisant. Vagueness of covenant requirements, however, has generally saved both Borrower and the Bank from the embarrassment of deciding what to do." Little more has been achieved by sectoral and structural adjustment loans which, like IMF credit, are supposedly advanced specifically to change borrower policies. Bank consultants Elliot Berg and Alan Batchelder report that these loans had no measurable impact on borrowers' GNPs and suffered from a number of crippling problems, including an unwillingness to cut off countries that failed to perform. It is no wonder, then, that James Burnham, former U.S. executive director of the Bank, wrote that policy-based credits have been turned into "unconditional balance-of-payments financing and, in effect, a subsidy to cover up problems caused by a borrower's poor economic policies."

Put bluntly, the constant flow of foreign funds, however targeted or conditioned, has given governments sufficient resources to allow them to implement policies that have often wrecked their economies. True, the time of reckoning finally came not only for the communist states but also for many collectivist regimes throughout the developing world, including Africa. But Western assistance unnecessarily prolonged the process. Even lavishly bribing leaders of borrowing states not to strangle their economies will never be as effective as cutting them off, simply allowing statist regimes to bear the consequences of their disastrous policies. Until now Third World debtors have been treated like drunks who were handed a wad of cash and told to drink no more. They are more likely to do the right thing when the industrialized West stops subsidizing their profligacy, leaving them no other choice.

## Can We Make Aid Work Any Better In The Future Than It Has In The Past?

So great has been the waste of foreign assistance, so mismanaged the programs, so perverse the impact on borrowing governments, that even many officials active in the aid community have had to acknowledge that past efforts have been ineffective at best and completely counterproductive at worst. Their response, however, is to request another chance—so that now they can use assistance to promote the reform process. This premise led the once-critical Reagan administration to support a general capital increase for the World Bank and the Bush administration to approve a 50 percent hike in the IMF's resources. This is also the justification for the ever-growing lending programs to Eastern Europe and the former Soviet Union.

Yet very little has changed with foreign aid in practice. Both donors and recipients remain biased towards increased lending and new projects. Huge loans continue to be made to governments and state entities. Aid officials remain reluctant to cut off nations that fail to implement promised reforms. Aid transfers still strengthen the political public sector. And Western assistance continues to relieve the pressure for domestic reform by ameliorating the consequences of past failed policies.

Indeed, this is precisely what the World Bank's experience with its adjustment lending program should have taught us. Ultimately governments have to be committed to adopting a broad range of market reforms because they are right, not because Westerners are willing to offer a little more money for them. Warn World Bank consultants Elliot Berg and Alan Batchelder: "It's almost never enough to make one-time changes in producer prices, subsidies, exchange rates. Successive adjustments are required, to account for price changes and other new factors. So it is a policy adjustment *process* that is needed." So frustrated were Berg and Batchelder with the failures of adjustment lending—and the fact that "difficulties of implementation are frequently treated in an extraordinarily cavalier way"—that they proposed shifting back toward project lending. Doing so would at least have the benefit of publicly acknowledging that it is next to impossible to buy the necessary political courage for foreign governments to adopt politically painful reforms. The belief that new lending can accomplish what nearly five decades of aid has failed to achieve is an expensive delusion.

## Conclusion

The catastrophe enveloping Somalia and the serious problems involving so many other poor nations should move hearts worldwide. With the end of the Cold War, the frustrating persistence of poverty amid plenty may be our most serious, and seemingly intractable, international problem. Citizens of wealthier nations should approach this issue with sensitivity, realizing that, as sociologist Peter Berger has observed, "immense anguish and pain, physical as well as moral, have been associated with the entry of [poorer peoples] into the common history of our age."

But continuing to treat foreign aid as an answer to Third World underdevelopment is neither sensitive nor compassionate. While the West does have much to answer for regarding its meddling in smaller states—arbitrary colonial line-drawing is an important cause of much of the conflict in Africa—financial transfers are no answer. Even America's AID now admits that many of its programs have failed: "much of what has haphazardly evolved as development assistance over the past four decades has not worked, has sometimes not even been aimed at the correct objectives, and, above all, has been overtaken by events." Thus, African states need to look inward to find the solutions to the tragedy of poverty and underdevelopment. In the end, it is domestic political leaders who pursue policies that stifle economic incentive, confiscate personal earnings, deter private investment, and oppress their own people, not foreign taxpayers who have contributed tens of billions of dollars internationally year after year, who bear the moral responsibility for international stagnation. Only after Third World peoples replace those officials and transform those policies will they achieve their potential.

July 1993

# 13

# World Bank: Servant of Governments, Not Peoples

Although the international debt crisis has received wide attention around the world, the institutions most concerned with Third World development, such as the World Bank, have operated largely outside the glare of unwanted publicity. The lack of critical attention has allowed them to generate a wide base of political support. Thus, when Bank president Barber Conable declared in September 1986 that "the Bank's role is to lead," there were few who disagreed. For the Bank, at least, more is always better.

Given its apparent success, the World Bank, created in 1944, has spawned a host of smaller imitators, most recently the European Bank for Reconstruction and Development. The EBRD was intended to help Europe's former communist states move towards capitalism and democracy. Yet after just two years of operation, the EBRD had little to show for its efforts other than $300 million in overhead expenses. As of 1993 the EBRD had spent $80 million on its headquarters building alone. Indeed, when then-President Jacques Attali found the Travertine marble in the lobby to be inappropriate, he spent $1.1 million to replace it with Carrara marble. All told, the EBRD's per employee cost was an astounding $237,000. Explained Attali, he felt a "duty to provide [Bank employees] with a very good environment."

While the EBRD's excesses seem extreme, it has followed the example of the World Bank, which has long cared more about the people working for it and the governments to which it lends than the peoples around the globe it is supposed to serve. The Bank's headquarters in Washington, for instance, is well-furnished, if not full of Carrara marble. The Bank's Board of Executive Directors, for years perfectly supine as the Bank funded projects that displaced millions of people and destroyed thousands of hectares of rain forest, rose up in horror in 1991 when the newly created EBRD decided to pay Attali an annual salary of $290,000, exceeding that of Bank president Conable, then earning $225,000 a year. The Bank's directors promptly approved a $60,000 pay hike, automatically raising the pay ceiling of other staffers by $36,000 to $190,000 as well. Bank staff are also eligible for a full range of perquisites: a salary supplement for spouses, a cash grant for each child, money for childrens' education, subsidized meals, and generous support for travel—first class or business—for home leave. And most employees fly first class while traveling internationally, a privilege jealously guarded. All told, Bank staffers cost $207,000 each.

Even employees who depart are treated very well. In 1987 Bank President Barber Conable initiated a $148 million reorganization. Eighty staffers left voluntarily, with "golden handshakes" averaging $134,000. Another 418 employees were fired—after collecting an average of $291,000. Conable's intent was to reduce the Bank's staff of 6200 and administrative budget of $816 million. By early 1993 the Bank employed more than 7000 people at a cost of $1.25 billion.

But the real scandal of the Bank is not that its staff members live well off of middle-class taxpayers in the industrialized countries. Rather, it is that the Bank serves the interests of foreign governments rather than peoples, encouraging poor nations to overdose on expensive loans that ultimately yield only debt and stagnation. As developing states have suffered, the Bank's only response has been to demand more money. In 1986, after decades of piling tens of billions in bad, new loans on top of bad, old ones, Bank President A.W. Clausen advocated a new financial infusion, explaining that "the Bank should not be constrained by lack of capital in meeting future demand." In 1993 Bank president Lewis Preston was pressing for yet another increase in funding: "Nothing less than the lives of millions of the poor" were at stake, he explained.

## A New World Order

The World Bank, officially the International Bank for Reconstruction and Development, was established along with the International Monetary Fund as part of the reordering of the global economic system in the aftermath of World War II. The Bank, presently owned by 155 member nations, was envisioned as a conservative public bank, a financial institution to help developing countries where the global capital markets proved inadequate. The articles of agreement explicitly directed the Bank, which relies both on capital infusions from member nations and commercial borrowing, to be only a "lender of last resort."

The Bank soon expanded its authority, however, by creating two separate, more specialized institutions. The International Finance Corporation was established in 1956 to lend to private entities in order to promote private investment. Four years later came the International Development Association, which was seeking in 1993 an $18 billion increase in funding, to act as a "soft lending window," providing heavily-subsidized loans, for poorer nations. Collectively these organizations are known as the World Bank Group.

Nevertheless, in its early years the Bank was a careful lender. In its 1948–1949 annual report, the Bank observed that "money alone is no solution.... Perhaps the most striking single lesson which the Bank has learned in the course of its operations is how limited is the capacity of the underdeveloped countries to absorb capital quickly for productive purposes." Equally important, the Bank required loan applicants to settle private defaults before extending credit, refused to lend to nations that expropriated property without adequate compensation, and would not back industrial projects that were not intended to be transferred into private hands. While such an approach may appear cold-hearted, it protected lender and borrower alike: projects were likely to yield some economic benefits, loans would not be provided if the borrower actively discouraged private investment, irresponsible governments could not look to Bank for open-ended subsidies, and lavish lending did not underwrite authoritarian regimes for which development was manifestly less important than maintaining power.

The Bank's policy began to change in 1960, however, with the creation of IDA. Even then the Bank felt no pressure to constantly increase lending, however, and the Bank's management tended to eschew lending that would result in debt service obligations exceeding ten percent of a borrower's export earnings. (In contrast, during the 1980s the Bank upped lending to Latin America despite a regional debt service ratio of 40 percent.)

## The McNamara Years

Bank presidents, traditionally selected by the United States, the largest Bank shareholder, have always dominated their boards of executive directors. Robert McNamara, Lyndon Johnson's Secretary of Defense during the Vietnam War, was no exception. In a sense, McNamara, named in 1968, turned the Bank into an international extension of President Johnson's "Great Society," attempting to solve serious, long-term economic and social problems with ever-larger cash transfers. Two decades later Third World peoples are still paying for his policies.

Between 1968 and 1981, when McNamara retired, total Bank (IBRD and IDA) lending jumped from $954 million to $12.3 billion, almost as much as the Bank had lent from its founding to McNamara's hiring. Admitted one Bank official at the time: "We're like a Soviet factory. The push is to maximize lending. The quantity control mechanism means that in May and June [before the end of the fiscal year] the pressures to lend are enormous and a lot of people spend sleepless nights wondering how they can unload projects. Our ability to influence projects in a way that makes sense is completely undermined."

But McNamara was not interested in designing fiscally sound projects. To the contrary, he was reported to be "almost obsessed with redistribution of income" and was determined to remake poorer societies into his preferred image, irrespective of the cost to Western taxpayers and desire of Third World citizens—by reducing birthrates, fostering industry, building dams, moving populations, and much more. Loans for social service projects, such as education, population, and urbanization, jumped from 3.6 percent in 1968 to 14.5 percent in 1981. Moreover, agricultural lending, long a critical part of the Bank's portfolio, increasingly turned from projects, such as irrigation systems, that were expected to help generate economic growth, to more nebulous "rural development" projects that seemed more like American social programs.

McNamara combined a commitment to top-down social change with a devotion to state-led development strategies. During the 1970s the Bank committed roughly 80 percent of its funds to public enterprises. In its 1975 annual report the Bank declared the existence of an overriding "need, at the national level of government, for a strong commitment to rural development policies." Having demanded that borrowing governments manage the economies, however, McNamara's Bank refused to judge their efforts, stating that it was "in no position, nor would it want to be, to dictate the design of such programs." In short, if a borrowing government decided that peasants should be forced out of ancestral villages into state collectives—as they were by Julius Nyerere's coercive "ujamaa" program, which brutalized peasants and devastated the nation's agricultural economy—the Bank would underwrite it.

As the 1980s dawned even the Bank could not help but notice that events were not turning out as it had planned: international debts were rising and borrowers' incomes were stagnating or falling. Yes, admitted the Bank in its 1980 annual report, there had been setbacks—a rather mild term to describe growing Third World poverty, indebtedness, and social collapse—but "lessons were learned and experience was gained." The Bank went on to explain that some countries were planning "to define the role of the public sector more selectively than before; elsewhere, however, it will be necessary to rationalize the policy framework of parastatal entities and revamp institutional relationships so that public enterprises might achieve the objectives for which they were created." In short, the Bank's strategy for the future was simply a little better implementation of its previous approach—along with more lending, of course.

## A New Era?

The appointment of A.W. Clausen as president in 1981 dramatically changed the institution's official rhetoric. For instance, Clausen stated that: "In their dialogue with governments, aid organizations, both multilateral and bilateral, have been less concerned with promoting private sector growth than with assisting the development of an effective public sector. That emphasis, in my view, is misplaced; aid agencies ought to be making, and must take, a more balanced approach." In 1987 the Bank discussed its willingness to tackle what had once been the great unmentionable—borrowers' domestic economic policies, such as price controls, regulations, distorted financial policies, and protectionist trade rules.

Yet actual lending practices changed little. Loans in 1991 ran $22.685 billion, nearly twice the $12.291 billion a decade earlier. When lending dipped in 1985, for the first time since 1968, the official Bank reaction seemed to be one of profound embarrassment; the annual report explained why the organization was prevented from lending more. Before he left office Clausen was emphasizing the importance of upping Bank lending to $20 billion by 1990, a goal achieved with the help of his successor, Barber Conable, who successfully pressed the industrialized nations to approve a $74.8 billion increase in the institution's capital.

Nor has the Bank abandoned its support for inefficient Third World industrial enterprises or social development projects. The bulk of lending still goes to public enterprises—$1.34 billion in the field of energy exploration and power production in 1991, for instance—that often act as fiscal black holes, draining away otherwise productive resources. Further, the Bank continues to attempt to reorder Third World societies. In 1985, under Clausen's leadership, the Bank was actually devoting a larger share of its funds to social purposes—education, population, urbanization—than it did in 1981. By 1991 these projects accounted for $6 billion, or 27.8 percent of Bank funds.

Not surprisingly, the benefits of the billions in new Bank lending have proved to be as fleeting as before. Indeed, the Bank's single-minded dedication to lending ever more itself resulted in significant numbers of project failures: an internal Operations Evaluation Department audit in 1987 conceded that "the Bank's drive to reach lending targets" had led to "poor project performance." Even more pernicious, expansive Bank loans encouraged countries to borrow and spend more than they could use wisely. And the Bank knew better. Its 1984 *World Development Report*, for example, repeatedly criticized the economic policies of the very nations that were borrowing most extensively from the Bank. Officials singled out Brazil, Ivory Coast, Nigeria, Peru, and Turkey, for combining "negative real interest rates with overambitious or inefficient investment programs." *In the very same year*, however, Brazil borrowed $1.604 billion for ten different projects, using fully 10.3 percent of the Bank's entire credit line. Turkey collected $794.3 million, Nigeria $438 million, the Ivory Coast $250.7 million, and Peru $122.5 million. In these cases and more, the Bank was promoting debt, not development.

Failed lending strategies like this persist because the Bank continues to be run for the benefit of governments, not peoples. And while it is pro-business, benefiting firms throughout the industrialized world that provide many of the goods and services purchased by Bank borrowers, the institution is not pro-capitalist. A freely competitive international marketplace, in contrast to the Bank's carefully controlled and subsidized one, is anathema to would-be economic and social engineers in both the Bank's Washington headquarters and the planning agencies in Third World capitals.

The basic problem is simple: the Bank is a government institution that deals with other governments and primarily relies on a professional staff largely headquartered in Washington, backed by a cohort of "experts," people who make their lives selling advice, not growing crops or starting businesses. In the minds of many Bank officials development projects affect things, not people, at least not people capable of deciding on their own futures. After a group of development officials toured one Senegalese village, a peasant commented that "They do not know that there are living people here."

After decades of large-scale lending programs, two Bank researchers admitted that the lack of citizen participation was an important cause of failure: "Project planners have repeatedly made unduly optimistic assumptions about the likely outcome of projects by overestimating the local people's interest in a project, their recognition of a need for it, the resources available to them for implementing the project, and economic and social incentives to do so, and the rate at which change in their social condition can take place." But despite these sort of criticisms, the project review process continues to run from capital to capital; those with the most at stake, such as peasants likely to be forced off of their land, are still never consulted. For instance, India's massive Sardar Sarovar dam complex, projected to displace 240,000 people, was arranged as if people simply didn't exist. Concluded an independent review of the Bank-funded project:

> In 1985, when the credit and loan agreements were signed, no basis for designing, implementing, and assessing resettlement and rehabilitation was in place. The numbers of people to be affected were not known; the range of likely impacts had never been considered; the canal had been overlooked. Nor had there been any consultation with those at risk. Nor were there benchmark data with which to assess success or failure. As a result, there was no adequate resettlement plan, with the result that human costs could not be included as part of the equation. Policies to mitigate those costs could not be designed in accord with people's actual needs.

## Human and Environmental Costs

It should come as no surprise, then, that Bank lending has failed in its essential purpose, of promoting economic growth. At the same time, however, Bank projects have harmed the lives of many Third World peoples—sometimes by its general support for venal dictatorships, at other times by subsidizing individual projects in both democracies and autocracies that have had disastrous social and environmental consequences.

For instance, Bank policy towards Ethiopia, ruled throughout the 1980s by a murderous dictator who consciously starved hundreds of thousands of people, is inexplicable. After the 1974 communist revolution the Bank doubled its support for the East African country; Bank support hit $166 million in 1985, with the money to be used to purchase fertilizer, promote agricultural research, improve education, and expand telecommunications services. Similarly indefensible was the Bank's decision to lend to Ceausescu's Romania, a regime bizarre even by communist standards. Over the years Romania received 34 loans worth $2.4 billion for everything from cattle and pig farming to the production of chemicals, pipe, and steel to oil recovery and power generation. As he cashed his Bank checks Ceausescu busily brutalized and impoverished his people.

In fact, the Bank appears to have never found an authoritarian government or coercive social program that it did not like. The Washington, D.C.-based Environmental Defense Fund estimates that during the 1980s some 95 Bank projects displaced more than two million people, almost all poor. Projects that would evict more than a million more remain under consideration for the future. The worst Bank-supported programs, particularly Tanzania's ujamaa movement, Vietnam's New Economic Zones, and Indonesia's transmigration program, *had as their purpose* the forcible removal of people. Their consequences were deaths, massive violations of human rights, social disruption, and economic deterioration.

Many others projects necessarily forced out local populations. Road construction, for instance, has regularly displaced surrounding peasants, and was used by Ethiopia as an excuse to seize the property of local peasants. Roads are often integral to larger development efforts, such as Brazil's $1.6 billion POLONOROESTE project, which developed an area of the rain forest larger than California. The Bank-financed project pushed out thousands of indigenous peoples and cleared large sections of the rain forest in both Rondonia and Mato Grosso provinces. Concluded one Bank assessment, the initiative proved to be "an ecological, human and economic disaster of tremendous dimensions."

Dams and irrigation systems have proved to be even more devastating. Construction of the Kariba Dam in Zambia during the 1970s, for instance, led to violent resistance and some deaths. Ghana's Akosombo Dam forced the displacement of some 80,000 people, many of whom never received compensation for their land. China's Ertan and Daguangba Hainan projects together will force the removal of more than 50,000 people. All told, over the last two decades some 400 water projects have moved millions of people.

Perhaps the most celebrated Bank project is India's Sardar Sarovar dam in the Narmada River. Under pressure to safeguard the interests of local residents, India announced in early 1993 that it would not request the $170 million remaining of the Bank's $450 million loan (originally approved in 1985). The system of more than 3,000 dams will submerge 37,000 hectares of land and displace an estimated 240,000 people. So strong was the criticism of the project that in 1991 outgoing Bank president Conable appointed an outside advisory panel, which found the Bank to be guilty of "gross delinquency" in its handling of the project. Sardar Sarovar also illustrates the almost complete impotence of the Bank's executive directors, since representatives of the U.S., Germany, and several other nations requested in October 1992 that the Bank halt the project, only to be ignored.

All of these projects have harmed the environment as well as transgressed human rights. The Indonesian transmigration program, for instance, destroyed tropical rain forces. Complains Bruce Rich of the Environmental Defense Fund, Western aid agencies, including the Bank, funneled three-fourths of their "forestry assistance" through the very same agencies that were "simultaneously financing the deforestation, watershed erosion and land deterioration that is occurring in many transmigration sites." Livestock promotion in Africa, particularly Botswana, has caused overgrazing and desertification, as well as disrupted the migration of wild animals. Mining projects, such as the Bank-supported Companhia Vale do Rio Doce iron ore mine in Brazil, helped spur surrounding development that has encouraged deforestation, desertification, and flooding. The devastating consequences of scores of hydro projects are equally obvious. Even seemingly innocuous industrial subsidies, to state power firms, for instance, have "adverse environmental consequences," admits the Bank—after pouring billions of dollars into public power sectors for decades.

Under pressure from American environmental groups, which were opposing Bank efforts to win American congressional approval of a general capital increase, in 1987 the Bank created an environmental division, added three score environmental staffers, and promised to be more sensitive to environmental concerns in the future. Three years later the Bank established the Global Environment Facility to lend for environmental management and other purposes. In 1992 the institution declared that it had "embarked on a major effort to incorporate environmental concerns into all aspects of its work."

These steps sounded good, but the Bank's basic orientation—aid for government economic projects irrespective of the costs or consequences—did not change. Indeed, some Bank "environmental" initiatives proved to be anything but that. One forestry and fisheries project in Guinea, for instance, was touted as part of the Bank's Tropical Forestry Action Plan to protect forests but, complained the EDF's Rich, "actually amounts to a deforestation scheme: the Bank's money will help support the construction of 45 miles of roads in or around two forest reserves totalling 150,000 hectares, of which some 106,000 hectares are still pristine rainforest." It should perhaps come as no surprise, then, that even the Bank acknowledged that TFAP's "results have fallen short of expectations."

In any case, a few environmental projects, even if genuine, cannot counteract tens of billions of dollars in development subsidies. The Bank has started placing environmental conditions on loans, but its modest restrictions will not eliminate the enormously destructive effect, in both human and environmental terms, of multi-million dollar development projects. Moreover, the Bank's conditions are often ineffective. In 1993 officials admitted that the results of environmental covenants were disappointing: "conditionality has been formulated without adequate regard for the context in which it would be applied."

## Why Underdevelopment?

The problem of the Bank, ineffectual at promoting self-sustaining growth but effective at causing environmental and social harm, can be fully understood only if one comprehends the actual causes of underdevelopment and overindebtedness. The basic premise of the Bank—and other foreign aid programs—is that poor nations lack access to capital. Yet borrowers would not have been able to amass an international debt of $1.7 trillion had this been the case. The real problem is that a lot of developing nations have grossly mismanaged their economies, in turn wasting otherwise ample aid transfers.

In many cases borrowing governments have enacted economically counterproductive policies because the maintenance of power, rather than economic growth, has been their priority. In other instances, whether out of ignorance or for reasons of ideology, countries have adopted ruinous economic policies—restrictions on prices and production, perverse monetary, fiscal and trade policies, disincentives to foreign investment, and bloated public sectors—that have denied their peoples economic opportunity and the ability to choose their own economic future. If anything became clear during the 1980s, it was that market economies outperform command systems. The importance of market-oriented policies has become so obvious that even unregenerate communist nations like China and Vietnam are adopting marketplace reforms.

At the same time, the lack of a correlation between foreign aid and domestic development has become increasingly evident. National growth rates do not match aid flows. Some heavy aid recipients—such as India and Tanzania, for instance—remain among the world's poorest nations. The actual legacy of decades of Bank lending, then, has been debilitating debt rather than self-sustaining development.

Nevertheless, the Bank continues to push for ever larger loan programs. Why? The institution desperately desires to play a leading role in the international economic process. The Bank's funders, particularly the United States, hope to use the organization to support their foreign policy goals by underwriting favored governments, as well as helping their commercial banks by securing the repayment of past loans to poorer nations. Finally, some Bank officials may really believe, despite all of the evidence, that they can help alleviate international poverty.

## Debased Lending

More lending will not help, however. Although many factors, such as First World protectionism and recessions, have contributed to the Third World's economic problems, the lack of a real return on the $1.7 trillion in foreign funds is the primary reason that borrowers have been left not only poor, but also heavily in debt. This poor economic result also demonstrates that the Bank's lending strategy has been seriously flawed, reflecting a: substitution of welfare for development, uncritical acceptance of statist development theories, preference for state enterprises over private companies, and focus on projects in disregard of borrowers' economic policies.

*Substitution of Welfare for Development*

In its efforts to help the poorest of the poor, what was to have been an economic development institution has increasingly funded quasi-welfare activities. Spending for population control, for instance, jumped from $40 million in 1975 to more than a half billion dollars a decade later. Urban development, too, became a favorite project category: World Bank funds went for everything from home improvement loans to upgrading squatter settlements to formulating "an integrated approach to regional and urban development." The Bank is spending even more on these sort of projects in the 1990s.

The basic goal of such programs, of course, is genuinely humanitarian. But many recipient governments have been anything but humane. In 1985, for instance, the Ethiopian government, involved in a bitter civil war, borrowed $30 million for "relief and rehabilitation services to alleviate the impact of drought and famine on human welfare," according to the Bank's annual report of that year. The money was to finance, among other things, the purchase of trucks. Yet trucks were the primary means used to implement a forced relocation program that the French organization Medecins sans Frontieres estimated killed up to 100,000 people. The Mengistu regime promised not to use the funds for its relocation program, but the president of the Ethiopian Refugees Education and Relief Foundation, Yonas Deressa, complained that "they just take the money and laugh." One Bank employee called it "genocide with a human face."

Less odious but more pervasive is simple abuse and corruption. The Bank loaned Bangladesh money to provide 3,000 mechanical wells for small farmers. Researchers found that local citizens of wealth and political influence gained control of most of the wells. Admitted one Bank official, "If any wells are left over, the local authorities auction them off. The big landlords compete and whoever offers the biggest bribe gets the well."

In any case, the Bank is not a good manager of these sort of projects. In its 1985 World Development Report, the Bank justified social subsidies on the basis that investment in, for instance, education and agricultural research can yield very high returns but that "these yields may be realized over a period of thirty to forty years, with no returns at all in the early years. This makes them unsuitable for private markets, so official help is needed at least during the initial stages of development." If this analysis is true, such "investments" would seem best left to traditional aid agencies rather than a "bank" that expects to be repaid, usually with interest.

Far more important, however, is the fact Bank-funded social programs have exhibited wretched long-term viability. While foreign transfers can increase local services in the short-term, thereby helping to meet the "human needs" of the recipient nations' citizens (assuming the programs are actually created with their interests in mind), such initiatives risk forcing debtor governments to choose between abandoning the programs once the original aid package terminates or maintaining the programs, even though that may require additional loans and more debt. In fact, internal Bank reports have consistently questioned the "sustainability" of such projects. For instance, in a 1987 study the Bank's Operations Evaluation Department reported that a lack of local funds had delayed implementation of education projects in Brazil, Guatemala, the Dominican Republic, Sudan, Tanzania, Trinidad and Tobago, and Zaire. More generally, the study concluded that "of the 31 poverty-related projects in 1985, 13 (42%) were failures. [O]f the 47 area development poverty projects evaluated, 24 have been failures."

Similarly, a 1987 study of two decades' worth of rural development programs—accounting for roughly 50 percent of all the Bank's projects—found a failure rate of 37 percent. Average rates of return fell below projections, cost overruns were pervasive, and two-thirds of the projects had problems with basic design as well as staff and management. The failure rate of non-poverty projects, in contrast, was significantly lower at 21 percent. "Some of the early failures have proven to be expensive," admitted the Bank, but, it added, "many valuable lessons have been learned."

Alas, such lessons haven't seemed to help the Bank in designing or managing projects. In its 1990 annual evaluation report the Bank reported a *48 percent* unsatisfactory rate for agricultural and rural projects. Including hundreds of earlier projects yielded a failure rate of 40 percent. And sustainability remained a great concern. Of 114 agricultural and rural projects, the Bank rated just 38 percent likely to be sustainable. Similar results were reported in the evaluation review for 1991, published in 1993. Just 53 percent of agricultural and rural projects were termed satisfactory. Moreover, allowed the Bank, "performance in relation to the sustainability of project benefit flows was also poorer than that registered for the combined 1989–90 cohorts."

The Bank's experience demonstrates that it is unrealistic to believe that poorer nations, even with ample international loans, can offer the many social services that predominate in richer nations. Rather, the Bank and its borrowers need to focus on promoting self-sustaining economic growth that will, in the long term, better enable poorer peoples to meet basic human needs.

*Uncritical Acceptance of Statist Development Theories*

But the Bank has not done so, preferring to back statist development strategies ever since its creation. "By the time the World Bank made its first loan outside Europe in 1948," write Bank staffers Warren Baum and Stokes Tolbert, "it found many develping countries committed to or already engaged in some form of centralized economic planning." Rather than trying to change their statist approaches, the Bank subsidized them.

Why should it have considered alternative strategies, however, since most of its staff seemed to believe in the "structuralist" theory of development, which assumed that Third World peoples could do little to advance their own lives but instead had to accept development programs imposed from above by a strong central regime? Stanley Please, who worked for the Bank for two decades, before retiring in 1983, observed that he was "a committed socialist" when he arrived at the Bank, but that: "I was surprised and shocked by the emphasis which the Bank at the time gave to the public sector in general and to the government in particular. Here was an institution which had the reputation of being ultra free enterprise and market-oriented, yet had more confidence in the rationality, morality and competence of governments than I ever had."

This orientation intensified during the McNamara years and persisted even during the 1980s, despite the popular perception that the Reagan administration made the Bank into a cheerleader for capitalism. Indeed, in 1987 Bank President Conable stated that "obviously, while I have some prejudice in favor of market resolution of difficulties, an institution like the World Bank cannot take a rigid position on such things." Thus, in the same year the Bank lent Ethiopia $39 million to augment its Ministry of Agriculture—the very bureau to blame for exacerbating the famine. Other beneficiaries of Bank financing in 1987 were Ghana's agricultural bureaucracy, China's Ministry of Chemical Industry, Guinea-Bissau's Ministry of Rural development and Fisheries, Tunisia's Agency for Energy Conservation, and Zaire's economic planning agencies. And the Bank continues this policy. Most of the Bank's $22.7 billion in loans in 1991 went through the hands of government agencies that were directing large segments of their nations' economies—India's petrochemical industry, for instance, China's industrial and urban development bureaucracies, Cyprus' industrial sector, a host of nations' development finance companies, and parastatals in Argentina, Colombia, and elsewhere.

Perhaps the fundamental problem is that the Bank itself is a public institution and tends to favor its own kind. One senior Reagan administration official complained that "it's hard to expect a government-owned multilateral body not to be primarily responsive to other governments and take the view that government-sponsored, government-owned, government-guaranteed projects are the best thing going."

*Preference for State Enterprises over Private Companies*

Given its *dirigiste* philosophy, it is no surprise that for years the Bank primarily underwrote public entities. The Bank subsidized many of the large, money-losing enterprises that have proved to be so debilitating economically for borrowers. Argentina, Brazil, and Mexico, as well as China and India, have all borrowed heavily for years, pouring billions of dollars of Bank credit—as well as other domestic and foreign funds—into their growing state sectors. Indeed, complains economist Shyam Kamath, it was their preference for state-led development that caused several nations to be Bank favorites. Of them "India received the most world Bank aid...from 1951 through 1989. Most of that...went to public-sector projects."

Today the bulk of Bank lending continues to go to public enterprises, subsidizing an excessive state economic presence and crowding out private investment. It is true that lending by the IFC, which is supposed to support private projects, has more than trebled over the past decade. But the resulting $15.9 billion in IFC loans compares to $162.4 billion from the IBRD and IDA over the same period. Moreover, not all IFC loans go to truly private enterprises; many have significant if not controlling government ownership.

The disappointing results of the Bank's preference for state enterprises should come as no surprise. First, public sector loans often fail to attain their objectives. In 1991 a Bank report on parastatals concluded that "experience has also shown nonmarket approaches to be less effective than had earlier been hoped and market failures to be more tractable than alleged." In 1993 the Bank acknowledged that "the performance of public enterprises—in mining, steel, DFCs, telecommunications, or transport—was disappointing." Rather than proposing less lending for such entities, however, the Bank argued that "this suggests that the Bank, when supporting such enterprises, should insist on proper and accountable management working to commercial objectives, free of government interference."

Perhaps an even more pernicious effect of Bank subsidies for an ever-growing state sector in borrowing nations has been to legitimize government-led development plans despite their consistent inability to deliver either equity or prosperity to Third World peoples. Nor is the Bank ignorant of the risk: in 1987 a Bank report warned that "foreign loans have reinforced the heavy public sector bias of African investments." Yet the Bank has continued to make large-scale loans to government industrial projects throughout the world, including in Africa.

In fact, even as many developing countries started moving away from *dirigiste* economic strategies in the late 1980s, the Bank was busy pumping money into parastatals. In 1988 the Bank provided $2.2 billion for largely state-controlled foreign industrial projects, a dramatic increase over the previous high of $821.1 million in 1986. Mexico alone borrowed $400 million to restructure its steel industry and another $265 million for the government fertilizer monopoly. China, Ghana, Hungary, India, Jordan, and Pakistan also collected Bank loans for public industrial projects. The pattern continues to recur. In 1991 there was $300 million for Argentina to "either privatize *or restructure*" [emphasis added] government energy, rail, and telecommunications firms. Colombia received $304 million to improve the management of its agricultural-market, housing, port, rail, and shipping firms. Smaller loans also went to Madagascar and Mauritania for similar purposes.

Equally pernicious has been the Bank's energy lending program. For years, the Bank enthusiastically underwrote inefficient state enterprises in countries such as Mexico, India, the Ivory Coast, and China, relieving pressure on those countries to allow private investment in the energy field. In 1991 loans in this area ran $1.34 billion. Indeed, in early 1993 the Bank announced more than $500 million in credit for Russia to help increase its output of oil. Yet if there is any area where the private sector has proved itself capable of operating successfully it is energy exploration and production.

Development finance companies (DFCs) constitute another major loan category. Most are state-owned, and, explains the Bank, owe their existence primarily to "an initial World Bank commitment, and continue to exist largely as favored channels for Bank financing." Under the supposedly market-oriented Preston regime DFCs absorbed $1.85 billion of Bank resources in 1991. Bangladesh, Bolivia, Brazil, Central African Republic, China, Colombia, Jamaica, Kenya, Lesotho, Malawi, Mexico, Morocco, and Poland all received money through this program. These loans not only usually increase the power of statist governments, they also waste money: a 1983 audit revealed that nearly half the DFCs had at least 25 percent of their loans in arrears. And to what end? A 1986 Bank study calculated that DFCs spent as much as $540,500 to create a single job in a poorer nation.

Given these sort of lending policies, examples of which could be multiplied endlessly, it is no wonder that an internal Bank audit from 1987 found that Third World states had done little to shed public enterprises. Why should they, so long as they can count on more Bank loans? There has subsequently been more progress, but in recognition of economic reality, not in response to Bank lending. Explained the IFC in its 1992 annual report, "The root cause, particularly in Eastern Europe and in Latin America, is the realization by governments that state enterprises are generally much less efficient than private companies in making products and providing services. Even in utility sectors that are so-called 'natural monopolies,' where regulation is important, it has been demonstrated that companies with private ownership deliver services more efficiently."

*Focus on Projects in Disregard of Borrowers' Economic Policies*

The Bank's willingness to fund individual projects, irrespective of the character of the borrowers' overall economic policies, effectively rewards the most authoritarian and irresponsible regimes. In this way the Bank helped Third World borrowers prop up mismanaged and failing economies and postpone critical economic adjustments, resulting in a larger debt, longer period of slow growth, and more dramatic economic crash.

The Bank certainly should have known what it was doing. In merely one of the more egregious examples, a 1981 Bank report devoted to the problems of Sub-Saharan Africa observed the collapse in agricultural production and exports by Ghana and Tanzania due to heavy taxes on farmers; yet that same year the Bank was lending the latter country $6.88 million "for the rehabilitation of the coconut industry." The previous year Ghana borrowed $29.5 million to help train farmers while Tanzania received $77 million for four different agricultural projects, including to improve research and construct storage facilities.

This curious lending philosophy, of deploring borrowers' overall policies while underwriting projects rendered ineffective by the same policies, has been implemented around the world. Stanley Please complained that "in country after country and year after year, the Bank had continued, during the 1970s and earlier, to have active and, in most cases, rising programs of project lending to agriculture and industry in the very countries in which it was asserting to the governments that their policy frameworks were distorted—not marginally distorted but distorted in major ways." Alas, Bank policy changed little during the 1980s and 1990s.

## Faulty Projects

The most obvious result of the Bank's enthusiasm for welfare over development, support for state-led development plans and public enterprises, and indifference to borrower economic policies has been consistently and dramatically poor loan performance. First, some of the Bank-funded projects are simply bad ideas. As the Bank observed in a 1984 report on Sub-Saharan Africa, much borrowing by poor African states "went to finance large public investment, many of which contributed little to economic growth or to generating foreign exchange to service the debt." Added the Bank, "Too many projects have been selected either on the basis of political prestige or on the basis of inadequate regard for their likely economic and financial rate of return."

Who funded many of these projects? The Bank, of course. And the results are not hard to predict. The Bank's 1990 annual review rated 36 percent of projects to be unsatisfactory. A year later the failure rate had increased to 37 percent, and the record continues to worsen. In late 1992 a Bank task force completed a study (the so-called Wapenhans Report) warning that there had been "a gradual but steady deterioration in port-folio implementation," with a doubling of loans with "major problems" over the preceding decade. The Task Force pointed to numerous prob-lems, including poor design, inadequate emphasis on implementation, too little supervision, undue emphasis on new lending, and a refusal to be firm with borrowers.

Probably more important, however, are borrowers' economic poli-cies. The Bank's major rural project evaluation concluded that borrow-ers' policy failures were to blame for many of the project failures: 54 percent of agricultural projects between 1979 and 1984 were adversely affected by price controls and similar misguided forms of economic in-tervention. Concluded the auditors: "It has become clear that it is not possible to implement viable projects in an unfavorable policy environ-ment." Similarly, in an evaluation survey released nearly a decade later the Bank noted that "of equal importance" in causing projects to fail was "the policy and regulatory environment (e.g., exchange rates, trade policies, investment codes, taxation regimes, etc.), which should con-front industries with the correct incentives and competitive pressures."

Bad though the Bank's assessments of its success rate are, they prob-ably overstate the Bank's record. The Bank has generally been repaid, irrespective of the outcome of particular projects, because most borrow-ers desire to keep their World Bank loans current to protect their credit-worthiness with commercial banks as well as the Bank. Also making it harder to evaluate the benefits of Bank lending is the fact that money is fungible. Thus, foreign governments may request loans in the name of the most internationally saleable projects, ones which they would un-dertake with domestic resources if necessary. Then they use any foreign credit acquired for the other purposes, which remain unknown and there-fore unevaluated by the Bank.

## Policy Reform

One Bank response to criticism has been to declare that the Bank's record compares well with "that of many other development agencies." But to argue that the Bank has been more successful than, say, the African Development Bank is not saying much. The more serious approach has been to *propose more lending.*

For years the Bank engaged in what it called a "policy dialogue" with borrowers. Yet gratuitous advice provided after the checks had been written has had little perceptible effect. Indeed, the obvious institutional pressure on Bank managers to lend undercuts their suggestions for policy reform. Robert McNamara, explained one former bank employee, "started by borrowing much more money than his predecessor and afterwards instructed his staff to find ways to spend the money. The increased availability of loanable funds has thus generated demand for more projects." With Bank staffers desperate to loan money, borrowers knew that their projects would be funded whether or not they acted on the Bank's advice.

Alas, the problem seems to be as serious as ever. The 1992 Wapenhans report contended that inadequate project implementation stemmed in large part from "the Bank's pervasive preoccupation with new lending." This reflects in part the natural bureaucratic incentives at the Bank, the fact that, as Bank consultant Elliot Berg argues, "higher visibility attaches to achievements in loan processing than in project performance management." But Bank officials also rationalize their efforts, believing that they must retain a "presence" in order promote good policy in the future. To cut off lending, explained one former Bank staffer, "may harm the execution of sound investments and lead to confrontation, which hardly fits a longer-run relationship of constructive cooperation." In short, the Bank is committed to lending, period.

Exacerbating the problem is the fact that the Bank relies so heavily on project loans, meaning that any conditions must be relatively minor and limited to the specific project. Admitted the Bank's Twelfth Annual Review, "past experience [is] that formal covenants on individual projects alone have been of limited value in influencing sectoral or economy-wide policies, or even in maintaining agreed policies."

Equally important, as the review further indicated, the Bank often doesn't enforce the few project covenants that it imposes. In its Tenth Annual Review the Bank admitted that "Where failure to comply with covenants has occurred, the Bank has generally been complaisant. Vagueness of covenant requirements, however, has generally saved both Borrower and the Bank from the embarrassment of deciding what to do." The Bank simply gave up trying to enforce agreements with Ceausescu's

Romania, even when, it admitted, the borrowers' practices were "substantially different from Bank norms." Years later nothing has changed. The Wapenhans Report concluded that staffers were reluctant "to take a firm stand with Borrowers," prefering to ignore or waive non-compliance. As a result, "the high incidence of non-compliance undermines the Bank's credibility."

A profusion of project loans with unenforced covenants makes serious policy reform unlikely. Why should countries change counterproductive economic policies when the Bank will generously fund projects throughout their economies, all the while ignoring many of the conditions set for the loan? This is the most logical reason for the phenomenon chronicled in the Bank's 1984 annual report: "the number of countries adopting measures of policy reform is inadequate to meet the crisis. Inadequate, too, are the extent and speed with which reforms are being implemented." Yet in the very next paragraph the Bank went on to declare that "increased external assistance, especially assistance on concessional terms, is critical to the process of policy reform."

The only way increased funding could conceivably encourage policy reform is to promise additional money to "buy" the cooperation of borrowing nations. So the Bank, explained Clausen in 1985, was upping its "lending in support of overall policy reform by developing new lending instruments such as structural and sector adjustment loans." The latter, SECALs, are predicated upon policy changes in a particular economic sector, such as agriculture. The former, SALs, are broader, being based on macro reforms, such as trade liberalization, tax reform, and deficit reduction. Between 1980 and 1989, the Bank made 187 adjustment loans worth $28.5 billion.

As impressive as these statistics may appear, however, they actually demonstrate the severe limitations on the Bank's approach. Through 1989 SALs and SECALs accounted for just 16 percent of Bank lending. The share in 1991 was roughly one-quarter, but that is unlikely to increase any further, for the Bank says that it "remains a development institution that commits the majority of its funds in support of specific investment projects." As long as most loans are extended for projects—and especially as long as other sources of aid and credit are available (during the latter half of the 1980s Bank adjustment loans ranged between four and six percent of total international capital flows to the Third World)—

policy-based lending will have little impact since even countries unwilling to make serious reforms will have access to foreign loans.

Consider Mexico, which enjoyed lavish Bank funding for its huge, money-losing public industrial sector during the 1970s, and which survived its 1982 debt crisis only through increased borrowing. In 1986 Mexico again teetered on the brink of default. The country had borrowed $4.1 billion over the previous six years alone for a variety of development projects, yet proved "reluctant to accept repeated Bank offers of project and sector help" in terms of "rationalizing public sector investment, subsidies, and state enterprises," warned one Bank assessment. But why should Mexico have adopted painful reforms when the international money was still flowing? Not until 1987 did Mexico accept its first policy-based loan. Only the subsequent election of Carlos Salinas de Gortari caused Mexico to switch to a reform course.

## Future Promise of Adjustment Lending?

Still, would so-called adjustment loans, particularly SALs, make sense if project funding did not undercut pressure for reform? Introduced in 1980, SALs basically offer to pay borrowers to improve their economic policies. The goal of SALs—economic freedom for people in developing states—is worthwhile. And despite the often traumatic experience of nations embarking upon adjustment programs, surveys consistently find that countries which adopt economic reform programs do better than those which do not. The reason is simple. Adjustment must eventually occur; delaying it only makes the process more painful.

However, this does not mean that Bank SALs have substantially advanced the reform process. One early Bank study warned that "the theory of reform on which the SAL rests is not clearly spelled out." How exactly are SALs expected to buy change? Moreover, there are potential countervailing risks: necessary reforms may be identified with unpopular foreigners, for instance. Yet if SALs do not result in meaningful economic adjustment, admits Bank staffer Moeen Qureshi, "it has largely been money down the drain."

A variety of surveys raise serious doubts about the efficacy of SALs. A 1986 Operations Evaluation Department review found that none of the ten major SAL recipients had implemented its reform program on time. Two countries failed almost entirely and four other had serious difficulties in meeting the conditions. The auditors reported that "the impact of the structural adjustment programs on a countries economic performance has generally remained below expectations." In 1991 Senior Vice President Stern admitted that "Time and again the best of policy intentions, the best of policy letters solemnly agreed to and signed by the finance minister and the Bank, broke down."

Some at the Bank argue that recent adjustment lending has been more successful. A 1990 Bank review, for instance, concluded that six of every ten loan conditions had been fully met and another 24 percent had been "substantially fulfilled." Even if true, however, such compliance statistics may mean little. Not all conditions are equal: some are formalistic and superfluous, which means their fulfillment increases formal compliance figures without improving the borrowers' economic performance. And surveys show that the highest degree of compliance tends to occur on the least important conditions.

In any case, the Bank's optimistic assessment is not shared by outsiders. A major study underwritten by Great Britain's Overseas Development Administration estimated the overall compliance rate for adjustment loans to be around 54 percent. Moreover, the researchers observed slippage even in the best of cases and found other SALs to be almost complete failures. The major achievement in the Philippines, for instance, was to get the Marcos regime "to consider liberalization of any sort," not to actually do anything. As for Kenya, explained the report, "of all the policy conditions attached to its money,... it is difficult to name a single one *during the SAL period* which was implemented because of its pressure."

One of the most serious flaws in SALs is weak policy requirements. Bank consultants Elliot Berg and Alan Batchelder, for instance, contend that preconditions for SALs "look hard, but the conditionality involved is mostly illusory." Even real restrictions are often ambiguous, and therefore open to subjective judgments as to whether or not they have been fulfilled.

Alas, the pressure then is to state that the covenants have been met, irrespective of the facts, since Bank staffers face powerful incentives not enforce SAL covenants. Argue three British researchers, loan officers "are under intense pressure to meet country commitment targets whatever the negotiating posture adopted by the recipient government, and to meet country disbursement targets however unpromising that government's subsequent implementation performance" It is presumably for this reason that, report Berg and Batchelder, "the main generators of SALs are within the Bank." In fact, one reason the Bank moved from project lending to SALs was because the latter *more quickly got more funds* to borrowers, allowing the Bank to lend twice as much per staff-hour as project loans. The unmistakable message to borrowers therefore continues to be: you will receive most of the money you want whatever your policies.

As a result, the Bank regularly ignores even severe SAL breaches. Concludes the British survey: "Even in those cases where almost none of the second tranche [or loan disbursement] conditionality has actually been fulfilled, ... all the money has eventually been handed over by the Bank." The Bank has cancelled only two loans, to Argentina and Panama, because of non-performance, and denied approval of a follow-up tranche in one other case, to Senegal. In other cases the Bank has at most delayed release of later tranches and, it claims, not approved additional future SALs. Yet in many cases, such as Ecuador and Kenya, project loans were forthcoming soon after disappointing experiences with adjustment loans. The Bank simply has no credibility in enforcing its loan terms.

Perhaps most important of all, conditions will not be fulfilled unless the borrower possesses the political will to comply. As the Bank recognizes, covenants are most likely to be kept if the programs are "owned" by the borrowers. Such a commitment is evident in Chile, now cited as a success by the Bank. However, admits one Bank researcher, "It must be emphasized that much of the success observed in Chile during 1987–89 is rooted in the major structural reforms implemented in the mid-1970s"—*before the creation of SALs.* The earlier government adopted economic reforms because it recognized that they were necessary, not because the Bank offered it bribes to do so. (To the contrary, at that in time the Bank was still committed to a largely *dirigiste* development strategy.) In the case of Thailand, researchers concluded that "it should be clear that the Thai Government in 1980 had a strong intention to restructure its economy even before" applying for a SAL. Other countries often counted as successes by the Bank include Colombia and Turkey, but both seemed ready to adopt reforms irrespective of Bank lending. In short, borrowers serious about change are likely to adopt some, if not most, of the SAL policies even in the absence of the SALs—particularly if other aid funds are not available. And borrowers would have had a good reason to do so. As the Bank acknowledges, countries like Korea and Turkey have attracted significant outside credit after enacting adjustment programs.

The necessity of borrower commitment to any reforms is perhaps the most fundamental weakness in the theory behind SALs. Nations that understand neither the substance of a Bank-initiated SAL nor the need for policy reform are unlikely to implement stringent loan conditions; equally important, such regimes are unlikely to make the many ancillary and related reforms that will almost certainly be necessary for the reform program to succeed in the long-term. While a SAL might spur passage of a particular set of reforms, what is really required is a commitment to an ongoing process of reform. Without it, SALs are likely to do little more than further boost the borrower's foreign debt.

Indeed, there is a real risk that by ameliorating the very economic conditions that forced the borrowing government to choose a reform path SALs may discourage governments from taking the necessary next steps. As the Bank itself pointed out, "When a country has a severe economic and balance-of-payments crisis and there is an imminent political crisis or upcoming election, the government is sometimes unwilling to adopt a sufficiently comprehensive adjustment. In such cases...the Bank wisely refused to make exceptions in the design of programs. As painful as they may be, crises can increase the likelihood of reform by raising the perception within and outside the government that policies must change, by weakening anti-reform interest groups and by increasing the willingness to rely on technocrats." True enough, but this is also a good reason to reduce the flow of aid funds rather than to use SALs to try to buy reform.

Although scores of developing states are now experimenting with market economics, their path has not been a straight one. Countries as diverse as Brazil, India, Jamaica, Mexico, Nigeria, Peru, and the Philippines have moved first one way and then another. The only constancy has been continual World Bank lending—and its apparent lack of impact on borrower's economies.

## Solving the Debt and Development Crises

There is hope for poorer countries, but there are no easy answers. Borrowers and lenders alike have overdosed on aid and loans and therefore face a painful future. Developing states need to adopt serious reform programs, commercial lenders need to write off nonperforming loans, and official aid agencies, like the Bank, need to abandon their efforts to restructure Third World societies and reduce their lending.

Doing so would provide the most powerful inducement possible for policy reform. Until now the Bank has essentially handed alcoholic borrowers a fistful of 100 dollar notes and told them to drink no more; after the money was squandered the Bank then demanded repayment. A better reform model is provided by Vietnam, which remains excluded from IMF and World Bank loans. In its 1991 annual report the Bank noted that Vietnam had adopted economic reforms that had resulted in private sector growth despite "difficult external conditions: Soviet aid is declining rapidly, and there is no immediate prospect of official financing from traditional donor countries to take its place." In fact, Vietnam almost certainly acted *because* Soviet aid levels were falling and there was no rising tide of Western assistance to fill the gap. Vietnam's program—like that in China and others elsewhere—is homegrown and had nothing to do with the Bank, SALs, or other sources of foreign aid.

In fact, the Bank's record is no better elsewhere. In 1992 Bank President Lewis Preston told the United Nations Conference on Environment and Development, "The Bank's effectiveness in combatting poverty, while protecting the environment, is the benchmark against which our performance as a development institution should be judged." It's a good standard, but the Bank flunks. For years, in the face of awesome failure, the international aid community has done little other than demand more. Yet the primary consequence for the Third World of the resulting hundreds of billions of dollars in aid and loans has been higher debt and lower growth. That might not bother those who hire the limousines and host the parties at the annual Bank-IMF extravaganza held in Washington, the "lords of poverty" in the words of journalist Graham Hancock. Not as lucky, however, have been the supposed beneficiaries of their efforts: the displaced peasants in India, murdered farmers in Ethiopia, impoverished city-dwellers in Zaire, and billions of others like them around the world. It's time the Bank remembered who it was supposed to be serving.

June 1993

# VI

# The Regulatory State

# 14

# America's Regulatory Dirty Dozen

## Introduction

In July, 1992 15-year-old Regina Orozco was fired from her part-time job at the Arby's restaurant in San Marcos, Ca. She was a model employee, explained her supervisor—hard-working, honest, and friendly. But the rules governing child labor are complex and even a single innocent violation can cost as much as $10,000. After an Arby's in Seattle was fined by the Labor Department for inadvertently breaking the law, the restaurant chain decided to discharge all 15-year-olds. Gina is a "wonderful employee," explained Jill See, vice president of operations for the firm that owns the San Marcos Arby's. "But we were severely fined...and I don't know anybody who would take those risks." McDonald's and Taco Bell have similar policies, for the same reason.

Similar was the experience of Jennifer Crafts in Chicopee, Massachusetts, who opened a restaurant called A.J.'s Place shortly after the birth of her son, A.J. Crafts kept A.J. in a playpen near the kitchen and patrons enjoyed the arrangement: "Everybody likes to see him. He's an adorable child," explained customer Richard Reynolds. Alas, city health inspectors soon descended upon the restaurant. They feared that A.J. might get hurt and that Crafts might not know enough to wash her hands after changing his diapers. So they ordered her to keep him home. Crafts had to go to court to remain in business.

The problem in these cases is not the intentions of the regulators. Rather, it is the results: ham-fisted interference that needlessly costs businesses and customers money and puts people out of work. Indeed, unnecessary federal rules have played an important factor in both slowing economic growth and harming the nation's international competitiveness.

## The Dirty Dozen

There is no shortage of rules that impede not only economic progress, but also health and often life. Even where the goals are legitimate, people could be better protected at less cost. In this way government not only wastes taxpayers' money through direct expenditures, but also the money of those being regulated.

### 1. The Delaney Clause

Drugs cannot be released until the FDA has certified not only their safety, but also their efficacy. As a result, tens of thousands of people have unnecessarily died while waiting for the heart-attack drugs streptokinase and TPA and the gastric-ulcer drug misoprostol. Families with Alzheimer's sufferers have been frustrated by the agency's refusal to authorize the use of the drug THA, despite evidence that it has helped four of ten patients who have tried it. Equally costly has been the delay in bringing anti-AIDS drugs, such as AZT, to the market. Only enormous pressure from AIDS activists and Vice President Dan Quayle's Competitiveness Council caused the FDA to speed up trials of potentially life-extending drugs. What was once a ten-year average development time for new drugs has been cut to 5.5 years for products meant for life-threatening diseases and 7.5 years for other substances. But these delays are still too long: the FDA should be restricted to monitoring safety, while leaving the question of effectiveness to pharmaceutical companies, doctors, and patients. Even FDA Commissioner David Kessler acknowledges that "Back in the 1960s and 1970s, post-thalidomide, the agency's mission was to keep unsafe products off the market. But in dealing with AIDS, we have learned in no uncertain terms that our job is not only to keep unsafe drugs off the market but to get safe and effective drugs to the market."

Another perverse consequence of the Delaney Clause is that, according to a recent Appeals Court ruling, the amendment requires the Environmental Protection Agency to ban any food additive, including pesticides, that are "found to induce cancer when ingested by man or animal," even if the risk is *de minimis*. Alas, the Clause was passed in 1958 when tests for carcinogens were far less sophisticated. Thus, the law now apparently requires the government to outlaw potentially scores of beneficial substances that pose no health danger and are far less carginogenic than dozens of natural substances consumed every day. Warns Elizabeth Whelan, president of American Council on Science and Health, "The bad news is that a lot of useful agricultural chemicals will be banned, the crop yields of some fruits and vegetables will decline, and food prices will rise."

## 2. *Corporate Average Fuel Economy (CAFE) Standards*

Similarly deadly is CAFE, which forces automakers to meet a minimum federal gas mileage standard or pay substantial fines. In 1990 then Transportation Secretary Sam Skinner refused to lower CAFE from 27.5 to 26.5 mpg in a decision declared to be arbitrary by the D.C. Circuit Court of Appeals earlier this year (1992). Nevertheless, environmentalists remain active on Capitol Hill supporting legislation to up CAFE to 40 mpg and candidate Bill Clinton suggested eventually upping it to 45 mpg.

It has long been known that, all other things being equal, bigger cars better protect their occupants than do smaller cars. Unfortunately, CAFE has caused automakers to downsize their products since that is the cheapest and most effective way to improve gas mileage. The result, according to a Brookings Institution/Harvard University study, has been between 2200 and 3900 dead drivers and passengers for each additional mandated mpg per model year. The rule is also grotesquely inefficient, pushing manufacturers to make cars that people don't want. Indeed, CAFE, after costing so much, may save little gas, since consumers are likely to drive more miles in cars with a better gas mileage (which lowers the marginal cost of driving). CAFE should be killed, rather than strengthened.

## 3. *Marketing Orders*

Equally perverse when hunger and malnutrition stalk hundreds of millions of people around the globe are marketing orders, imposed by the Agriculture Department (USDA) at the behest of citrus and nut producers. An anachronistic outgrowth of Depression-era legislation intended to stabilize farmer incomes by establishing federally-backed cartels, over the years the orders controlled the production of billions of dollars worth of specialty crops, including hops, lemons, oranges, raisins, and walnuts. Industry boards set quotas on what portion of his crop a farmer may sell; the rest usually rots in the orchards or fields. In many years USDA has destroyed more oranges and lemons than have harsh winter freezes.

Marketing orders have raised consumer prices but done little to stabilize farmers' incomes, according to USDA and Office of Management and Budget surveys. Moreover, periodic episodes of deregulation—oranges in 1985 and 1992, lemons in 1991 and 1992, for instance—increased farmers' incomes. All controls over production, which could be tossed out by USDA tomorrow, should be ended.

## 4. Sugar Import Quotas

Congress killed sugar price supports in 1974, but the Reagan administration revived them in 1981 as part of an ugly political deal for the votes of several southern Democratic congressmen. The price supports, in the form of nonrecourse loans, are only rarely used, however, for Congress imposed tight import quotas which raise domestic prices well above the loan levels. And far above world levels as well.

Thus, while the program's budget cost is relatively small, the consumer cost is horrendous, as much as $3 billion in higher prices, all to benefit about 12,000 domestic growers. At the same time, sugar demand as fallen, causing soft drink manufacturers, among others, to shift to high-fructose corn syrup. As a result, the sugar refining industry has suffered a depression: numerous plants have closed, many are operating at reduced capacity, and thousands of employees have been thrown out of work.

## 5. The Davis-Bacon Act

Passed in 1931, Davis-Bacon mandates payment of "prevailing" (or union) wages on federally-subsidized construction projects. A huge windfall for construction unions, the law wastes a billion dollars a year, according to the Congressional Budget Office. The law also likely causes additional hidden costs by discouraging many contractors from even bidding on federal projects, reducing competition.

However, the most pernicious impact of the measure is on workers trying to break into the job market. Since contractors must pay union wages, they cannot afford to hire less skilled and experienced people. In practice, this means Davis-Bacon projects are overwhelmingly white projects—which was, in fact, the law's original purpose. It was originally backed by legislators who publicly decried the competitive threat of "cheap colored labor." Even inner-city rehabilitation projects today cannot offer neighborhood young people jobs because of this perverse and wasteful law. The result is greater unemployment, with the consequent increase in federal social spending and the equally serious erosion of hope in distressed urban areas for a better future.

### 6. Wetlands Controls

Based on dubious statutory authority, the EPA imposed wetlands rules requiring federal approval for even the most basic uses of an estimated 100 million acres of land, much of which was ordinarily dry. Landowners have been prosecuted or threatened with prosecution for removing trash, adding fill dirt, repairing a levee, installing a tennis court, plowing land, and planting crops without an Army Corps of Engineers permit. (John Pozsgai, for instance, is serving a three-year term for cleaning up a trash dump ruled to be a wetlands.) All told, as much as five percent of U.S. land, including about 75 percent of Alaska and half of all farmland, arguably fell within federal jurisdiction under the EPA's original regulations. Intervention by the Quayle Council forced a rules rewrite, reducing the amount of land subject to federal rules, but the issue remained unresolved when President Clinton assumed office.

At issue is not the importance of protecting genuine wetlands. Rather, it is the inefficient extension of federal power over land with little environmental consequence and the failure to compensate landowners whose property is effectively seized through regulation.

### 7. The Minimum Wage

In 1989 Congress approved a compromise measure, signed by President Bush, that upped the minimum wage from $3.35 to $4.25 over a two-year period. There is no doubt that the minimum wage simultaneously raises business costs and puts less-skilled employees out of work; the only question is how many jobs are destroyed. The congressionally-created Minimum Wage Study Commission, for instance, estimated that every ten percent wage hike cuts youth job opportunities by between one and 2.5 percent. Other studies suggest that an equal number of young people stop looking for work. In short, the minimum wage is one of the most perverse and inefficient methods of trying to help the poor. The 1989 legislation did include a temporary "training wage" for new workers, but that only slightly ameliorates the destructive effects of government pay-setting.

## 8. The Nutrition Labeling and Education Act

Existing food-labeling law was dramatically overhauled by the Nutrition Labeling and Education Act, which ran some 700 pages. The law requires companies to use FDA-approved terms, list nutritional information in a FDA-specified manner, and only make FDA-backed claims. The law is expected to force changes in 257,000 different labels and could cost firms an estimated $3 billion or more. The Agriculture Department followed the lead of the FDA, proposing similar requirements for the products that it covers.

## 9. The Pollution Prevention Act

Also approved in 1990 was this statute, which requires manufacturers that use one or more of 300 specified chemicals to prepare an annual report on the use of the chemical or chemicals, the amount recycled or released into the environment, pollution-reduction efforts, future projections, and more. Writes Murray Weidenbaum, head of the Center for the Study of American Business, "ecologists should mourn for the trees that will be cut down to provide the paper for all the reports that will be prepared, in triplicate at least," under this law.

## 10. The Civil Rights Act of 1991

The Civil Rights Act was agreed to after two years of nasty debate. The regulation at issue—the legal standard for convicting firms of discrimination—goes back to a 1971 Supreme Court case in which the Court ignored the law's explicit language and legislative history and ruled that Title VII did not require proof of discriminatory intent. That is, a firm could be successfully sued if its practices had the *effect* of discriminating against minorities. In 1989, however, the Court ruled that a plaintiff had to specify a particular employment practice when alleging disparate impact and to prove that the policy was not legitimate—and therefore that the firm was guilty of discrimination. In short, the ruling set an eminently reasonable standard: to collect damages, a plaintiff had to prove that he had been discriminated against.

Critics in Congress, however, preferred the "guilty until proven innocent" standard of *Griggs*. The 1991 legislation shifted the burden of justifying employment practices back onto the firm. The result will not be better protection of those who have been discriminated against, since they were entitled to relief under the Supreme Court's standard. However, the inevitable result of the recent amendments will be economic losses from dropping legitimate business practices to avoid litigation, the expense of defending against baseless lawsuits as well as paying erroneous judgments, and lost economic productivity due to hiring less well-qualified workers in order to meet numerical quotas. The high social costs of increasing racial polarization would be additional.

The law also increases likely litigation from cases involving discrimination on the basis of disability, religion, and sex. Among its most bizarre provisions is a limit on punitive damages that varies by the size of the firm. Observed then-*Wall Street Journal* columnist L. Gordon Crovitz, "damages for sexual harassment would increase with ... the size of the workforce, not with the heinousness of the offense." While increasing potential damages for sexual harassment, the law leaves the offense largely undefined. The inevitable result is going to be more wasteful litigation and judgments.

## 11. The Americans with Disabilities Act

Promoted as a natural extension of the Civil Rights law, the ADA, as the disabilities law is known, was passed with little opposition. Yet the ADA could have a truly dramatic impact on U.S. business. Current estimates are that the law, which is intended to benefit those with a documented "physical or mental impairment that substantially limits one or more of the major life activities" will cost about $2 billion annually, but the number could go far higher because the ADA combines two different regulatory approaches: redesign for physical plant and quasi-affirmative action for disabled applicants and employees. Notably, what the

ADA does not do is simply bar discrimination on the basis of disability, as would an analogue to traditional Civil Rights laws. Rather, the law requires firms to undertake potentially expensive "accommodations" for disabled applicants and employees. Consultant Robert Genetski figures that the physical modifications alone could eventually cost as much as $65 billion.

Moreover, the statute, even more ambiguous than most civil rights laws, will prove to be a lawyers' full employment act. Edward Potter, president of the Employment Policy Foundation, told the *Washington Post* that "no one really knows" how many lawsuits will be generated, but he offered a "back of the envelope" prediction of 12,000 annually. Evan Kemp, chairman of the Equal Opportunity Commission, projected 12,000 to 15,000 new complaints before his agency, a 20 to 25 percent increase in its caseload. But even these estimates may be far too low: Exceptions to the bill's provisions, for instance, vary by size and type of firm, ensuring that most disputes will end up in court. And the Association of Trial Lawyers of America has formed the Automatic Door Litigation Group to help promote liability suits relating to the ADA's requirements.

To criticize the ADA is not to dismiss the obstacles faced by those with disabilities, of course. But the plight of these Americans does not itself justify forcing others to undertake potentially very expensive remodeling and employment assistance programs. In the words of then-congressional staffer Robert O'Quinn, "the ADA pursues, with zealous disregard for economic costs, its stated goal of mainstreaming disabled individuals. The provisions of the ADA and the regulations derived from it are frequently outlandish." And unfair to firms that, of course, bear no responsibility for the fact that someone is disabled.

## 12. The Clean Air Act

The first Clean Air Act was passed in 1963 and has been amended several times. The latest version, signed into law by President Bush in November 1990, ran nearly 800 pages (twenty times the length of the original law!) and was incomprehensibly complicated. The law explicitly called for the development of 400 sets of new regulations—which are expected to fill up at least 7,000 pages—and requires every state to revise its existing "implementation plan." It is perhaps no surprise, then, that the Bush administration boasted that its 1993 budget "provides an all-time high level of funding and staffing for EPA's operating program: nearly $2.7 billion and more than 14,000 employees. Since the Bush Administration took office, EPA's operating program will have increased by 54 percent, and the workforce involved in research, regulatory, and enforcement responsibilities will have expanded by 22 percent."

To try to discuss the bill in much detail risks putting readers to sleep. Suffice it to say that the statute, which consists of seven separate titles, tightened up existing law across-the-board. The law is hideously ineffi-cient, relying on command-and-control dictates, attempting to eliminate minimal risks at very high costs, and requiring ever more businesses to get ever more permits for ever more modest changes in their facilities and operations. Estimates of the cost of complying with the law range up to $40 billion, which will come on top of what the EPA today figures to be $155 billion in annual compliance costs. Unfortunately, however, these direct costs do not take into account the price increases of various goods and services throughout the economy; as a result, the real cost of environmental regulation may run twice as high as is commonly thought. In particular, autos, electricity, and gasoline will all cost more; a large number of oil refineries and steel plants are expected to shut down.

Although some cost to protect the environment is obviously inevi-table, the gross inefficiency of a command-and-control system is not. While the U.S. spends roughly 2.1 percent of its GNP on compliance with environmental laws, most Western industrialized states spend only between .8 and 1.5 percent of their GNPs because they rely more on performance-based standards, which require firms to achieve certain results but leave the method of doing so up to individual companies. Studies suggest that relying more heavily on market-oriented systems could reduce compliance costs by anywhere between 1.1 and 22 times. Yet, observes Brookings Institution scholar Robert Crandall, "The inef-ficiencies in most federal environmental programs are well known as the result of decades of research. But most environmentalists and their supporters in Congress appear uninterested in redesigning these pro-grams. The new Clean Air Act looks distressingly like the old one— with the exception of the acid-rain program," which allows limited trading of emissions rights.

These are merely a sampling of some of the worst, most inefficient rules imposed by the federal government. Today there are few aspects of both the workplace and home with which government is not con-cerned. And the cost to the economy has been high.

## The Federal Regulatory Burden

Government regulation is obviously not a new phenomenon. Yet the sort of activities covered and restrictions imposed in the republic's early years were far more limited than what we see today. "There was a time, long ago, when the average American could go about his daily business hardly aware of the government—especially the federal government," observes Robert Higgs of Lafayette College. But the massive expansion of the central government during the Civil War and especially the major crises of this century—World War I, the Great Depression, and World War II—led to the massive regulatory state that we see today. "Virtually nothing remains untouched by the myriad influences of governmental expenditure, taxation, and regulation, not to mention the government's direct participation in economic activities," writes Higgs.

Alas, the continuing expansion of government control benefits no one. The government already effectively makes more and more decisions for private firms. Observes Ron Utt, a former official at the Office of Management and Budget (OMB):

> The typical business in America, confronting a vast array of federal, state and local mandates, is required to fulfill provisions of the clean air and water acts, provide a minimum standard of living to workers, engage in recycling, carry an expensive insurance policy against product liability, ferret out illegal aliens, provide a costly package of medical benefits to employees that may have to include acupuncture, wigs, pastoral services and drug treatment, provide special accommodations to disabled employees, and promote equal opportunity as determined by race, sex, and sexual activity.

Federal controls, often supplemented by state laws and regulations, raise costs to business, both destroying jobs and hiking prices paid by consumers. All told, figures Thomas Hopkins, an economics professor at the Rochester Institute of Technology and former deputy administrator of OMB, regulation is costing roughly $400 billion a year, or about $4,000 per household. Utt figures the cost may be greater, as much as $500 billion, or $5,000 per household. That comes to a 14 percent reduction in standard of living on the average household income of $32,000. Even higher is the estimate of William Laffer, then at the Heritage Foundation, of between $881 billion and $1.656 trillion. (Laffer's estimate is larger because he includes more indirect costs, such as lost production, of regulation.)

The largest single source of regulatory costs is what Hopkins terms "process regulation," particularly due to paperwork and reporting requirements that are neither exclusively social nor economic in origin. In 1990, compliance with tax laws and regulation, the requirements of federal medical programs, particularly Medicaid and Medicare, and federal mandates to state and local governments ran about $122 billion (in 1988 dollars). And even these estimates may be too low. Leon Transeau, who became the Interior Department's paperwork manager during the the Reagan presidency, has estimated that the public spends about 12.6 billion hours dealing with government paperwork, roughly seven times the official estimate. Some two-thirds of that burden falls on business; valuing time at, say, $20 an hour suggests that this amounts to an extra $166 billion annual tax on business alone.

Environmental controls, which run about $99 billion, account for the second largest regulatory burden. (The EPA itself estimates environmental regulation to be substantially more expensive, $155 billion, compared to $110 billion, Hopkins' estimate in the same 1990 dollars.) Almost as costly is economic regulation, such as trade barriers and entry restrictions in particular industries. These sort of federal rules cost about $95 billion (again, in 1988 dollars) in 1990. Lost efficiency from regulation, as distinct from the formal cost of complying with federal dictates, ran another $46 billion. Finally, social regulation—implemented by such agencies as the Consumer Product Safety Commission—came to about $29 billion in 1990.

In effect, this $392 billion in federal regulatory spending operated as a tax on individual citizens and the society as a whole. In 1990 the federal government spent $1.251 trillion, 23.2 percent of GNP. Regulation, at about $430 billion (Hopkins' estimates in 1990 dollars), raised that burden by more than one-third, making the real federal share of the nation's economy above 30 percent.

Unfortunately, much of this cost is pure waste. One recent survey suggests that costs for consumer products, discrimination, drugs, energy, and occupational safety all exceed the benefits. Only highway safety regulation appears to unambiguously deliver more good than it costs. Estimates on environmental regulation vary wildly, with analysts divided over the net benefits. And there is little doubt that the costs of the latest Clean Air Act greatly exceed the benefits, perhaps by tens of billions of dollars. Understandably, then, Bush's Council of Economic

Advisers Chairman Michael Boskin complained that "over-regulation is one of the major impediments to a growing economy."

## The Bush Regulatory Record

Unfortunately, however, the regulatory burden grew, and grew rapidly, since Boskin's boss, George Bush, took office. The decade of 1978 to 1988 saw significant deregulation in a few narrow fields, particularly banking, energy, and transportation. The benefits were significant, but the process was often incomplete—Savings and Loans were freer to invest but enjoyed *expanded* federal deposit insurance, encouraging them to make a large number of unduly risky loans, since taxpayers were responsible for any losses. Although deregulation was more spotty in other areas, the Reagan administration did manage to bring down the number of pages in the *Federal Register*, essentially a catalogue of federal regulatory activity, from nearly 90,000 in 1980 to below 50,000 in 1986.

In many areas regulation remained a particularly serious problem, however. And despite the ample opportunity for positive regulatory reform, the Bush administration seemed unconcerned about the issue during its first three years. In 1990 the president did empower the Competitiveness Council, chaired by Vice President Quayle, to review new federal rules, and the Council was vigorously denounced by regulatory activists. But the Council had just six full-time employees and by its own estimate reviewed only 50 to 60 regulations (out of nearly 5,000) in 1991. Thus, the Council never had the resources to seriously evaluate the flood of regulations emanating from Washington. As a result, the *Federal Register* contained the third most pages in its history that year, despite the Council's activities.

But with the economy floundering and his poll ratings dipping President George Bush used his 1992 State of the Union speech to declare "a 90-day moratorium on any new federal regulations that could hinder growth." He later extended the moratorium. The irony was that George Bush's moratorium was directed against his own administration. Unlike President Reagan's moratorium imposed after that president's inauguration in 1981, which affected regulations proposed by his predecessor, the Bush moratorium affected only measures initiated by members of his own administration.

Why did President Bush feel it necessary to take on his own administration? Although he served as head of his predecessor's deregulatory task force, Bush's officials were busy—very busy, in fact. As of the end of 1991 59 different agencies were working on 4,863 regulations, of which 919 were new additions to their agencies' agendas. Over the preceding decade the government typically had about 4,000 regulations in process at any one time.

In fact, 1991 saw the sharpest increase in more than a decade in the number of pages in the *Federal Register*, up 26 percent to nearly 68,000, the most since 1980. But even this may have understated the breadth of reregulation under the Bush administration, since it was not just length of rules, but also who and what they affected. All told, wrote Jonathan Rauch, "there is little doubt Bush's first term has witnessed the broadest expansions of government's regulatory reach since the early 1970s."

But the increased activity should come as no surprise given the fact that regulatory spending and the number of regulators increased sharply. In 1992 more than 122,000 federal bureaucrats, about 20 percent more than during the mid-1980s, and higher even than in President Jimmy Carter's record-setting year of 1980, were drafting regulations for 59 different agencies. Federal regulatory spending, too, grew steadily, up roughly 9.7 percent in 1991 and 5.6 percent in 1992, to more than $13 billion annually. While President Reagan actually cut regulatory outlays during three of his eight years in office, expenditures rose steadily under his successor.

## A Deregulatory Agenda

The Bush moratorium was never capable of having much long-term impact. First, it could not affect statutory requirements, other than to encourage officials to slow down their implementation of laws approved by Congress. Second, the administration had no authority over independent agencies, such as the Federal Communications Commission, which in 1990 successfully resisted direct White House pressure to eliminate some intrusive special interest regulations. Third, the moratorium did not apply to "emergency" rules. Finally, the moratorium was conducted largely by the same officials who originally decided that the regulations were necessary.

Thus, President Bill Clinton—who actually criticized Bush for overregulation during the 1992 campaign—must go much further in stemming today's regulatory tide if he is genuinely committed to improving the climate for entrepreneurship and productivity. The administration should embark upon a four-point deregulatory program. First, it needs to stop new regulations, not only within the administration, but also from Congress. Second, it needs to attack a number of long-standing rules bequethed it by past administrations and Congresses. Third, the president needs to press for the repeal or amendment of many of the most onerous regulatory statutes recently initiated by the Bush administration and/or passed by Congress. Fourth, the administration and Congress need to more accurately balance benefits and costs, and seek less wasteful ways of achieving the often positive ends.

*One: Stop New Regulations*

Among the more serious regulatory burdens now being seriously proposed on Capitol Hill are so-called mandated benefits. In early 1993 Congress passed and President Clinton signed into law legislation, previously vetoed by President Bush, requiring employers with 50 or more employees to provide up to 12 weeks of unpaid leave in the event of a birth, adoption, or serious illness. Although sold as a largely costless measure, forced parental leave will disrupt firm operations, hike costs by requiring the hiring of a replacement, and reduce other employee benefits. Nevertheless, the National Research Council, an arm of the National Academy of Sciences, published a 260-page study recommending that employers be forced to provide *paid* leave.

Even more significant are proposals for mandatory health care benefits, something already required by some states. Such a provision would obviously have an even more negative effect on firms. It would, warns Simon Rottenberg, an economics professor at the University of Massachusetts at Amherst, "reduce the number of jobs available, reduce money wages, and reduce the availability of other fringe benefits. These negative effects would fall disproportionately on the less-skilled, whose wage is close to the minimum wage." Indeed, the latter would be most likely to end up unemployed.

Congress is seriously considering legislation to expand the power of the Food and Drug Administration. A bill—the Comprehensive Occupational Safety and Health Reform Act—has been introduced that would mandate the establishment of joint employee-employer safety and health committees to review firm plans and procedures, inspect worksites, challenge employer-OSHA agreements, and more. The Indoor Air Quality

Act would direct the EPA to create an indoor pollution plan and order OSHA to create an indoor air-quality standard.

Nor is this all. Writes Weidenbaum, a former Chairman of the Council of Economic Advisers:

> Other regulatory programs on the congressional agenda include the proposed "workplace fairness" act (making it illegal for an employer to hire permanent replacements during a strike), a revised Clean Water Act, an expanded toxic wastes law (the Resources Conservation and Recover Act or RCRA), renewal of the Superfund statute (the Comprehensive Environmental Response, Compensation, and Liability Act or CERCLA), and perhaps a redo of TOSCA, the Toxic Substances Control Act.

## Two: Repeal Long-Standing Regulations

The administration and Congress could start by dropping the older members of the Dirty Dozen. The introduction of life-saving drugs should no longer be delayed while the FDA judges efficacy. Citrus products and other foods should not be destroyed in order to establish a marketing cartel for farmers. The federal government should no longer push drivers into smaller, more dangerous cars. Congress needs to lift quotas on imported sugar. And federally-supported projects should be able to make use of less expensive neighborhood labor in local housing rehabilitation projects, for instance. Once policymakers have dealt with the Dirty Dozen, they should systematically take on the many other wasteful rules that permeate the federal government.

## Three: Abandon or Amend Recent Onerous Regulatory Initiatives and Statutes

Congress needs to reconsider many of its most recent, foolish legislation. For instance, Washington needs to dramatically reshape the Clean Air Act and similar regulations in order to balance benefits and costs and better achieve environmental goals in a less inefficient manner. The meaning of the ADA needs to be clarified and the law should be changed to prevent discrimination, not require expensive and inefficient affirmative measures. The Civil Rights Act should be amended to require clear proof of discrimination before a plaintiff can recover damages. And the new food labeling requirements should be cancelled.

Other rules, too, should be changed. One complicated regulation, issued by the IRS in spring 1992 after three and one-half years of work, barred "discrimination" against lower-paid employees. The IRS gave less than four months for most companies to comply with detailed requirements on adjusting pensions for retirement age.

In the same year, the Federal Aviation Administration approved regulations phasing out noisier aircraft, which will raise airlines' costs and act as a barrier to new entrants. The Occupational Health and Safety Administration issued regulations, over the objections of the Quayle Competitiveness Council, which believed the need for them to be unproved, limiting workers' exposure to formaldehyde. The 1990 budget package included a sevenfold hike in fines by OSHA. Fines under the Mine Safety and Health Act were quintupled.

*Four: Reform the Regulatory Process to Emphasize a*
*Balance Between Benefits and Costs and Promote*
*More Cost-Efficient Means of Achieving Goals*

Today there is an inevitable incentive to regulate within the federal bureaucracy. After all, agencies exist to act, and employees are normally rewarded for initiating, not quashing, regulations. President Clinton needs to start appointing as administrators people who recognize that the burden of persuasion for economic intervention lies with those who want to initiate action. The point is not that there are no market failures, but that there are far more government failures. Thus, would-be regulators should have to make a clear and convincing case that there is not only a serious problem, but also that one or another government program will solve the problem, before the state intervenes.

Moreover, rules should be imposed only if their costs exceed their benefits. Too often the regulation's few benefits are visible, while the costs are hidden, biasing the government's decision to act. To speak in terms of cost-efficiency is not to ignore the importance of other values, but to recognize the trade-offs necessarily involved. Observes Robert Hahn of the American Enterprise Institute, "Sensible regulation should balance concern for the environment, health and safety with concern for an economy that can provide jobs, a high standard of living and the resources to attack pressing domestic problems like crime, drug abuse and inner-city blight. These issues are more important to the health and welfare of the people than squeezing the last virtually undetectable part per billion of an offending substance from the air."

Further, increased wealth will help advance the objectives that regulation normally seeks to promote. That is, richer countries, for instance, are more concerned about and better able to protect the environment. OMB's Office of Information and Regulatory Affairs (OIRA) was sharply criticized for attempting, during the Bush years, to force agencies to consider the indirect impact of regulations on people because of their cost, yet, explains Daniel Mitchell of the Heritage Foundation, "economic growth does lead to higher living standards, better diets, improved sanitation, and other changes which reduce mortality and improve overall health."

The incoming administration should also elevate OIRA into an independent agency. The new, expanded OIRA should be charged with reviewing all proposed regulatory initiatives—something the Quayle Council on Competitiveness, disbanded by President Clinton, was incapable of doing. The president should instruct all members of his administration to look for more efficient, market-oriented strategies where regulation is still deemed necessary. An environmental approach relying on goal-setting rather than command-and-control regulation, for instance, would provide far better environmental protection at far less cost.

Congress, too, should act. Legislation should be approved to create an independent agency with the duty of monitoring and blocking unnecessary regulation. Moreover, Congress should require executive branch officials to better balance the benefits and costs of regulation. Indeed, Senators Orrin Hatch and Dan Coats, among others, have crafted the Regulatory Accountability Act of 1992, which would require agencies to document the expected benefits and benefits, consider alternative approaches, choose the most cost-effective strategy, and offset costs through revision of existing rules.

## Conclusion

There seems to be an almost inevitable quality to the increase in regulation—rolled back for a time in certain areas during the Carter and Reagan years, but now advancing again as it did in the early 1970s. Alas, unless President Clinton takes charge and changes the course of government, the burden on the public is going to continue to grow heavier every day.

Of course, we do face many very serious problems. But expansive federal regulation has proved that it almost always creates more problems than it solves. As AEI's Carolyn Weaver observed in the context of the ADA:

> In thinking about the role of government in promoting the employment of the disabled, it is easy to overlook the government's wider responsibility to ensure a sound and growing economy. Economic growth may well be the single most potent weapon for creating new jobs and new opportunities for some of the nation's most disadvantaged citizens. Let us hope that the burdens imposed by the ADA on American businesses do not undermine the achievement of sustained growth.

If we are going to provide the expanding economy necessary to provide opportunities to all, both the executive and legislative branches need to embark upon a large-scale deregulatory campaign to emphasize less inefficient and wasteful means of achieving the laudable goals that today animate much government rulemaking. It's time that officials realized that businessmen will create more jobs only when government stops penalizing them for doing so.

October 1993

# 15

# Whither Health Care in the Age of Clinton?

Debate over health care "reform" is not new, but President Bill Clinton has demonstrated yet again the ability of the holder of the national bully pulpit to dominate Washington's political agenda. The president, through his sharp attack on the present system, emotional appeal to those whose care has been uncertain or adequate, and proposal to revolutionize the way Americans receive care, has given an immediacy to the health care debate never before present.

During the 1992 campaign Bill Clinton claimed to be a "new Democrat." As for health care, candidate Clinton proposed a "New Covenant for change" that "provides real incentives to lower costs and improve quality, increases access, and emphasizes a more educated, responsible citizenry." Despite some mandatory aspects, he eschewed price controls and seemed more friendly towards markets than had Sen. Kennedy, among others. But once Bill Clinton was elected he quickly veered left in a number of areas, including health care. He created a panel of more than 500 experts, headed by his wife, to remake one of America's most important industries. The tenor of their deliberations was reflected by Wall Street analyst Kenneth Abramowitz's comment that "Right now, health care is purchased by 250 million morons called U.S. citizens." It was necessary, he explained, to "move them out, reduce their influence, and let smart professionals buy it on our behalf." Not surprisingly, then, the resulting program maintains little more than the rhetoric of the New Democrats. At virtually every juncture the program relies on traditional Democratic approaches: government bureaucracies, employer mandates, price controls, controls over choice, legislated benefit packages, and spending limits. It is perhaps for this reason that Sen. Kennedy exhulted after the President's speech: "We've never had a better opportunity to achieve our goals."

## A Crisis?

In his State of the Union speech the President stated that "our government will never again be full solvent until we tackle the health-care crisis." But he sees the problem as far more than financial. If one took his rhetoric seriously one would think that people were dying in droves due to inadequate medical care. The theme of "crisis" has been repeated endlessly by Clinton aides, legislators, journalists, and analysts.

Yet there is demonstrably no crisis. Problems, yes. Serious problems, yes. But a "crisis," no.

Indeed, if you become seriously ill, there is no better nation in which to become sick than the U.S. America's death rate, perhaps the best measure of access to and quality of care, is among the lowest, and often the lowest, for most major illnesses. In some cases the differences are quite dramatic: you are twice as likely to die from a hernia or intestinal obstruction in Sweden than in the U.S., three times as likely to die from an ulcer in Great Britain than in America, and seven times as likely to die from prostrate disease in Sweden than in the U.S.

This is not to say that American *health* is equal to that elsewhere. Infant mortality and life expectancy lag behind those of many other industrialized states, but that reflects serious social pathologies absent from many other nations. For example, the U.S. has many problems characteristic of Third World states in its inner cities. Moreover, explains Dr. Leroy Schwartz of Health Policy International, "we have a large number of people who indulge in high-risk behavior." That is, overall health figures are dramatically affected by America's high rates of homicide, drug use, and AIDS.

American medicine is particularly good at treating the injured and sick because it rewards research and innovation, and utilizes the latest techniques and technologies. The pharmaceutical industry, for instance, is one of America's most competitive businesses internationally. Compared to other nations the U.S. is also awash in high-tech devices and procedures. This technical and technological superiority is expensive, of course. But to artificially restrict patient access to such care is also costly. Britain does not provide kidney dialysis for those over the age of 55; the Kidney Patient Association estimates that 1500 people die every year as a result.

## Problems?

Still, the problems are real. Cost is the most obvious concern. Last year the nation spent $838.5 billion on health care, 14 percent of GNP, up from 13.2 percent in 1991. In the latter year the comparable percentages were 6.6 in Britain and Japan, 8.5 in Germany, and 9.1 in France. And the Commerce Department expects medical costs to continue racing ahead at 12 percent a year.

However, spending/GNP ratios alone do not demonstrate the existence of a problem, let alone a crisis. There is no "right" amount of money to spend on health care and comparisons with other nations help little. Based on purchasing power parities (rather than misleading exchange rate measurements), America has the highest standard of living in the world: the U.S. gross domestic product per capita is more than 55 percent higher than that of Western Europe, 35 percent more than in Australia, 28 percent greater than in Japan, and 11 percent higher than in Canada. There is nothing strange, then, about Americans devoting an increasing share of their incomes on medical attention as they grow more prosperous. Surely there is at least as much justification for spending a marginal dollar on health as on a nicer car, more recreation, or another beer.

The problem, then, is not that people are spending too much in a absolute sense, but that people are paying more than necessary for the care that they are receiving. Reform efforts, therefore, should be directed at changing underlying incentives rather than reducing simple expenditures. After all, the American people might want to devote 14 percent of GNP to health care even after cost-cutting reforms were adopted, if they believed the benefits that they were receiving were worth the expense.

Rising costs have, however, contributed to the problem of inadequate insurance. Some number of Americans—probably between six and 16 million rather than the commonly cited 37 million—are chronically uninsured. They generally receive poorer attention and are more vulnerable to medical emergencies.

The other serious problem area involves stresses to particular parts of the system. Upward spiraling government expenditures have exacerbated federal and state budget deficits; Medicaid and Medicare are both delivering steadily lower quality care despite runaway spending. Their inadequacies, combined with some people's lack of insurance and the steady flow of illegal aliens, have created an epidemic of cost-shifting onto patients with private insurance and overloaded municipal hospitals, which are estimated to suffer as much as $10 billion in unrecovered expenses. As serious as are all of these problems, and they are serious, it is noteworthy that the worst difficulties and greatest overspending afflict *public* aspects of the health care system. This should raise at least some doubt as to the ability of the federal and state governments to manage the rest of the health care system.

## The Call for Reform

The unrelenting campaign by the President and continuous media barrage have led to an almost hysterical demand for action. Indeed, nine of ten people polled believe the system to be in "crisis." Yet the vast majority of Americans are pleased with their health care. Opinion polls consistently find that 70 percent or more of Americans are satisfied with their care. Even six of ten of those with incomes below $20,000 are content.

Unfortunately, public officials, usually enamored of their own skills and distrustful of the seeming "chaos" of the marketplace, are more inclined towards radical forms of intervention. In particular, the administration would: limit total health care spending; create a National Health Board to control premium rates; establish a standard benefits package for consumers; require firms to pay 80 percent of the cost of employees' health insurance premiums; mandate coverage for part-time employees as well; establish regional "Health Alliances" to negotiate insurance coverage and collect premiums; bar most individuals from going outside "their" Health Alliance for coverage; allow states to penalize large firms that self-insure; authorize states to create Canadian-style single-payer systems; prohibit employers and insurers from reducing coverage for expensive illnesses; and subsidize coverage of the currently uninsured.

The proposal is breath-taking in scope and radical in intent. It would dramatically reshape the medical marketplace and make Uncle Sam the nation's Doctor-in-Chief. If the Clinton program is passed, Washington will end up determining what insurance benefits people can buy, what kind of care they can receive, and how much they can spend. In perhaps no other area of their lives would Americans be ceding the government so much authority.

## Clinton Plan Pitfalls

The administration proposal suffers from several serious flaws. Although well-intentioned, the proposal must ultimately be judged on its likely results. For it will do patients little good if the President meant well or not if they end up paying more for less.

### The Fatal Conceit

Some advocates of nationalized medicine apparently believe that the most important problem with health care is that no one has specifically designed and managed today's system. Rather, medicine is responding to the whims of 250 million "idiots," as Kenneth Abramowitz put it. What is therefore needed, in their view, is essentially central planning— a National Health Board, for instance, along with Health Alliances, legislated benefits, federal mandates, and the like.

This position is hardly new. To the contrary, it motivated generations of apparatchiks and bureaucrats throughout Eastern Europe and the former Soviet Union. Indeed, for more than 70 years often dedicated and occasionally even well-intentioned people assumed that they could reshape human institutions to fit their abstract visions of utopia, irrespective of economic forces, individual desires, social mores, cultural traditions, and the like. The experiment clearly failed when it came to making computers, steel, and similar products; it was no more successful in providing health care. Only the much greater wealth of the Western industrialized nations that socialized their medical systems allowed them to avoid the catastrophe that overtook the poorer communists. But whatever the exact rhetoric, the belief that an intricate process like medicine can be ordered through the political process reflects what Nobel laureate Friedrich Hayek called "the fatal conceit."

Of course, many medical decisions are more complex and wrenching than the question of, say, which car to purchase. But the very complexity of the questions enhances the importance of decentralized decision-making. However smart, the seven members of the administration's proposed National Health Board cannot substitute for a complex process involving millions of patients, doctors, hospitals, insurance companies, and other participants involved in more than 1.3 billion medical "transactions" a year. In the health care marketplace, like any other industry, freely moving prices transmit valuable information to be acted on by participants. The outcomes, however imperfect, are far more likely to advance the interests of patients than edicts based on bureaucratic whims of a central organization. A person may still have to rely on information and advice provided by others in determining the best care for oneself or one's family, but in one case he is a thinking decision-maker and in the other he is an inanimate input.

It is true, of course, that today's nominally private system is disturbingly bureaucratic. But that unsurprisingly reflects the fact that patients directly pay so little of their bills: On average, five cents on the dollar for hospitalization, 19 cents for doctors' care, and 24 cents for other services. Write Goodman and Musgrave, "Patients therefore have an incentive to purchase hospital services until, at the margin, they're worth only 5 cents on the dollar and to purchase physicians' services until they are worth only 19 cents on the dollar." At the same time, those who pay the rest of the bill have an even more powerful incentive to try to restrain that spending. Which has led to the bureaucratization of the medical process. So long as patients control such a small percentage of outlays, they will have a limited role in making medical decisions. Rather than empowering political officials and health administrators by nationalizing the health care system—forcing patients to elect the right president and Senators to choose the right national health board members in order to make the right medical decision—the government should restore to patients the authority and responsibility to control their medical destinies.

## Cost Explosion

By even its own estimates the Clinton program would be expensive, at least $700 billion over five years (1994 to 2000). However, the administration initially claimed that spending cuts and tax hikes would result in a *reduction* in federal outlays of $91 billion; these estimates were "not debatable," explained Council of Economic Advisers Chairwoman Laura D'Andrea Tyson, at least they weren't before the administration downgraded the expected savings to $70 billion and then $58 billion. Lest the administration seem confused, White House aide Ira Magaziner promises that the latter forecast is accurate: "We've discussed this thoroughly, and I don't think there is disagreement now on what the numbers should be."

But no one familiar with the federal record, let alone that of public health care programs, should take their claim on faith. Medicare, Medicaid, renal dialysis coverage, and the short-lived catastrophic health care initiative all suffered from soaring costs almost the moment after passage. For instance, within eight years after Medicare's passage its tax rate was running at twice the initial projections; the program now spends roughly 50 times what it did in its first full year. The *initial* costs of Medicare's kidney dialysis program, passed in 1972, were more than twice projected levels. The problem is endemic to third-party payment programs, which naturally inflate demand and thus expenditures.

Of course, the mere fact that others have failed does not mean the administration might not be right. Yet consider what the administration proposes to do: include 37 million more people on insurance, provide an expansive basic benefit, promise all Americans coverage for prescription drugs, increase Medicare benefits, and effectively upgrade Medicaid coverage. Perhaps it is no surprise that barely one week after Hillary Clinton testified before Congress, the administration began revising its cost estimates.

Rep. Pete Stark, chairman of the House Ways and Means Subcommittee on Health, says "This is like cold fusion. You get all these wonderful results with no effort, no problem." Senate Finance Committee Chairman Patrick Moynihan (D-N.Y.) calls the estimates a "fantasy." He adds: "These numbers all come out of their computer in that way. They won't last, they mustn't last."

The supposed Medicare/Medicaid savings are particularly dubious. Hillary Clinton testified before Congress that "we are thinking zero growth in costs," but Rep. Stark argues that five to six percent annual increases is the best achievable. Indeed, the Reagan and Bush administrations used explicit price controls throughout the 1980s cut both programs' rates of projected growth, but between 1980 and 1990 federal outlays jumped from $35 billion and $14 billion, respectively, to $98 billion and $41 billion. Three years later spending ran *$133 billion and $80.5 billion.* And even this rather modest success has been achieved primarily at the expense of other patients. Since Medicare and Medicaid are estimated to only cover 87 percent and 46 percent, respectively, of actual costs, many physicians effectively shift many of the costs onto their other paying customers. (Some, of course, simply refuse to see patients under the two plans, but those that do are not content with the low reimbursement rates.) The Colorado Hospital Assocation estimates that the average hospital bill in its state is $2,300, or 50 percent, higher because because of cost-shifting (due to the uninsured and members of prepaid plans as well as Medicare/Medicaid recipients). All told, Hewitt Associates, a consulting firm, figures that cost-shifting is responsible for almost half of insurance premium increases not attributable to inflation generally. While the administration's attempt to limit all health care expenditures might restrict future cost-shifting, this would make it even harder to make dramatic new cuts in outlays since doctors would have no means of recouping lost revenues and would be more likely to refuse to see Medicare and Medicaid patients.

But in the end, the administration, despite its protestations to the contrary, doesn't seem to think the numbers to be too important. Bill Clinton told an audience in Tampa, Florida: "All of you have to be prepared to face the consequences if the cost savings don't materialize," namely that the administration would have to "slow down the benefits, or raise more money." In short, trust him. But if there's a problem—you'll pay.

## Global Budgeting

In order to cut spending, the Clinton program originally envisioned "global budgeting," whereby the National Health Board would impose maximum budgets on the Health Alliances. Sharp criticism of global budgeting, which has led to huge waiting lists abroad, caused the administration to retreat from formal restraints on outlays. Nevertheless, the administration expects to achieve its ends in other ways. Explained HHS Secretary Donna Shalala to Congress, the administration now expects its limits on premiums to limit national health care expenditures: "we believe premium caps are a substitute for global budgeting."

Alas, global budgeting is flawed in principle. As noted earlier, there is no "correct" level of health care spending. Medicine is an art, not a science, and one cannot program exact health care expenditures over the upcoming month, let alone year. Nor is there any reason why outlays should climb a set amount—such as the overall consumer price index— instead of matching people's perceived needs. Indeed, why should Americans be prohibited from spending more on their health but not more on, say, automobiles or entertainment?

Equally important, it is impossible to meet an arbitrary target without making arbitrary cuts in services. In setting spending limits the Board is supposed to consider expenditures in other states, actuarial area ratings, "current per capita health care expenditures for the guaranteed benefits package trended forward to 1996 based on projected increases in private sector health care spending," as well as "adjustments for expected increases in utilization by the uninsured and under-insured and to recapture currently uncompensated care." Meeting actual patients' needs, however, seems not to be an important factor.

The desire to cut expenditures that are truly unnecessary—that is, which are undertaken because perverse incentives have distorted the normal balancing of costs and benefits—is legitimate, but can be best achieved by changing the health care system's incentives. If Washington merely demands cuts without changing the structural environment, particularly the degree of third-party payment, within which medical services are demanded and supplied, it will inevitably degrade the quality of care and reduce the freedom of choice currently enjoyed by most Americans. This has, in fact, been the result in Great Britain, Canada, and Sweden, all of which employ global budgeting. In the former one million and perhaps even more people are on waiting lists for medical attention at any one time. Canada's waiting lists are smaller—just 250,000 people—but our northern neighbor spends 50 percent more than Britain on health care, 9.0 percent of gross domestic product in 1990, compared to 6.2 percent.

## Price Controls

Equally dangerous is the means by which the administration plans to ensure that its budgets are met. The premium limits, like the budgetary limits, are wholly arbitrary: premiums will initially be set to fit within the budget and then could rise only according to a set formula, the consumer price index plus 1.5 percent in 1996 down to the simple CPI (one-fourth the current rate of increase) by 1999. The administration's hope, of course, is to foster efficiency by limiting how much people can pay for insurance. But admitted one Cabinet officer anonymously: "When you go to tight caps, you are going to something like price controls."

Thus, the president and his staffers are smoking—and inhaling—strange substances if they believe that they can arbitrarily cut rates without cutting services. To the contrary, the easiest way to absorb a premium reduction is by reducing quality. Warns the Congressional Budget Office: "insurers would probably take a variety of actions—increasing utilization review, avoiding potentially high-cost enrollees, reducing benefits, and cutting payments to providers are the most likely."

To avoid these effects, the administration would prohibit discrimination against high-cost enrollees and mandate a minimum benefit package. As a result, insurers would have to increasingly rely on utilization review and payment cuts, essentially price controls. As the pressure of being caught between arbitrary government premium limits and rising costs rose insurers would have to ever more fervently dispute bills and demand fee reductions, as well as perhaps lobby Congress to impose direct price controls on providers. "It gets kicked back to provider income in one way or another," admits Ira Magaziner. Even if reaming doctors was fair, it would certainly have an impact on services. "Yes, you will have universal access," observes James Todd, senior vice president of the American Medical Association, "but to what will you have access?"

Moreover, the administration presumably plans to employ some form of price control in order to make major "savings" in Medicare and Medicaid. Past cuts have been achieved by simply, and arbitrarily, reducing reimbursement rates. For instance, the official Medicare formula for physicians is "Payment = $(\{RVUw_s \times GPCIw_a\} + \{RVUpe_s \times GPCIpe_a\} + \{RVUm_s \times GPICm_a\}) \times CF$." All of these letters and acronyms represent something, but quality care is not among them. Today, as noted earlier, Medicare pays roughly 87 percent of standard fees and Medicaid allows only 46 percent. The result is two-fold: patients essentially wear a red letter when seeking medical care, discouraging doctors from treating them, and physicians who see poor and elderly patients shift much of the cost onto other consumers. New reductions by the Clinton administration would exacerbate these trends, saving the nation little money while further degrading medical care for the elderly and poor.

Indeed, for more than a decade both the corporate sector and government have been trying to limit costs. Alas, reports Dr. Joshua Wiener of the Brookings Institution, "costs are still going up at very high rates." A whole panoply of programs have been created—Health Maintenance Organizations, Preferred-Provider Organizations, Professional Standards Review Organizations, Utilization Review, and more. Some, like HMO's, have lowered base health care costs. But the rate of increase, perhaps the problem that has most captured Washington's attention, has remained largely unchanged. Concluded the National Academy of Science's Institute of Medicine in 1989, although UR, widely used by business, "probably has reduced the level of expenditures for some purchasers, utilization management—like most other cost containment strategies—does not appear to have altered the long-term rate of increase in health-care costs" over the previous decade. In fact, "employers who saw a short-term moderation in benefit expenditures are seeing a return to previous trends."

*Regional Monopolies*

The bureaucratic key to the administration's plan is the Health Alliances, which are to negotiate with providers and hold down insurance rates. Although considered to be part of the "managed competition" strategy advanced by many moderate Democratic supporters of the president, the HA's would be almost all management and no competition. Either monopoly government or quasi-government agencies, they would do nothing to spur market forces; rather, they would operate as yet an additional administrative layer on top of an already over-burdened system. For this reason many advocates of "managed competition," including some Democrats active in the 1992 Clinton presidential campaign, are either opposing or remaining publicly neutral towards a proposal that would be better called managed coercion.

Indeed, the prime characteristic of the HA's is a lack of consumer choice. It would be *illegal* for most people other than the elderly, servicepeople and their families, and employees of large companies to purchase insurance outside of a HA. People would not be allowed to purchase plans that cost 20 percent more than the average of all of the HA's plans. Nor could people agree to pay doctors any supplement above the HA-approved fee schedule. Indeed, likely to disappear are many fee-for-service plans since "annual ceilings and the 20 percent rule will make it virtually impossible for some alliances to offer choose-your-own-doctor health insurance," warns Elizabeth McCaughey of the Manhattan Institute. And despite the president's promise that Americans will be able to choose fee-for-service coverage, the administration would grant the National Health Board the authority to give HA's waivers to not offer fee-for-service plans.

Further, the HA's would arbitrarily impose high medical costs on lower-risk consumers. This reflects three factors: the prohibition against insurers adjusting premiums to reflect age and health (making the young subsidize the middle-aged and old, who use far more medical services), the bar against taking behavior into account (making the health-conscious underwrite the risk-takers, who are hospitalized 40 percent more often), and the use of community ratings (making the lowest medical consumers subsidize the highest medical consumers). The latter is critical. States would have to create health alliance regions, within which all residents would be pooled. Thus, suburban residents grouped with central cities would pay far higher rates than more distant neighborhoods. The Clinton plan purports to forbid what McCaughey calls "medical gerrymandering," but the process could become as politically divisive as electoral redistricting. It will also unfairly stick random groups of consumers with the bulk of the bill for extending insurance to the uninsured and expanding Medicaid coverage.

*Job Destruction*

Equally serious is the administration's apparent failure to recognize that raising the cost of employment will reduce the number of jobs. The keystone of the health care proposal is requiring employers to provide insurance for their workers. Although superficially appealing as a means of expanding access to health insurance, such a mandate actually would hurt its intended beneficiaries. Warn economists Dwight Lee and Ronald Warren, "the connection between legislation mandating noble objectives and the actual accomplishment of those objectives is far more tenuous than most people seem to realize."

Most workers at major firms are already covered by employer-health care plans; fully 90 percent of companies that don't offer health insurance have fewer than ten workers. Thus, a federal edict would primarily affect smaller enterprises, which are most vulnerable to added regulatory costs. Even at businesses which do not presently offer a health care plan, most employees are not denied access to care. Some are covered through the benefits of other family members. The poorest workers are eligible for Medicaid or receive charity care from nearby clinics, doctors, and hospitals.

Still, for some inadequate and costly care is a problem. But mandates would do little to help them; more likely they would either find their incomes reduced or their jobs destroyed.

The basic problem is that firms, especially little ones in a competitive marketplace, rarely have bountiful cash balances to meet regulatory requirements. In response, the administration has promised to underwrite smaller companies' medical benefits. Alas, such aid may be only temporary—before the plan's unveiling one White House aide said that the subsidies would end after eight to ten years. Even if the financial support is provided as promised, it would only moderate the problem. Moreover, the payments will burden *other* firms that would be indirectly paying for their competitors' employee benefits. And if the administration's cost estimates prove to be the "fantasy" predicted by Sen. Moynihan, then Uncle Sam would have little money to assist small business. One of the first places this or a future administration might attempt to cut, once the overall health care program was firmly fastened into place, would be these subsidies.

Which means that the plan's impact on private firms could eventually be devastating. Most companies that do not offer health care benefits can't afford to do so; many are start-up operations that provide an important entry into the marketplace for their employees but possess only a limited capacity to increase compensation. Since mandated benefits do not make workers more productive, they do not encourage firms to add compensation. Rather, mandates tell companies to *substitute* benefits. That is, most firms would comply with new requirements by lowering, or reducing any future increase in, cash compensation and other fringe benefits, such as family and sick leave. A 1990 study for the National Bureau of Economic Research estimated that almost 90 percent of the cost of mandated health care benefits is likely to fall on workers.

Other workers will be even less lucky, losing their jobs. Particularly vulnerable are workers at the margin—minimum wage employees, for instance, whose monetary compensation cannot be reduced by law. While a firm cannot pay them less, it can not pay them at all, by firing them. The number of people at risk in this way is enormous: more than one third of employees who lack health insurance earn the minimum wage. In this way mandated benefits would most hurt those currently without health insurance. Although estimates vary dramatically, depending upon the likely premium cost, availability, amount, and permanence of any subsidy, "elasticity" (or price sensitivity) of the demand for labor, and appearance of the administration's promised health care cost savings elsewhere (thereby reducing premiums), the total job loss could be significant. A Joint Economic Committee study has estimated that a health care mandate that imposed a seven percent tax on payroll could eliminate more than 700,000 jobs; a nine percent hit would destroy over 800,000. The CONSAD Research Corp. estimates that losses under three different forms of employer mandates could exceed one million. The consulting firm figured that the proposal closest to that of the Clinton administration could cost between 390,000 and 650,000. Another 6.6 million jobs would be "at-risk," according to CONSAD, which means they would "experience the highest probability of elimination or layoff" and "substantial losses in wages and benefits." A more recent study by economists June and Dave O'Neill of Baruch College comes to similar conclusions, warning that "3.1 million jobs will be lost, with more than 75 percent of these losses concentrated in low-wage, labor-intensive sectors of the economy."

Even Hillary Clinton has acknowledged that some job loss was unavoidable, given how many firms do not presently provide insurance. But the administration simply doesn't seem to care. In response to a congressman's question on the impact of the administration plan on small business, Mrs. Clinton responded that "I cannot be responsible for saving every undercapitalized entrepreneur in America." But these "undercapitalized entrepreneurs" provide millions of people with satisfying employment. They also often grow into the larger enterprises that she seems more fond of—at least they do if they are not strangled at birth by Washington.

In his State of the Union speech President Bill Clinton warned that his entire economic program could fail if Congress did not enact health care reform. Alas, the economy will suffer far more if Congress approves job-destructive health care reform.

*Pernicious Potpourri*

While it is hard to dislike the President's soaring rhetoric before Congress, it is easy to question many of the details in the administration's 239-page blueprint of its plan. For instance, while HHS Secretary Shalala told an audience of doctors that the president did not want "a centralized bureaucratic health care system run from Washington," that is precisely what the National Health Board would be. Made up of seven appointees and attended by bountiful staffers and advisory committees, the Board would oversee the states, make recommendations on the standard benefit package, set budgets, badger pharmaceutical companies, and run the "National Quality Management System." In short, a single body in Washington would direct the course of an industry made up of 650,000 doctors, 1.6 million nurses, more than 30,000 hospitals and nursing homes, thousands of allied firms, and patients who make 1.3 *billion* visits to physicians annually.

The proposed expansions of coverage—some whole-hearted (pharmaceutical and long-term care), some timid (substance abuse and mental health)—along with reduced deductibles and copayments would further reduce the nexus between patients and payments, concomitantly cutting consumer incentives to use health care more responsibly. Combined with HA's and the requirement that insurers use community ratings, which bar differential premiums based on health and risk-taking activities, the program would make patients almost irrelevant to their own care.

The plan to subsidize early retirees' medical coverage appears to be a sop to large manufacturers rather than a logical social policy. The administration's estimated cost of $6 billion is regarded by most experts as unrealistic since the federal benefit is likely to encourage firms to offer more and more generous early-out programs, swelling the number of people eligible for federal aid. CEA Chairwoman Tyson puts the number of early retirees at as many as 600,000; some administration officials privately worry that depopulating the work force in this way would exacerbate the funding problem for Social Security.

The proposal to mandate coverage for part-time workers would destroy even more employment opportunities. In fact, the administration program actually discriminates against part-time work, a flexible opportunity that many people, including mothers seeking to spend more time with their children, increasingly desire. President Clinton, however, would treat anyone working 30 hours a week as a full-time employee. Thus, a firm that hired two part-timers for 20-hours each would be responsible for two-thirds of the standard health care premium payment for both employees, totaling one and one-third health care policies for the equivalent of one full-time position. Businesses would likely drop even more part-time than full-time jobs.

## Is There a Way Out?

If the Clinton program doesn't live up to its billing, what is the answer? It is not nationalized medicine, which generally offers substandard care everywhere in the world. It's not the Canadian system, which provides poorer service and more limited technological access. Perhaps even worse, Canadian medicine does not even live up to its reputation for being cheaper. After accounting for differences in population and including costs of tax collection, health care in Canada is as expensive as that in America. As a result, conclude Jacque Krasny and Ian Ferrier, two Canadian health care consultants, "A fair comparison of the two systems suggests that wholesale adoption of the Candian system will not result in a satisfactory decline in U.S. health care costs." Ironically, one of the things that makes Canada's system "work" is the presence of the U.S. as a safety valve. Even Quebec Premier Robert Bourassa, a fervent supporter of his nation's single-payer system, flew south when he was diagnosed with a potentially deadly skin cancer.

Nor is the solution a purer form of "managed competition"—creating HA's without the global budgeting and insurance premium caps, for instance—which almost inevitably involves more management than competition. For many Americans one form or another of managed competition is already a reality, since they are employed by firms that have chosen HMOs or PPOs or which offer competing plans; alas, as noted earlier, this approach has not solved the health care system's problems. Unfortunately, most proposals for managed competition envision more controls and less freedom, including a national regulatory board and legislated minimum benefits package. Most would push consumers into cheaper, prepaid plans and limit a patient's choice of doctors and treatments. Most would also probably rely on increasing restrictions on prices and services. And all would ignore the fundamental problem of pervasive third-party payment, thereby limiting their effect on future price increases.

Rather, the solution lies, first, in enhancing market forces, particularly by empowering medical consumers. Second, it involves incremental reform of counterproductive policies, all the while building on the strengths of the existing system.

*Enhancing Market Forces*

The most critical difference between medical insurance and real insurance is that the former covers virtually every expense, even small procedures that could easily be paid by the insured, while the latter involves a pooling of the unlikely risk of catastrophic loss. The result is what John Goodman and Gerald Musgrave call a "cost-plus" system for medicine. As they write, "The major reason costs are rising is that when patients and physicians get together, they are spending someone else's money rather than their own." The share of all medical services covered by third parties, either private insurers or the government, rose from 48.4 percent to 76.7 percent between 1965 and 1990. Coverage of doctors' fees increased from 38.4 percent to 81.3 percent and hospital charges edged up from 83.2 percent to 95.0 percent over the same period. Thus, the average patient directly pays just one-fourth of the cost of his treatment.

The effect on medical prices should be obvious. Imagine a system under which third-parties covered three-fourths of the cost of buying a new car. Demand for cars, especially luxury autos, would soar. It has, of course, been argued that medicine will never respond to market forces in the same way as will, say, auto repair. However, while a patient may may have little discretion in deciding how he wants to be treated after a serious automobile accident or heart attack, he can easily choose not to see a doctor is he has a common cold or minor cut. And prices matter in making that decision, because if health care was costless there would be little reason not to visit the hospital for the most minor ailment, or not to have one's physician perform every one of the 900 different blood tests that could be done.

Adjusting the financial incentives facing patients would encourage them to take a greater interest in their care, learn more about their conditions, and consider less expensive treatments. For instance, the Rand Corporation found that people with free care (a zero deductible) incurred 50 percent higher medical bills, visited physicians 50 percent more frequently, and were admitted to hospitals one-third more often than those with a deductible of $1000 (worth about $2500 today). Lest there be fear that greater patient responsibility leads to poor health and death, Rand found no significant difference between the health of people based on their deductible (other, oddly, than in the care of their eyes). In short, patients, advised by their doctors, are at least as capable as administrators and legislators in balancing the costs and benefits of additional medical treatments.

Pervasive and generous medical insurance has also generated a blizzard of paperwork. Much of the administrative burden is simply filing forms and cutting checks for even the smallest expenses; increasingly important in recent years is the role of insurers' "gate-keepers" as part of UR and other cost-containment procedures and physicians' staff to negotiate with the gate-keepers. Again, consider the effect on auto or home insurance if every repair required submission of a form, approval of the procedure by a company representative, and issuance of a check. One estimate of the share of medical spending devoted to administration is 19.3 to 24.1 percent. That would be $202 billion last year siphoned away from patient care.

The administration claims that it will address the problem of administrative expenses by standardizing forms. The health care plan would not, however, reduce *the number of pieces of paper* flooding doctors' and insurers' offices. To the contrary, by extending coverage to more people while still handling small claims, the Clinton program could exacerbate the problem. Only moving people away from full coverage and toward catastrophic insurance would markedly reduce the paperwork burden.

The federal role in severing the connection between consumers and providers is obvious enough with Medicare and Medicaid. Washington also bears the bulk of the responsibility for driving private medicine and insurance towards "cost-plus" care. Starting in 1942, when the War Labor Board ruled that fringe benefits were not subject to wage controls, the government has encouraged the expansion of generous private insurance, especially by offering employers tax deductions for a form of compensation that is not treated as taxable wages. Because of this de facto subsidy of health insurance compared to simple salary, employers provide more employees with richer policies.

Thus, a first step for Congress would be to end its tax preference for lavish insurance policies. This could be achieved by taxing health care (and other fringe) benefits, though any such hike should be paired with an equivalent reduction in tax rates. Rationalizing the health care system should not become yet another excuse for government to raid taxpayers' wallets. Or Washington could preserve tax deductibility, but only for policies that restore some nexus between patients and payments—ones that act like real insurance, covering catastrophic expenses but leaving routine expenses to patients.

Such a step would dramatically reshape the health care marketplace. Patients would take a more active role in questioning doctors about their options and be more careful about seeking the most cost-effective routine, non-emergency treatment. Doctors, too, knowing that their patients would be picking up the tab, would be less promiscuous and lavish in their recommended treatments. Moreover, by dropping many of the $50 office visits, which cost as much to reimburse as $10,000 operations, such an approach would cut administrative expensives by reducing providers' time spent on paperwork and insurers' costs of paying (or refusing to pay) claims.

Better, however, would be the more far-reaching proposal for medical IRAs, or medi-save accounts. This approach, what the Cato Institute's Brink Lindsey calls the "Patient Power plan," would empower consumers—whether high-income, middle-class, poor, or elderly. Today employers in urban areas with an average cost of living spend about $4500 per employee for health care. Rather than paying that $4500 for a standard insurance policy, a company could instead purchase a catastrophic policy for $1500 and give the employee the extra $3000 to cover his deductible (94 percent of families have annual medical expenses under $3000). This is not an option today because the $3000 would be treated as income and taxed; at the same time, the self-employed are allowed to deduct only one-fourth of their health insurance premiums and medical expenses only when they exceed 7.5 percent of adjusted gross income. (Some cafeteria-style fringe benefit plans include flexible savings accounts, but any unused funds revert to the employer, the opposite of the result intended by medical IRAs.) Again, the tax law could be changed in one of two ways. Catastrophic policies, with large cash payments for deductibles, could be made fully tax deductible. Or health care benefits could be taxed, with a full credit available for the purchase of insurance.

Congress should apply the same principle to both Medicare and Medicaid. That is, rather than have Washington (in conjunction with the states for Medicaid) run mammoth fee-for-service insurance plans for the poor and elderly, the government should either provide vouchers or refundable tax credits towards a participant's purchase of an approved policy. Such an approach, while it might increase federal budget costs, would both help moderate overall medical expenses and improve participants' care.

*Reducing Unnecessary Costs*

While states cannot reach such issues as the federal tax deductibility of health care insurance, there is still much states could do to help reduce health care costs. In fact, one of the virtues of federalism is that states can operate as laboratories for policy experimentation. States could helpfully act in several areas. With federal approval they could use medical savings accounts as a model for vouchers to replace Medicaid, as proposed by the American Legislative Exchange Council. They should revise occupational licensure laws to end unnecessary restrictions on nurses, nurse practitioners, and similar professionals. States should also eliminate (or Washington preempt) expensive mandated benefit laws, which force private insurers to cover nearly 1000 specific conditions. The cost of these benefits vary widely, but some are quite expensive: Goodman and Musgrave estimate that the percentage of uninsured who lack coverage because mandated benefits have priced them or their firms out of the market ranges from 15 percent in Arkansas to 64 percent in Connecticut, and about 25 percent overall. Moreover, states should address an important cause of rapidly rising doctors' fees—the runaway liability system. Lawsuits per 100 physicians more than trebled between 1981 and 1985 alone; observes Peter Huber of the Manhattan Institute, "more medical malpractice suits were filed in the decade ending 1987 than in the entire previous history of American tort law." The problem is not only rising malpractice premiums—which increased more than threefold between 1982 and 1989. The threat of litigation causes doctors to perform more procedures and tests than necessary, or "defensive" medicine—estimated by the AMA to have cost $15 billion in 1989. Finally, excessive litigation, including product liability, hinders medical innovation, particularly within the pharmaceutical industry.

## Conclusion

Our health care problems are real and serious reform is necessary. Alas, the president's approach, rather than fulfilling his soaring rhetoric, is far more likely to simultaneously reduce personal choice, increase costs, and degrade the quality of care. Therefore, if Congress is serious about solving America's health care problems, it will eschew the Clintons' ideological crusade, choosing instead to strengthen rather than uproot a system that, despite its manifold faults, still provides quality care to the vast majority of the American people.

November 1993

# 16

## The Pharmaceutical Industry:
## Problem or Solution?

In his 1993 State of the Union speech President Bill Clinton warned that his entire economic program could fail if Congress did not approve serious health care reform. Alas, his economic program could also fail if Congress approves the wrong sort of health care reform. The result could be a simultaneous medical failure and fiscal disaster.

Unfortunately, the administration seems to be moving in the wrong direction with a tax- and regulation-heavy reform proposal. One of the reasons that it is more likely to hurt than help is that fact that its proponents seem as interested in punishing supposed villains as in improving the lives of patients. Doctors and insurance companies have long been popular targets of populist wrath; so, too, are pharmaceutical companies. For instance, during the 1992 presidential campaign President Clinton promised to "stop drug price gouging." His wife's task force had little more regard for the drugmakers, complaining of their "sins of the past," including charging thousands of dollars a year for some drug therapies. Worries one industry lobbyist, "administration officials have made a political calculation that they need to go to war with us."

Task force members responded to analysts who spoke of market-oriented health care reforms by arguing that the marketplace would not limit prices "of single-source drugs for which there is no therapeutic equivalent," as if the purpose of patents was something other than allowing inventors to earn a generous reward for their labors. But the administration apparently shied away from formal price controls because of opposition from even liberal Democratic legislators like Senate Majority Leader George Mitchell. In the end, the president's advisers seemed to lean towards creating a federal board to collect industry information, set price guidelines, and browbeat offending companies. Explained one task force document, such a commission "would collect information about prices, and it would establish guidelines as to a reasonable price for prescription drugs that have no therapeutic alternative. It would have the authority to publicly condemn any companies that violated the guidelines."

Congressmen, too, are pressing for controls over prescriptions and prices. For instance, Sen. David Pryor (D-Ark.), chairman of the Special Committee on Aging and close friend of President Clinton, has long used his committee to press for limits on pharmaceutical prices. He testified before the President's Task Force on Health Care Reform, complaining that "manufacturers can essentially set the launch price, without the health care system having any idea of whether the price is 'fair' or even 'reasonable'." Yes, continued research and development is important, he acknowledged, but "that does not mean—as a matter of public policy—that the manufacturer should be able to charge whatever the market will bear." Indeed, he argues, the companies will gain an unwarranted windfall from the Clinton program's inclusion of pharmaceuticals, which alone warrants regulating the industry.

Other congressional critics of the drug industry include Representatives Sonny Montgomery (D-Miss.) and Pete Stark (D-Ca.), and Senators Byron Dorgan (D-N.D.) and Sen. Edward Kennedy (D-Mass.). For instance, Rep. Montgomery proposes limiting the prices of drugs purchased by Veterans Affairs hospitals. Rep. Stark, supported by the American Association of Retired Persons, suggests creating a U.S. equivalent of the Canadian Patented Medicine Prices Review Board to slow drug price increases. Sen. Dorgan wants to cut pharmaceutical tax credits and create a Prescription Drug Policy Review Commission. Sen. Kennedy hopes to force drugmakers to provide their products for lower prices to entities funded under the Public Health Service Act.

Even some doctors contend that pharmaceutical prices are too high. Columbia University's Paul Meier, a consultant to the Food and Drug Administration, says that "There's a limit to how much we should play the market." As he explains, "If someone who finds a pill that would save babies from some dreadful fate says, 'I'm charging an outrageous amount but it's worth it,' I would say that's morally corrupt." How to set a "fair" price? Dr. Peter Arno of New York City's Montefiore Medical Center proposes establishing prices based on those of comparable products or drugs in other nations.

In short, the average American could be forgiven for thinking that the drugmakers deserve to be damned. Yet all the attention being given to pharmaceuticals seems odd, given their relatively small role in the health care crisis. Prescription drugs accounted for roughly eight percent of total health care expenditures, half that of three decades ago and *far lower than in most European countries.* The average consumer doesn't know that, however, because the government covers a smaller share of drug costs in America, meaning consumers pay more of the expense directly and therefore complain more vociferously to their elected officials. In fact, this goes a long way to explaining why President Clinton and many congressmen are so busy attempting to develop well-publicized "solutions" to the nonproblems in this area.

Before the government "reforms" pharmaceuticals, it needs to recognize some important facts about the industry. First, it is one of America's most successful economic sectors: U.S. firms developed roughly half of the drugs marketed worldwide during the 1970s and 1980s. According to the General Accounting Office, pharmaceuticals is the only one of the 11 high-tech industries that it studied which did not lose ground internationally during the 1980s, but rather "maintained their strong position over the decade." Between 1973 and 1986 American firms accounted for ten times as many drug patents as Germany and Japan, 16 times as many as Great Britain, and 20 times as many as France. U.S. research and development spending has grown 15-fold from 1970, to more than $9 billion. R & D also rose significantly as a percentage of revenues during the 1980s—at a time when companies were being accused of price-gouging.

Second, while drugs may be expensive, the lack of drugs is also expensive. That is, drugs often replace higher priced medical operations and treatments. Actigall dissolves gallstones, for instance, and thereby saves an estimated $2 billion annually precisely *because* 350,000 patients use it. Surgery for ulcers usually runs more than $25,000, while taking medication may run just $1,000 annually; the resulting savings totals at least $3 billion, not counting the economic gain of workers not incapacitated by surgery. Medicine for arthritis and osteoporosis permits some elderly patients to avoid institutionalization. Patients who spend $300 a year on drugs to treat angina can thereby avoid coronary bypass surgery running $40,000 or $50,000. The beta-blocker Timolol reduces the number of second heart attacks by 16 percent and saves about $2 billion every year. The Battelle Institute estimates that for just eight leading diseases between 1968 and 1989 drugs saved 671,000 lives and $83.8 billion.

Thus, a drug's price tells us nothing about its value. Explains Dr. Herbert Gladen at the Baltimore Veterans Administration Medical Center, "higher-priced drugs may actually be more cost-effective if they have greater efficacy, wider therapeutic range and are less costly to prepare and administer." Indeed, because even expensive prescription drugs are so cost-effective, limitations on their use actually increase total medical outlays. A 1988 Louisiana State University study, for instance, warned that if Medicaid, the joint federal-state program for lower-income people, restricted drug coverage, overall costs were likely to rise between 4.1 and 15.5 percent. Just such an attempt by New Hampshire to limit the number of prescriptions for Medicaid recipients caused an upsurge in doctors' visits, hospitalizations, and nursing home admissions. The legislature dropped the ill-consider regulations within a year.

Are drug prices nevertheless too high? Sen. Pryor, for instance, complains that pharmaceutical prices rose far more swiftly than the general inflation rate during the 1980s. Drug prices are higher here than in other nations, he contends, and new drugs are extraordinarily expensive. "While these new drugs helped to reduce hospital stays, and in many cases avoided more costly medical interventions," he acknowledges, "there was no indication that the prices for these drugs had any relationship to their costs of production and development, or were priced reasonably."

One should always be skeptical of the partisan use of statistics, since, when tortured, they will confess to anything. Warns Robert Goldberg of the Gordon Public Policy Center, the Bureau of Labor Statistics has failed to incorporate changes like the greater availability of generics into its figures, meaning that the reported drug price index may be inflated by as much as 50 percent. In any case, for most of the 1960s and 1970s drug price increases remained *below* the overall inflation rate, as well as the rise in the cost of medical care. As inflation waned in the 1980s drug prices followed the overall trends but fell less quickly.

Moreover, by the mid-1980s generic substitutes for brand name drugs were entering the market more speedily as a result of legislation passed in 1984 reforming the FDA approval process. While this step reduced the cost of older medications, it had the opposite effect on new releases. Firms found the effective life span of their brand name products to be shorter, forcing them to focus more on the introduction of new products, which typically cost the most, and *charge more when the drug was released in order to recoup development costs.*

Moreover, the price hikes of the 1980s are not carrying over into the 1990s as competition has intensified. "The market for drugs has changed dramatically since 1981, particularly in the last three years," reports Robert Goldberg. According to the Boston Consulting Group, industry-wide average discounts quadrupled to 16 percent in 1992 over 1987. New drug prices in 1991 and 1992 were 14 percent lower than comparable products in the past. Some of the cuts were drastic—36 percent for new heart drugs, for instance. HMOs, hospitals, and drug mail order firms were also gaining an increasing share of drug sales and simultaneously winning discounts of up to 30 percent from list prices. And the pressure for price-cutting will increase as larger numbers of drugs lose their patent protection. Observes Dr. Goldberg, "by 2000, 200 drugs with $22 billion in sales will be off patent."

In any case, politicians today are likely to do no better than those who tried over the past several thousand years to set "reasonable" prices for any number of goods and services. Prices respond to supply and demand, not moral fervor. There is no objective standard by which Sen. Pryor or anyone else can call one price reasonable and another unreasonable. Nor is there anything about the market that gives participants the power to "price-gouge."

After all, the market is competitive—there are some 22 major drug firms, and no company has no more than a 7.2 percent share. (The industry was even more fragmented in 1962, before more stringent federal regulatory standards, passed in the aftermath of thalidomide-induced birth defects, drove out of business smaller companies. The new FDA "regulations created pronounced economies of scale for drug innovation, which steadily increased over time," reports author Terree Wasley.) The only way a firm can gain "monopoly" power is by developing a good product protected by a patent. Patents, however, are required to induce firms to spend money on research and development. After all, the average cost of developing a drug runs $359 million, according to the Office of Technology Assessment (OTA).

Much of this expense is due to the federal drug approval process. Companies must convince the FDA that prospective products are not only safe but effective; separate applications, which typically run 100,000 pages long, are required for different treatments by the same drug. Since

1962 both the total cost of bringing drugs to market, and the length of time devoted to testing and review, effectively cutting a product's effective patent protection, have more than doubled. In 1984 Congress passed a measure extending drug patent lives, but that step only ameliorated, rather than solved, the problem.

The costs of a process that averages 12 years would be high enough for any industry. But, notes Michael Ward, staff economist at the Federal Trade Commission, "the very nature of the lengthy drug development process makes the pharmaceutical industry susceptible to harm from unnecessarily stringent regulations."

Most importantly, the risks involved are enormous. Pharmaceutical companies find many more dry holes than gushers: 70 percent of new drugs *that reach the market* are estimated to lose money. Most never get beyond the research stage. There are typically 30,000 to 45,000 medical articles on drug therapies a year. Government patent grants for drugs usually range between 2,000 and 4,200 a year; companies list about half that number as investigational new drugs with the FDA. Another half fall out by Phase Three of the testing process and companies usually end up filing applications for 80 to 250. The FDA then approves between 20 and 60. Concludes Ward, "In all, firms will market about one out of a hundred of the products for which they have developed patents."

Studies suggest that the 1962 amendments have had little impact on the introduction of ineffective drugs—companies never liked duds because they don't make money if their products don't work—but have reduced the rate of introduction of new drugs by two-thirds and the speed with which they enter the market by one-half. The U.S. has also lost some of its edge over other industrialized states, which permit the sale of safe and effective drugs still prohibited by Washington. Because patients suffer when they receive no medicine as well as when they receive bad medicine, on net the tightened federal regulation has made more Americans sicker and allowed others to die.

Even so, some critics argue that the drug companies are making too much money. A widely cited OTA study contended that "returns to the pharmaceutical industry as a whole over the 12-year period from 1976 to 1987 were higher by 2 to 3 percentage points per year than returns to nonpharmaceutical firms, after adjusting for differences in risk." Average industry profits ranged between 13 and 14 percent during the 1980s.

This rate of return hardly seems unreasonable given the very high risks of both failure and regulation, which Robert Goldberg believes the

OTA has underestimated. In any case, this level of return is probably not sustainable, given the increasing competition within the industry and cost consciousness of consumers. In particular, OTA's future estimates overlook how dramatically generic products have been eroding brand name drug prices over the last decade.

Moreover, Dr. Steve Wiggins, an economics professor at Texas A & M University, suggests that "a common misstep by industry critics is to rely on accounting data to measure industry returns" when such figures are "unreliable because accounting conventions require the expensing of research and development." Wiggins contends that compared to the cost of capital drug company returns look far from impressive. He compares the industry's capital costs, which ran from 17.2 and 15.1 percent between 1980 to 1990, with an estimated return of between 13.5 and 16 percent, which, he says, indicates "competitive returns."

It is also important to recognize that the industry's profits were largely channeled into research. In 1992 the drugmakers spent more on R & D, $12.6 billion, than they earned in profit, $10 billion. Industry R & D grew by a 15 percent compound annual rate in the 1980s. As a percentage of sales industry R & D approaches 17 percent, nearly twice that for the rest of the health care industry and treble that for the electronics industry. Even the OTA acknowledged that its "findings on returns to pharmaceutical R & D and to the industry as a whole explain why R & D expenditures have risen so fast throughout the 1980s. Investors followed the promise of high returns on future innovations." But ignored by the OTA is the fact that a lot of this money, as much as one-third, according to Dr. Goldberg, is going into biotechnology, which is riskier than traditional drug research.

Where does all this effort produce? The Boston Consulting Group points to a score of new drugs expected to be approved later this decade to combat AIDS, allergies, Alzheimers, asthma, arthritis, cancer, depression, diabetes, glaucoma, Herpes, hypertension, obesity, strokes, and many more diseases. With these conditions costing untold lives and an estimated $400 billion a year, it seems foolish to begrudge the pharmaceutical industry a healthy return on its investment. Critics should be celebrating the industry's success rather than carping about an allegedly "excessive" percentage or two of profits.

Unfortunately, new federal restrictions would simultaneously raise the industry's cost of capital and reduce its rate of return, forcing firms to both cut R & D and distort their research efforts. Companies would skew their efforts to products that would more easily win regulators' approval for price increases and also shift money to unregulated investments, *such as marketing*, that would simultaneously offer less risks and better returns.

The exact form of price controls wouldn't matter. Any would hurt patients—not by denying them access to current therapies, since those drugs are already on the market, but by discouraging new treatments from appearing. The resulting cost, in both financial and health terms, to patients could be staggering. Between 1975 and 1989 American firms developed half of the 66 top drugs introduced in the marketplace. French enterprises, in contrast, created just three. The most important difference between the two nations is government policy. Observes P.E. Barral, "In France, the calibre of pharmaceutical research is seen as having deteriorated, because severe price control has encouraged French companies to give priority to small therapeutic improvements which are useful in price negotiations. Such systems tend to stifle originality and induce risk aversion." At the same time, drugs accounted for 16.7 percent of French health expenditures, twice America's level. Moreover, per capita spending on drugs is almost three times as high in France.

Health care reform should involve a search for answers, not villains. In the case of pharmaceuticals, the system is working: a highly competitive industry is leading the world in the discovery and marketing of new treatments and cures. Although drugmakers have an incentive to invest heavily in R & D, pharmaceuticals account for a lower proportion of total medical expenditures than in socialized systems, while at the same time helping to hold down overall medical expenses. If the administration and Congress nevertheless put ideology before prudence and tighten controls over the drug industry, they risk killing the golden goose that has provided so many benefits for so many patients.

February 1994

# 17

# National Service: Utopias Revisited

In his State of the Union speech President Bill Clinton proposed more than just higher taxes and additional spending as part of his curious approach towards deficit reduction. He also promised to make his vision of national service a reality. In the president's mind not only is Washington to take a larger share of people's earnings to use in more "appropriate" ways. The state is apparently also to guide the young into more "appropriate" pursuits as well.

National service has long been a favorite utopian scheme. Eight decades ago William James wrote of the need for a "moral equivalent of war," in which all young men would be required to work for the community. He argued that "the martial virtues, although originally gained by the race through war, are absolute and permanent human goods," and that national service provided a method for instilling those same values in peacetime. "Our gilded youths would be drafted off," he wrote, "to get the childishness knocked out of them, and to come back into society with healthier sympathies and soberer ideas." Anachronistic though his vision may seem today, his rhetoric has become the touchstone for national service advocates: In succeeding decades a host of philosophers, policy analysts, and politicians proffered their own proposals for either voluntary or mandatory national service. And some of these initiatives have been turned into law: military conscription, the Civilian Conservation Corps, the Peace Corps, and ACTION, for instance.

In 1988 the Democratic Leadership Council, to which Gov. Bill Clinton belonged, advocated a Citizens Corps of 800,000 or more young people to clean up parks and handle police paperwork. The system would be run by a Corporation for National Service, which would set the level of benefits for participants and offer an educational/housing voucher. Underlying the proposal was an assumption of mass moral decadence that had to be rectified by the federal government. We live in a "prevailing climate of moral indolence," contended the DLC, where "such venerable civic virtues as duty and self-sacrifice and compassion toward one's less fortunate neighbors are seldom invoked."

Candidate Clinton was too interested in being elected to criticize the voters in those terms, so he used more positive rhetoric to propose allowing perhaps 250,000 or so people annually to work off their student loans through approved government service (once in office he reduced the total to 150,000). His initiative, he explained, would allow everyone who wanted to go to school to do so, while having them give something back to the community. Superficially, at least, it sounded like a win-win proposition. In practice, however, his program, a more limited version of which was approved by Congress, will likely pour billions of dollars into make-work jobs while reinforcing the entitlement mentality that pervades our society.

## What Is National Service?

National service has always generated strong approval in opinion polls, largely because it means different things to different people. The concept of "service" to the nation seems difficult to fault, and everyone imagines that the "service" that results will be of the form and provided in the manner that they prefer. Thus, a century ago Edward Bellamy used his novel *Looking Backward* to propose drafting an industrial army of both men and women for life; in 1910 William James urged conscription of young men into the most unpleasant of work, such as construction, fishing, and steel-making. The so-called preparedness movement pressed for mandatory military training and service before the onset of World War I. Radical Randolph Bourne later proposed forcing young men and women to provide two years of service before the age of 20. Universal military training received wide endorsement after World War II, and Congress reimposed military conscription after only a one-year interregnum. Defense Secretary Robert McNamara advocated tying civilian service to the draft in the early 1960s. Sociologist Margaret Mead advocated a universal program that "would replace for girls, even more than for boys, marriage as the route away from the parental home."

Since then the proposals have come fast and furious. Don Eberly of the National Service Secretariat has spent years pressing for a service program, while carefully sidestepping the question of whether it should be mandatory. Charles Moskos of Northwestern University pushed a civilian adjunct to the draft before the creation of the All-Volunteer Force in 1973 and most recently has presented a detailed voluntary program. Moskos nevertheless retains a preference for civilian conscription, admitting that "if I could have a magic wand I would be for a compulsory system." (Also mandatory, though in a different way, is the service requirement for high school graduation now imposed by the state of Maryland and roughly 200 local school jurisdictions.) Dozens of bills were proposed in the 1980s to create commissions, hand out grants, reestablish the Civilian Conservation Corps and Works Progress Administration, initiate other new service agencies, and pay part-time volunteers. Most serious was the Democratic Leadership Council's initiative, which Congress turned into an omnibus grant program, along with the Commission on National and Community Service. The issue had largely died until earlier this year (1992), when the Los Angeles riots caused observers from the late tennis great Arthur Ashe to *Newsweek* columnist and former Col. David Hackworth to Bush campaign aide James Pinkerton to press for different forms of national service. More important, candidate Clinton began inserting the idea into his stump speeches.

## Clinton's Scheme

According to President Clinton, "you could bet your bottom dollar" that his program would "make it possible for every person in this country who wants to, to go to college." He proposed, as one of his top five priorities, creating the National Service Trust Fund. Everyone, irrespective of their parents' income, could borrow for their educations; they would repay their loans either through federal withholding from future wages or by "serving their communities for one or two years doing work their country needs." After the election some advisers, like Moskos, pressed the President to also consider an alternative approach, allowing high school graduates to earn college tuition vouchers through community service.

However, deficit concerns caused the administration to quickly back away from President Clinton's most ambitious campaign musings, even though, explained then-White House spokesman George Stephanopoulos, the president "intends to fulfill his commitment to build a national service plan." In a speech at Rutgers University, Clinton proposed to start with a pilot program, to be expanded to as many as 150,000 participants or more, who would receive two years of tuition for every year of work. Apparently students could work either before or after attending college. Total benefits—and whether participants' salaries would all be equal or would reflect the total amount of aid received and forgiven, which would obviously be much greater for someone attending an Ivy League school than for someone attending a state university—were originally unspecified. In return, explained President Clinton:

> We'll ask you to help our police forces across the nation, training members a new police corps, that will walk beats and work with neighborhoods and build the kind of community ties that will prevent crime from happening in the first place; we'll ask young people to help control pollution and recycle waste, to paint darkened buildings and clean up neighborhoods, to work with senior citizens and combat homelessness and help children in trouble.

Ultimately, the president offered a more limited initiative and Congress approved a further scaled-down version of the Clinton proposal. The newly created AmeriCorps will employ some 20,000 in its first year and up to 100,000 over three years. Full-time participants will receive minimum wage compensation plus fringe benefits and a tax-free educational voucher of $4725; part-timers' voucher will be half as large. The Corporation for National and Community Service, subsuming the Commission on National and Community Service and ACTION, will administer the AmeriCorps. The Corporation is to offer information, technical assistance, and, most importantly, money to state service programs. The Corporation will also promote service-learning programs for schoolchildren and initiatives involving the elderly. States must create their own commissions on national service to select the programs to be funded by the Corporation.

Congress authorized $1.5 billion over three years for the Corporation, and, in typical fashion, set aside grant money for favored interests and bureaucracies: labor, Indian tribes, the disabled, the elderly, state governments, universities, and state educational agencies. The Corporation set up shop on October 1, 1993 and is now soliciting proposals for well over $100 million worth of grants for 1994.

There is nothing compulsory about the Clinton proposal, but coercion could follow later. Of course, the president's avoidance of military service during the Vietnam War makes it difficult for him to ever propose such a step. However, such long-time enthusiasts of a mandatory, universal system, like Sen. John McCain (R-Ariz.), see voluntary programs as a helpful first step, and may continue pressing for their approach with a limited form of national service now the law of the land, especially if "too few" children of privilege and wealth joined. After all, Sen. Edward Kennedy exhulted that "in a sense, the passage of this legislation marks the end of the 'me' era in our national life." But what if the employment of a few thousand people in "public service" projects has no such effect, leaving unreformed the "moral indolence" denounced by the DLC a few years ago? Then he, along with the more conservative Democrats who make up the DLC, too, might be moved to support compulsion.

Service is obviously a good thing, which is why so many people feel warm and fuzzy when politicians propose "national service." The issue, however, is service to whom? All of these government programs ultimately assume that citizens are responsible not to each other, but to the state. The proposals suggest that as a price for being born in the United States one "owes" a year or two of one's life to Washington. Mandatory, universal schemes unabashedly put private lives at the disposal of the government, but most voluntary programs, too, imply a unity of society and state, with work for the latter being equated with service to the former.

Yet Americans have worked in their communities since the nation's founding and opportunities for similar service today abound. Some 80 million people, roughly one-third of the population, now participate in some volunteer activities. Businesses, churches, and schools have taken the lead in helping to organize their members' efforts. In a cover story *Newsweek* reported that "many of the old stereotypes are gone. Forget the garden club: today working women are more likely than housewives to give time to good works, and many organizations are creating night and weekend programs for the busy schedules of dual-paycheck couples. Men, too, are volunteering almost as often as women."

Much more could be done, of course. But it would be better for government officials to lead by example rather than to concoct multi-billion dollar schemes to encourage what is already occurring. True compassion is going to be taught from the grassroots on up, not from Washington on down. The underlying assumption of the Clinton program—that there is a debilitating dearth of service that can be remedied only through yet another raid on the taxpayers—is simply false. Moreover, the Clinton program, while cloaked in public spirited rhetoric, nevertheless relies heavily on economic incentives. Indeed, much of the President's pitch during the campaign was framed in terms of naked self-interest: earning credit towards college tuition.

A second bias held by national service advocates is that "public" service is inherently better than private service. Yet what makes shelving books in a library more laudable or valuable than stocking shelves in a book store? A host of private sector jobs provide enormous public benefits—consider health care professionals, medical and scientific researchers, business entrepreneurs and inventors, and artists. Working in a government-approved "service" job neither entitles one to be morally smug nor means one is producing more of value than the average employee in the private workplace.

## Entitlement Mentality

Still, national service proponents rightly point to the problem of an entitlement mentality, the idea that, for instance, students have a right to a taxpayer-paid education. Why should middle-class young people be able to force poor taxpayers to put them through school? The solution, however, is not to say that students are entitled to do so as long as they work for the government for a year or two, but to eliminate the undeserved subsidy. People simply do not have a "right" to a university education, and especially a professional degree, at taxpayer expense.

National service advocates respond with shock. Education, they argue, will be increasingly important in an increasingly technological age. True enough: the greatest divergence in incomes in the 1980s reflected the gulf between those with and without college degrees. That increased earning potential primarily benefits the student himself, however, and the likely lifetime gain of $640,000 should allow him or her to borrow privately. The interest rate may be higher than with today's federal guarantees, but that hardly seems unfair given the added earnings to the student.

Nevertheless, Sen. Chris Dodd (D-CT), an early supporter of the Clinton program, contends that even middle-class families can ill afford to send their kids to college. That's now accepted as a truism, but it is not obviously correct. More than three-quarters of the best students currently go on to higher education. Qualified students unable to get a college education because of finances are few. Policymakers need to acknowledge that not everyone needs a university degree, and one from a leading school, to find fulfillment in life. Some young people are not academically oriented or interested; others have found more satisfying ways to spend their lives. The federal government shouldn't be pushing them to go to college.

Anyway, the fact that higher education, especially at elite private universities, strains many family budgets is hardly surprising, since the dramatic increase in federal educational aid has helped fuel a rapid rise in tuition. Further flooding the educational system with money is likely to benefit administrators as much as students. The point is, if there's more money available for schools to collect, they will do so.

Moreover, it is because of free-spending legislators like Dodd that government now takes roughly half of national income, making it difficult for families to afford higher education. Politicians worried about middle-class taxpayers should therefore cut special interest spending, not hike costs by billions of dollars, through a national service program. In short, while the jump in federal educational assistance in the 1970s undoubtedly helped more students attend college, there is no reason to assume both that these marginal attendees benefited more than the cost of their education and that they could not have afforded school had tuitions not been artificially inflated by the influx of aid and their families' incomes been so sharply reduced by taxes.

The problem with national service is not just theoretical, however. Like every other proposed national service plan, the Clinton proposal is likely to break down in practice. Admitted the President shortly after his election: "I feel very passionate about" national service, "but there are a lot of factual questions that have to be asked. How much money should everybody be able to borrow a year? What contributions should people's families be expected to make, if any? If you put this into effect, how are you going to keep the colleges and the universities of this country from using it as an excuse to explode tuition even more?" Good questions all, and all go to the viability of any program. Alas, passage of his legislation has not really answered them.

The implementation problems are likely to be enormous. First, President Clinton says that he will not allow any job displacement, which guarantees that participants would not perform the most valuable work to be done. The Democratic Leadership Council's proposed program had the same feature—to forestall opposition from organized labor, the group promised that its program would neither impair existing contracts nor limit the promotion possibilities for existing workers. The latter, however, is virtually impossible to enforce: if AmeriCorps members end up at local school districts as teachers and teachers' aides, will the district hire as many other teachers and teachers' aides in the future? Almost any job that might be performed by a municipal union member is likely to be excluded from any national service program, or if not, generate significant political opposition.

Even assuming this problem can be overcome, national service is not likely to produce significant social benefits. What work would participants do? Past government "service" programs have always been very limited in scope. Advocates of national service like to point to the Peace Corps and VISTA, but these two programs along with more than 60 state and local programs involve some 18,000 people. Even during the military draft the government had little use for the labor of conscientious objectors, placing only 30,000 into service jobs from 1951 to 1965. What will tens of thousands a year more do?

Meet current "unmet social needs," national service advocates respond. Past proponents of national service have tossed around figures ranging up to 5.3 million as to the number of jobs that need to be done. According to one study, for instance, libraries require 200,000 people; education needs six times as many. But as long as human wants are unlimited, the real number of unfilled social "needs," as well as unmet business "needs," is infinite. Labor, however, is not a free resource. Thus, it simply isn't worthwhile to satisfy most of these "unmet" needs. One of the great benefits of the market process is that it balances benefits and costs throughout society, using wages as a signal to determine when activities warrant undertaking. National service would treat some jobs as sacrosanct, while ignoring disfavored alternative tasks that could be performed instead.

## Opportunity Costs

Indeed, this may be the crux of the national service debate: the role of opportunity costs. Paying young people their national service's generous compensation—they will receive tuition relief *plus* salary and health care benefits—to paint "darkened buildings," suggested by the President, or do police paperwork, proposed as part of the DLC's program, or perform other "service" entails forgoing whatever else could be done with that money. Moreover, it involves forgoing whatever else those young people could do. "Public service" has a nice ring to it, but there is no reason to believe, a priori, that a dollar going to national service will yield more benefits than an additional dollar spent on medical research, technological innovation, or any number of other private and public purposes. Indeed, the Clinton program will likely delay the entry of tens of thousands of people into the workforce every year, an economic impact that the President and his advisers appear not to have calculated. Yet the relative value of labor may rise in coming years as the population ages. As a result, the opportunity cost of diverting young people into extraneous educational pursuits and dubious social projects could rise sharply over time.

Another potentially important opportunity cost is diverting top quality men and women from the military. The end of the Cold War has sharply cut recruiting needs, but it has also reduced some of the allure of volunteering as well as the perceived national need. As a result, by summer 1992 the Army, which typically has a more difficult recruiting task than the other services, was about ten percent behind in signing up recruits for 1993. Observed Gen. Jack Wheeler, head of the Army's recruiting effort, "I'm not panicking, but the numbers are disturbing." The military has even seen recruiting fall off in such traditional strongholds as northern Florida and other parts of the South. Yet various programs of educational benefits have always been an important vehicle for attracting college-capable youth into the military. Providing similar benefits for civilian service may hinder recruiting for what remains the most fundamental form of national service—defending the nation. The military rightly fears the potential impact on a system that is working well. Observed Thomas Byrne of the private Association of the U.S. Army after the DLC proposal was unveiled, "we don't want high-caliber people who might otherwise join the Army off planting trees instead." The result, again, would be higher costs: economic, as more money would have to be spent to attract quality people; military, as the armed forces might become less capable; and moral, since military service would lose its preferred status, warranted by the uniqueness of the duties involved.

Still, there are undoubtedly many worthwhile tasks nationwide that people could do. The problem in many cases, however, is that government effectively bars private provision of such services. Minimum wage laws effectively forbid the hiring of dedicated but unskilled people and inhibit rehabilitation programs, like that run by the Salvation Army; restrictions on paratransit operations limit private transportation for the disabled. Licensing, zoning, and other unnecessary and often nonsensical regulations increase the price of day care. Similar sorts of restrictions harm private voluntarism as well. Health regulations prevent restaurants in Los Angeles and elsewhere from donating food to the hungry, for instance. In short, in many cases important needs are unmet precisely because of perverse government policy.

To the extent that serious problems remain, narrowly targeted responses are most likely to be effective. That is, it would be better to find a way to attract several thousand people to help care for the terminally ill than to lump that task with teaching, painting buildings, and a dozen other jobs to be solved by a force of hundreds of thousands. Talk of millions of "unmet social needs" is meaningless.

In any case, local organizations are not likely to efficiently use "free" labor from the federal government: staff members would have an almost irresistible temptation to assign hated grunge work rather than more suitable tasks to national servers. There are good reasons why many tasks that are not performed today are not performed, a fact ignored by national service advocates. In fact, a similar problem of perverse incentives has been evident in federal grant programs which allow states to use national money for projects without much local contribution. Observes David Luberoff, of Harvard's John F. Kennedy School of Government, "One of the lessons of the interstate project is that in general...if you don't require that states put up a reasonable amount of the cost, you run the risk of building stuff that is probably not that cost-effective."

Real voluntarism, in contrast, works because the recipient organization needs to offer valuable enough work to attract well-motivated volunteers. But the Clinton program will simply assign people, people whose motivation would as likely be working off a school debt as "serving." In fact, the government risks subverting the volunteer spirit by paying loan recipients too much. The DLC suggested that its program promoted sacrifice, yet University of Rochester economist Walter Oi estimated that the total compensation—salary, health care benfits, and untaxed educational/housing voucher—for "serving" was the equivalent of

$17,500 annually *after taxes*, well above the mean earnings for high school graduates. The Clinton administration will offer compensation of at least $15,000 annually, and perhaps closer to $20,000, after including salary, health insurance, child care, and tax-free educational voucher. Such a wage won't make AmericCorps participants rich, but will make "service" a much better deal than, say, pumping gas. As a result, some students will likely see national service as a financially remunerative job option, not a unique opportunity to help the community.

Further, imagine the bureaucracy necessary to decide which 100,000 jobs are "service." Someone will have to sort through labor union objections to "unfair competition," match participants to individual posts, and monitor the quality of people's work. Can national service workers be fired? What if they refuse to do the work assigned to them? What if they show up irregularly or perform poorly? At what point does their legal right to the educational voucher vest? And so on.

## Unwieldy Bureaucracy

These are not minor problems to be solved after the program is in place. To the contrary, the specifics go to the heart of the viability of any national service proposal. A Corporation for National and Community Service would make grants to states and local national service councils, and state governments would establish councils which will likely be composed of community groups along with local government officials, businessmen, and educational and union representatives. These groups will hire staff, prepare plans, and oversee their implementation.

This sort of unwieldy bureaucracy is not likely to promote inexpensive and innovative solutions to human needs. Unfortunately, controls and regulations will inevitably follow federal labor and money. It is fear of just such consequences that has led the Guardian Angels, cited by national service advocate Charles Moskos as one of the most "striking examples of civic-minded youth volunteers," to reject federal grants. So does Habitat for Humanity, the Christian organization, supported by former President Jimmy Carter, that constructs housing for poor people.

Even worse, federal involvement is likely to politicize much of what is now private humanitarian activity. Congressmen oppose efforts to close local government offices; interest groups lobby to twist social programs to their own benefit; labor unions mobilize to block proposals to contract out work. A program offering the free services of a hundred thousand young people will provide a massive honey pot attracting the worst sort of political infighting, with local and state officials demanding that "their" groups receive a "fair" share of the benefits.

Such battles could spill over into the courtroom. Religion pervades the volunteer sector—must churches and para-church groups eviscerate their religious focus in order to participate in the Clinton program? Equally problematic is the issue of controversial political, sexual, and social lobbies. One can imagine volunteers, backed by Democratic Party interest groups, wanting to treat work with Act-Up and Planned Parenthood as "service." The Clinton administration's attitude towards would-be volunteers at church day care centers and non-liberal public interest groups like the National Taxpayers Union would likely be quite different. This returns to the basic questions, what is service? and who decides?

The larger the federal program grows the more cumbersome it is likely to become. Small programs under charismatic leaders, like the San Francisco Conservation Corps, have performed well, but their objectives are more limited, better defined, and more manageable. Moving from a few hundred to a hundred thousand is no easy task. Alas, the incredible fraud, misuse, and waste endemic to other "public service" programs like CETA hardly augur well for yet another, even larger, federal effort at social engineering.

In fact, CETA, with its system of federal funding for local jobs, is an important model. Aside from the nonsensical waste, reports policy analyst James Bovard, was the political abuse: "In Philadelphia, 33 Democratic party committeemen or their relatives were put on the CETA payroll. In Chicago, the Daley political machine required CETA job applicants to have referral letters from their ward committeemen and left applications without such referrals piled under tables in unopened mail sacks. In Washington, D.C., almost half the City Council staff was on the CETA rolls." So awful was CETA that it became one of the few programs ever terminated by Congress.

Finally, money has to be an issue in a year when the President successfully pressed for massive tax hikes—three dollars for every dollar in spending cuts even by his own figures, and much more by more objective analyses. Unfortunately, national service will not come cheap. There will be more loans and thus more defaults, as well as the salaries and benefits paid to those who take government service jobs. The President acknowledged that his campaign program could more than double the cost of the current student loan program, between $4 billion and $5 billion, to some $12 billion. His more limited initiative, approved by Congress, will run less, but the political dynamic of concentrated beneficiary groups versus the larger taxpaying public tends to promote the constant expansion of benefits once they are established. Even if the program eventually costs only an extra few billion dollars, it will still be difficult to justify spending so much money in this way, especially when the President just backed large-scale tax increases. Hiking expenditures so that private individuals can go to school for private gain is a dubious use of public money. And using national service to effectively hire 100,000 or more young people to do jobs of questionable worth is an even bigger waste.

Like the mythical Sirens, national service retains its allure. Argues Roger Landrum of Youth Service America, "Clinton has a shot at mobilizing the idealism and energy of a very significant number of young people, as Roosevelt did with the Civilian Conservation Corps and John F. Kennedy did with the Peace Corps." Alas, President Clinton's scheme is likely to end up no bargain. It will probably create a nightmarish bureaucracy and increase an already out-of-control deficit. National service will also reinforce today's misbegotten entitlement mentality while siphoning tens of thousands of young people out of productive private labor and into make-work projects. Finally, if the program inflates tuition levels as has student aid in the past, it probably won't even benefit many participants, since it will fund college administrators more than students.

What we need instead is a renewed commitment to individual service. People, in community with one another, need to help meet the many serious social problems that beset us. There is a role for government: officials should commit themselves to a strategy of "first, do no harm." We need to eliminate public programs that discourage personal independence and self-responsibility, disrupt and destroy communities and families, and hinder the attempts of people and groups to respond to problems around them. But the private activism that follows needs neither oversight nor subsidy from Big Brother. Some of the voluntarism can be part-time and some full-time; some can take place within the family, some within churches, and some within civic and community groups. Some may occur through profit-making ventures. The point is, there is no predetermined definition of service, pattern of appropriate involvement, set of "needs" to be met or tasks to be fulfilled. America's strength is its combination of humanitarian impulses, private association, and diversity. We need service, not "national" service. National service is an idea whose time will never come.

November 1993

# 18

# Real Welfare Reform:
# An Idea Whose Time Has Come

For all of the partisanship and rancor in politics today, there is very little debate about the central reality of modern society: the welfare state. Originally developed in Germany and Great Britain in the last century, state social programs have arisen and expanded in every industrialized nation. Broadly defined (beyond a dole for the poor), "welfare" now accounts for not only the largest share of government spending around the industrialized world but also the fastest growing segment of outlays, greatly contributing to the rapidly accelerating fiscal deficits and crises that beset so many nations.

Welfare programs continue to expand because they tend to be politically sacrosanct, defended by conservatives and liberals alike. Nevertheless, in recent years dissatisfaction has been growing with programs specifically directed at the poor, with a consensus seeming to develop that such programs as Aid to Families with Dependent Children (AFDC) have "failed." In general, critics argue that these forms of welfare have not achieved their goals of poverty reduction and personal independence. To the contrary, an increasing number of observers charge that these programs have had the unintended effect of actually worsening poverty—both encouraging more people to end up poor and creating a class of people permanently dependent on the government.

In contrast, the traditional criticism of poverty programs by mainstream analysts and politicians is that they are underfunded or suffer from one or another technical problems. More recently, attention has focused on the perverse incentives created by government aid. Ongoing legislative reform efforts are now focusing on changing the behavior of welfare recipients—mandating job training and work, encouraging school attendance, discouraging additional pregnancies, and so on.

Some writers on both the right and left have gone further, however, arguing that the very design of the current system is flawed; indeed, some contend that no form of public subsidy can avoid the debilitating problems now so evident in the American inner-city. Examples of the latter more "radical" skeptics of welfare include Frances Fox Piven and Richard Cloward, who contend that the *unstated* objectives of the system are illegitimate, with the government intending to control and manipulate the poor rather than help them. Starting from a very different position is Charles Murray, who argues that control and manipulation is the ultimate outcome despite the generally good intentions of legislators and administrators.

Although a sharp debate over welfare policy developed in the mid-1980s, such criticism of government poverty relief efforts is familiar to social historians. This discussion has occurred before—in Britain in the 1830s, 1880s, and 1890s, and America in the 1880s and 1890s. Alas, each new debate cycle seems to take place in a historical vacuum, with participants apparently unaware of the previous discussion.

Moreover, the professional literature is full of controversies that are highly abstruse and technical. Although important, these sub-debates about a single policy tree all too often divert attention from efforts to better understand the welfare forest as a whole. It is therefore better to start from the other direction, first surveying the broad assumptions and objectives that underlie government welfare policy, before attempting to resolve narrower points.

Perhaps the most basic question, especially for those approaching the issue from a religious perspective, is why a welfare system? Do people have a duty to help those in need? Do individuals have a *right* to aid from their better-off neighbors? If they do, which individuals may enforce a claim to welfare? The proverbial widows and orphans? Teenage mothers who choose not to work? The unemployed?

Moreover, if "society" is to act, in what form should aid be provided? Today "compassion" is commonly equated with government social spending, yet, as Marvin Olasky details in his book, *The Tragedy of American Compassion*, compassion originally meant to suffer with another. In the early years of the American republic people created an effective, community-based, *voluntary* safety net, one that relied on personal involvement rather than bureaucratic action. Why did the nation move from private to state provision of poverty relief?

To help answer this question Murray attempts to explain the purpose of the welfare system: what do those who are paying the bills hope to achieve? The answers are many and complex. Some people simply hope to buy social stability; others want to promote economic equality; still others intend to enable people to participate fully in society and fulfill their potential as human beings. Whether or not these are good goals, and whether or not they warrant coercing taxpayers to pay for a welfare program, are ultimately moral questions. The purposes of poverty programs also raise numerous practical issues, particularly as to the best means of achieving the system's ends. Only after we decide what we hope to achieve can we design programs to meet those goals.

For instance, if our objective is social control rather than personal independence, then the current programs work pretty well. If, however, our primary objective is to relieve human suffering, then the system's effectiveness is much less clear: while AFDC ensures that fatherless families do not starve, it makes fatherless families more likely and displaces alternative sources of financial support. As for making poor people independent, the current programs are a dismal failure. Indeed, the federal "war on poverty," despite the expenditure of *$2 trillion* (on top of $1.5 trillion by states and localities) since 1965, does not even appear to have reduced the incidence of poverty.

It is probably for this reason that welfare has long been perhaps the least popular government program. Although most Americans want to help the less fortunate, they suspect that the government is more interested in spending money on an expansive bureaucracy than in making poor people independent.

The official poverty rate, now about 13.5 percent, fell during the early 1960s but has remained essentially unchanged since the advent of President Lyndon Johnson's "Great Society" and concomitant expansion of the welfare state. In terms of simple numbers, the welfare rolls have expanded across the nation since inauguration of the poverty war. The 1970s were years of growth, with the number of AFDC (Aid to Families with Dependent Children) recipients rising from nearly two million to more than 3.5 million. The number of welfare recipients dipped in 1982 before rising again. But by 1990 the number of AFDC recipients nationwide was 4.6 million. A variety of other welfare programs have also shown dramatic growth over the last two decades.

Welfare outlays, though not as great as many people assume, are still substantial. In 1990 the federal government spent $210 billion on a range of welfare programs, including cash aid and medical assistance. States and localities spent billions of dollars more. The problem is particularly serious in such states as California, Michigan, and New York. California, for instance, has twice as many welfare recipients as any other state. Welfare outlays absorb about ten percent of the state's budget and are growing 12 percent a year. With benefit levels almost twice the national median, California has been attracting welfare immigrants. (The state has 12 percent of the nation's population, but hosts 16 percent of AFDC beneficiaries and accounts for 26 percent of AFDC's costs nationwide.) Faced with a serious budget crisis two years in a row, welfare has become a prime target for cuts.

In fact, Governor Pete Wilson placed on the November 1992 ballot an initiative to cut general benefits by up to 25 percent, end the practice of paying recipients more for additional children, and require teenage mothers to live with their families and stay in school to collect checks. The measure also would have limited migrants to their old benefit levels for a year. Voters defeated the proposal, but out of concern over its enhancement of gubernatorial power, not its cuts in welfare benefits.

And California is not alone in targeting welfare. In January 1992 New York Gov. Mario Cuomo announced his intention to cut $1 billion in welfare costs. All told, through 1992 36 states had allowed inflation to reduce real AFDC benefits; seven states had cut payments while another nine had tightened eligibility standards for the program, which primarily serves single parents with minor children. Michigan ended so-called general assistance, for able-bodied single adults, dropping 82,000 from the roles. Another dozen states sharply cut these payments.

Moreover, in January 1992 New Jersey ended supplemental payments for larger families. The chief legislative sponsor, then-Majority Leader Wayne Bryant, explained that: "What this does is give welfare recipients a choice. They either can have additional children and work to pay the added costs, or they can decide not to have any more children." Several states are also considering joining New Jersey in tying behavior, such as accepting employment training or working in public service jobs ("workfare") and childrens' attendence in school ("learnfare"), to benefits.

The Bush administration, so disinterested in domestic policy, unlike its predecessor, generally avoided the welfare debate while pouring ever more money into federal social programs. Spending increases on AFDC, Head Start, and Medicaid were far greater than those under Jimmy Carter as well as Ronald Reagan. Despite Democrat Bill Clinton's professed support for welfare reform, during the primaries he denounced the New Jersey reform package, advanced by a black legislator representing the state's poorest district, stating that he would instead spend more money on education and child care. Although Clinton supported a modest work requirement for welfare recipients during the general election, he also proposed $6 billion in increased spending, including more money on the same sort of job training programs that have failed badly in the past. In contrast, New Jersey Gov. James Florio, a liberal Democrat, lauded the reform bill as he signed it into law. The current system, he argued, was "corrupt," "morally bankrupt," and "entraps our children in a cradle-to-grave cycle of dependency."

Serious reform of the public welfare system, a frequent goal over the last three decades, has proved to be extremely difficult, but it would offer many benefits—not only an important source of budget savings but also an opportunity to help break the debilitating cycle of dependency that has developed among many recipients. What the poor need more than anything else today is liberation from a system which ensnares and enfeebles them.

Yet the real answer is not likely to come from within the public sector. Unfortunately, the debate over welfare has itself been sadly impoverished. The conventional wisdom is that the only alternative to a government-run, taxpayer-financed system is private charity, an amalgam of idiosyncratic organizations and niggardly programs that would inevitably allow millions of needy to "fall through the cracks." Thus, the only "real" issues in the minds of most public officials involve what kind of government-run, taxpayer-financed system we should use: universal or targeted, with an insurance element or not, and so on.

Yet the private alternative is not nearly so limited as is commonly conceived. Many different forms of social organization have been used by different societies at different times to provide what is today called "welfare." In some societies the extended family or kin group is the primary locus of providing a "safety net." In other cases it comes through the church—the Mormons, for instance. Similarly, in Islamic society welfare is financed by alms-giving, mandatory for Muslims, but the program is organized rather than run by the state.

Perhaps the most interesting form of welfare institution in the West, at least to those concerned about individual liberty and personal independence, is collective self-help, or mutual aid as it is more commonly called. Coexisting with traditional charity, mutual aid was the dominant form of welfare up into the 1920s in the U.S. and its international cousins, Australia, Britain, and Canada. Although fraternal societies were the main sources of such assistance, churches, community associations (represented by the "Community Chest" cards in Monopoly), labor unions, service institutions (such as hospitals, which raised money through contractual contributions), subscription societies, and temperance and self-improvement groups also helped develop an extensive yet voluntary social network.

Not only was the plethora of mutual aid organizations effective and flexible, but the informal system had a positive moral impact both on individuals and the larger culture. In particular, these groups embodied the principle of personal responsibility, self-help, and cooperative community action. These values, along with productive labor and thrift, were popular at the time. Mutual aid as an institution highlighted the traditional distinction between deserving and undeserving poor, a difference further reflected in the practices and rules of most such organizations. Further, mutual aid was also essentially democratic and egalitarian, conflicting with both paternalism from state to citizen and from rich to poor.

Equally important, but little recognized today, mutual aid enhanced cooperation between unrelated individuals. Far from encouraging greed, selfishness, and isolation, mutual aid drew people into a system where responsibility for those in need was shared. Because the organizations were both smaller and more flexible than, say, the Department of Health and Human Services, their members necessarily had great involvement in the lives of those in need. The result was more of the real "compassion" that Olasky writes about, thereby encouraging independence, hard work, and self-respect among all parties. The existence of so many private aid institutions also played what many observers believe to be a major role in the "moralization" process in Britain and the U.S. during the 19th Century, a process that produced a 40-year decline in crime rates.

That mutual aid worked, and worked well, seems beyond dispute. Which is why Charles Murray contends that many, if not most, of today's state welfare activities could be better performed by local and voluntary institutions. Yet an important question remains: why did this system decline so rapidly after the 1920s? The answer is important because it will help us determine whether or not it is possible to rely more on private social services in the future. In theory, at least, a welfare system based on a mixture of charitable institutions and mutual aid societies would best promote the values of interest to a classical liberal, especially freedom and responsibility, thereby fulfilling the only proper objectives for a welfare state. But is it possible to get from here to there? To the extent that the decline of mutual aid was linked to the severity of the Great Depression, for instance, it may be possible to revive such private entities today. The obvious change in the public's sense of individual and state responsibilities might be reversed by patient educational efforts. If the process is a result of modernity, or one or another particular institutional features of today's industrial society, however, then the chances for change seem much more dim.

Few people are satisfied with today's poverty programs, yet this element of the welfare state remains almost as sacrosanct politically as Social Security and other benefit programs. History provides us with numerous effective and voluntary alternatives to today's system, but, unfortunately, it gives us fewer lessons how to gain popular acceptance for shifting the responsibility for welfare from the public to the private sector.

August 1993

# 19

# War on Drugs or America?

Drug abuse is a world-wide phenomenon, but no where is the problem more acute than in the U.S. One-third of the population above the age of twelve has used at least one illegal substance; violent crime is tearing apart inner-city neighborhoods; ever tougher law enforcement campaigns have sacrificed personal freedoms, and with little apparent effect on the drug trade. In short, current American policy is a failure. The country that has often set trends around the world has come to a point where it must choose between two different paths—peace or war.

## Urban Decay

America's drug problem may be most dramatically illustrated by the fact that its capital city of Washington, D.C., is literally awash in drugs. When Ronald Reagan took office in early 1981, open air drug markets operated within blocks of the White House. Along one nearby street, reported the *Washington Post*,

> it is dawn and cold on the dingy, trash-strewn street barely a mile from the White House. Despite the early hour, the street is busy. Men bundled in thick jackets and ski caps stand along the curb gesticulating strangely at slow-moving cars and chanting, "Bam-D, Bam-D, Bam-D." It is the incantation of drug dealers, the inner-city invitation to passing motorists to buy illegal drugs.

For much of the decade there were more such open air drug markets than food supermarkets. And the problem was little better at the end of the decade in Washington, or many other major cities. In an extensive investigation of the drug trade *Insight* magazine reported that "buying heroin in America's biggest cities is almost as easy as buying aspirin," with "sale days and bargains and shopping malls, where a buyer can select whatever drug he wants" as well as home delivery with "the drugs brought by children on bicycles."

The fact that drugs could remain so freely available after two presidents and several Congresses had devoted so much energy to stamping out the trade demonstrates that something was wrong with their basic approach. The lesson learned by many government officials, however, is not that current policy is flawed, but that the government hasn't been arresting enough people and the penalties for drug use aren't high enough. For example, in 1989 the chief federal drug official, or "drug czar," William Bennett, argued that "we haven't really tried law enforcement." New York City's District Attorney for Manhattan, Robert Morgenthau, made much the same argument less than a year later, claiming that "we haven't tried enforcement, so how do we know if it will work?" Yet neither Bennett nor Morgenthau could be ignorant of what had transpired during the 1980s: how few benefits were garnered for such great expenditures and after such pain and suffering.

Consider:

- Congress passed successively stricter anti-drug legislation in 1984, 1986, and 1988—usually in direct response to upcoming elections.
- Over eight years the Reagan Administration spent some $22 billion on anti-drug activities. In half as many years the Bush administration poured more than $45 billion in more of the same programs. Federal spending jumped more than eleven-fold between 1981 and 1991, and hit $12 billion last year (1992). Inflation-adjusted spending in 1988 alone was ten times the amount during the first decade of alcohol "Prohibition" in America earlier this century. More than 70 percent of current expenditures are for enforcement, otherwise known as "supply reduction."
- Cities across the country initiated special drug enforcement programs: Operation Clean Sweep in Washington and Tactical Narcotics Teams (TNT) in New York City, for example.
- Drug arrests nationally jumped from 162,000 in 1968 to 1.36 million in 1989, and remain above one million annually. There were 3.5 million arrests during the Bush administration's tenure.
- The number of drug busts tripled and the number of convictions doubled during the 1980s. Arrests of women for drug offenses between 1980 and 1989 jumped 119 percent, compared to 37 percent for other crimes. The respective figures for men were 85 percent and 19 percent. Drug violations in America's largest city, New York City, accounted for between 40 percent and 53 percent of felony indictments in the latter half of the 1980s, up from 25 percent in 1985 and 13 percent in 1981, respectively. So great is the flood that some cities and states created special "drug courts."

- Users as well as dealers have been punished. During the 1980s convictions in federal district court increased more than twice as fast for possession as for selling, 340 percent compared to 142 percent. Of the 1.01 million arrests nationally in 1991, only 337,340 were for trafficking; fully two-thirds were for possession.
- Congress and state legislatures steadily increased penalties, mandating jail time, imposing large civil fines, seizing property, denying federal benefits, and evicting tenants from public housing. So draconian have the mandatory penalties become—in Michigan possession of less than one and a half pounds of cocaine with intent to distribute results in a sentence of life without possibility of parole, a harsher penalty than imposed on most murderers—and so perverse is their effect, hitting a larger percentage of street-level operators than high-level importers, that conservative federal judges appointed by Republican presidents have publicly complained.
- America's prison population more than doubled between 1981 and 1988, from 344,283 to 573,565. By 1992 that number hit 856,058. Virtually every jail and prison system at every level is overburdened: for a time New York City was forced to place inmates on barges, a policy it abandoned only after it downgraded its special TNT program and reduced the number of drug arrests. Not only is one in every 292 Americans currently in prison, but an incredible *one of every 46* is under court supervision—in prison or jail, on probation or parole. Most of the increase is due to stricter drug law enforcement. At the federal level, for instance, the number of drug inmates rose by 600 percent between 1980 and 1991, and now account for 56 percent of the federal prison population. Even more important is state enforcement activity, since state sentences for drug crimes rose 73 percent, compared to a four percent decline for non-drug offenses, between 1986 and 1988. Reported the White House in early 1992, "Increasing sentence lengths for drug crimes, as well as increasing numbers of arrests for drug-related crime, have put an added burden on the ability of prisons and jails to meet this responsibility." While this would appear to most people to be a problem, enthusiasts of the Drug War view bulging prisons as a sign of seriousness and success.
- The armed services, Coast Guard, and Civil Air Patrol (an air force auxilary) have grown more involved, providing search and pursuit planes, helicopters, ocean interdiction, radar, and surveillance. Defense Department spending on the drug war ran $1.3 billion in 1992, more than six times the amount just four years before. The National Guard in every state and four territories is involved in drug enforcement. Military advisers and troops have been sent to Bolivia, Columbia, and Peru to assist them with their eradication efforts. The U.S. also invaded Panama in part to seize the dictator Manuel Noriega for his apparent involvement in the drug trade.
- The Central Intelligence Agency and National Security Agency have begun using spy satellites and communications listening technology as

part of the drug war. The CIA also created a special Counter Narcotics Center.

- The U.S. began indicting and kidnapping foreign nationals for their activities on foreign soil.
- The government also started monitoring the sale of legal products, such as indoor equipment and common chemicals that can be used to grow and produce drugs.
- The federal government imposed drug testing on public employees and required contractors and grantees to establish "drug-free" workplaces. Enthusiasm for drug testing spilled over into the private sector: In January 1992 75 percent of firms surveyed by the American Management Association said they tested employees for drugs, an increase of 247 percent over 1987. Although individual programs differ greatly, millions of U.S. workers in non-sensitive jobs are now potentially subject to drug tests.
- Traditional American civil liberties protections have been increasingly circumscribed. Criminal attorneys now talk about the "drug exception" to the Fourth Amendment, which prohibits unreasonable searches and seizures, as well as to the entire Bill of Rights. The number of wiretaps has increased sharply; now more than half of this form of court-authorized surveillance are drug-related.

    The government is making roughly 19,000 property seizures, worth $1 billion, annually. All told, the government has acquired $12 billion in private assets, including homes and even multi-million dollar yachts, because relatives, friends, and employees of property owners have been found with drugs. Only half of those from whom property has been expropriated have ever been charged with a crime. Lawyers are required to reveal the names of clients who pay large bills in cash; the city of Cleveland threatened to jail landlords who did not evict alleged drug dealers; several jurisdictions have imposed teenage curfews; the Coast Guard has blockaded harbors to search for drugs; and the police routinely search buses, cars, and airline passengers without warrants or any hard evidence of a crime.

- In its 1988 report on drug enforcement, the Justice Department touted its multi-faceted policy, including "Centralized Intelligence Network," "Multi-jurisdictional Task Forces," "Reverse Stings," "Financial Investigation Units," "Street Sweeps," "Saturated Patrols," "Walking Patrol Officers," "Drug Interdiction Program," "Airport Drug Interdiction Program," "Air Smuggling Program," "Canine Drug Detection Units," and "Marijuana Eradication Program." Five years later the White House issued a report with a similar listing of its many enforcement initiatives.

What has been the result of all of this activity? World cocaine and heroin production are up, and most of these drugs get to their intended destinations. Early in the Drug War the U.S. Coast Guard estimated that it successfully stopped just five to seven percent of incoming drug shipments; now, after tens in billions of dollars in spending and an endless array of programs, its estimate has edged upward to just 10 to 20 percent. Indeed, reports the Senate Judiciary Committee, "The simple fact of the matter is that after spending $5.9 billion on the interdiction effort more cocaine and more heroin enters the country today than before the [Bush] Administration's first drug strategy."

Thus, consumers have ever more access to drugs. Regarding cocaine, concluded an inter-agency panel in July 1992: "Average purity at all levels (gram, ounce, and kilogram) for the year increased from those observed in 1990—again suggesting ready availability." The committee went on to state that "the heroin abuse situation in the United States was a growing concern in 1991" and warned that circumstances appeared to be disturbingly similar to those involving crack before the explosion of that drug's use. In fact, in early 1992 the government acknowledged that heroin was purer then than at any other point over the previous decade, when the Department of Justice established its "Domestic Monitor Program." American law enforcement officials also admit that LSD "remained a popular drug with the high school and, to a somewhat lesser extent, college population in the United States." The percentage of high school seniors using LSD hit its highest level in five years in 1990. Indoor production of marijuana has risen sharply as the government discovered and destroyed more outdoor production and interdicted more foreign imports. All told, in 1992 the U.S. Justice Department implicitly admitted failure on almost all fronts:

> During the first three months of 1992, the price of cocaine remained low at all quantity levels, while cocaine purity for ounce and, in particular, gram quantities escalated. The prices and purity levels of heroin are more dificult to pinpoint. Prices have declined at the low end of the price range since the early to mid-1980's, but a wide variety of sources of supply led to documented extremes in purity levels. Simultaneously, marijuana prices increased during the past several years at virtually all levels of the traffic. Overall prices for LSD remained relatively low.

Police officers in the field also increasingly acknowledge that their special enforcement programs can do little to stop drug use. Enforcement against open-air markets has simply pushed more of the trade into apartment buildings and grocery stores. In 1990 two reporters reviewed the New York City Tactical Narcotics Teams and wrote that "today the notion that TNT would be the answer to the drug problem seems laughably naive. In the two years since TNT began in Queens [a neighborhood of New York City] it has become devastatingly obvious—especially to the police—that street-level enforcement doesn't make things better in the long term." Two years later the police department formally downgraded the TNTs. Explained Suzanne Trazoff, a deputy police commissioner, "We were making 100,000 arrests for narcotics, but we weren't solving the drug problem."

While casual drug use has been falling, the Senate Judiciary Committee warns that "more Americans are hard-core addicts, as 3 million Americans are addicted to cocaine or heroin." As of 1991 75.4 million Americans over the age of 12 had tried at least one illicit substance. Some 26.1 million, more than one-tenth of the entire population, had used one or more drugs that year. And 12.6 million had consumed drugs during the previous month. Moreover, even though use has trended down, other problems are rising: in early 1992 emergency room visits for cocaine and heroin problems had increased to record levels.

## An Ancient Social Problem

Substance use and abuse has been evident on earth for thousands of years. The Sumerians used opium as far back as 5000 B.C. The Spanish encountered coca when the colonized Latin America and introduced marijuana in Chile in 1545. The latter drug made its first appearance in the United States in 1649. Alcohol and tobacco have been used from time immemorial.

Different societies have dealt with the use of different substances differently. Opium and marijuana were legal in the United States until earlier this century; in fact, during the 19th century many doctors attempted to get patients to switch from alcohol to opium. Muslim nations have tended to ban alcohol but not opiates, and even today coca tea is widely available throughout South America. The United States' leading drugs of choice, alcohol and tobacco, have been prohibited at times—the first by the federal government during Prohibition from 1920 to 1933, the second by 14 states as of 1921. In both cases the drugs were relegalized quickly.

The failed attempt to suppress alcohol use provides a particularly appropriate lesson for today's prohibitionists. The costs of the "liquor war" were high: organized crime gained a lucrative revenue source, gang warfare spread across major cities, and honest citizens were penalized for engaging in acts that harmed no one else. Those who drank found their drug of choice to be more potent and dangerous, while other people turned to potentially more harmful substances, such as cocaine and opium. Not only was Prohibition a failure at the time but, argues Auburn University economist Mark Thornton, "the Eighteenth Amendment and the Volstead Act, which established the mechanism of the amendment's enforcement, would be decisive and negative factors in American life and culture for over a decade." Contrary to popular assumptions, the intense federal campaign did not even substantially curb the consumption of alcohol. In short, what has been called America's "noble experiment" yielded few benefits in return for very high costs.

Peoples around the world continue to struggle with the question of how to deal with drugs. There are at least some perceived benefits from their use, occasionally severe problems from their abuse, and almost always huge costs from trying to ban them. Since the decision as to what one ingests or inhales would normally appear to be one for the individual rather than the state, the burden for justifying restrictions on drug use should rest on those who would imprison drug users and their suppliers.

Among the justifications for drug prohibition are the desire to save drug users from themselves, protect children from temptation, prevent users from becoming addicted, help residents of inner-cities, and protect other nonusers from a variety of ills. However, none of these goals is realized by the ban on drug sale and use, and even if realized, the benefits would likely remain outweighed by the costs of current policy.

## To Protect Drug Users

One of the most important rationales for drug prohibition is paternalistic—that the government needs to prevent people from taking substances that can incapacitate and kill. Attempting to protect others from harm is a worthy goal, but drug prohibition is, at best, an imperfect vehicle for doing so.

First, though the legal ban on drug use presumably stops some people from using illicit substances, it has not prevented a large number of people from using them. Roughly 40 percent of Americans over the age of 12 have tried at least one illegal drug; one poll found that *half* of those between the ages of 18 and 29 had used illicit substances. At least 68 million people are thought to have experimented with marijuana and 24 million with cocaine. Roughly 20 million Americans used marijuana with some regularity in 1991. There were about 6.4 million cocaine users in the same year as well as 700,000 heroin addicts.

Why is this so? As noted earlier, drug interdiction is thought to block the shipment of less than one-fifth of drug shipments. It is virtually impossible to prevent smuggling in a large, free, and open country. Some 45.4 million people visit the U.S. every year; 4.4 million vehicles of all types enter the nation. Tens of millions of pieces of mail are sent to the United States annually. In 1992 618.8 million tons of goods came to the U.S. on ships and another 2.19 million tons on planes. More than 20,000 planes and 17,000 ships ply the routes along which traffickers send their illicit exports. From this huge inflow the U.S. government must stop the six to eight tons of heroin and 100 metric tons of cocaine needed to service the American market.

Even worse, drug traffickers have proved to be quite entrepreneurial, adjusting their practices to thwart changing enforcement trends. In 1992, for instance, a federal inter-agency panel expressed concern over smugglers' increased reliance on cargo ships and planes.

Moreover, the Rand Corporation, a government funded research organization, estimates that smuggling accounts for just one percent of drug street prices. Thus, even dramatically intensified interdiction efforts will have little effect on drug availability and prices, and will not keep drugs out of people's hands.

Nor are attempts to eradicate crop production any more likely to succeed. Most illicit substances can be produced around the world. Not surprisingly, then, increased Columbian efforts to crack down on the cocaine cartels led suppliers to shift production to Bolivia, Brazil, and Peru. Heroin comes from Mexico as well as Lebanon and South Asia; production and trafficking now appear to be rising in the former Soviet republics of Central Asia. Marijuana is grown all around the United States, as well as in Belize, Columbia, Jamaica, Thailand, and elsewhere. A number of countries formally prohibit drug production, but fail to effectively enforce their laws; drug profits are obviously an important "lubricant" in poorer nations. Moreover, admitted the U.S. government in 1992, "Even successful countries continue, however, to be plagued by the sheer volume of traffic; the diversion of legitimate chemicals, such as acetic anhydride, for illicit purposes adds to the plague." In any case, increased interdiction efforts, which prove relatively more effective against the relatively bulky marijuana, have caused greater production of pot in America itself, particularly through indoor "hydroponic" methods, as well as of synthetic analogues of such drugs as heroin from chemical labs.

In fact, the *Los Angeles Times* reported in late 1989 that: "In interviews over the past several months, numerous officials near the front lines of the South American war have underlined a common concern: The continent's rugged geography, weak institutions and needy peoples give cocaine traffickers almost unlimited opportunities for exploitation." Not surprisingly, international cocaine production increased in 1992 despite the best efforts of the U.S. government and its counterparts around the world. Complained the Senate Judiciary Committee: "the drug trade is akin to the Hydra of Greek mythology—growing two heads for every one cut off."

Another reason that drug prohibition fails in its goal of protecting users is that present policy affects only the least dangerous drugs. Tobacco kills some 435,000 people annually in the United States; alcohol's death toll approaches 150,000. Both of these substances also cause a number of serious maladies, ranging from emphysema to hypertension, and the latter has a particularly dramatic impact on nondrinkers, since some 40 percent of America's 50,000 traffic deaths are related to drinking.

In contrast, all illicit drugs combined account for about 5,000 deaths, most of which are actually due the perverse side-effects of prohibition. Thus, even dramatically higher usage rates would result in far less harm than is presently caused by alcohol and tobacco—per 100,000 users tobacco kills 650, alcohol kills 150, heroin kills 80, and cocaine kills 4.

This is not, of course, to suggest that illicit substances are safe, but that their dangers vary greatly. Marijuana, for instance, does not kill; it may still be responsible for a variety of health problems, but the evidence is less than definitive. Heroin can kill, but it usually does so only if dosages are mistakenly increased or impurities are mixed in. Even sociologist James Q. Wilson, who opposes legalization of heroin, has acknowledged that "there are apparently no specific pathologies—serious illnesses or physiological deterioration—that are known to result from heroin use per se." Synthetic heroin, in contrast, developed as a consequence of the ban on the natural substance, can have devastating side-effects, causing conditions akin to Parkinson's disease.

Cocaine and crack can kill, but they usually do so only rarely and usually as a result of inordinate concentrations or the presence of adulterants. They can also result in anxiety and depression, but do not have as deleterious an effect on drivers as does marijuana, which, in turn, causes less impairment than alcohol.

The mere fact that other dangerous substances are legal does not necessarily mean legalizing illicit drugs would reduce social costs, of course, but it certainly demonstrates that current policy is irrational and the attention of the criminal law devoted to such substances as cocaine and marijuana is disproportionate. Moreover, drug prohibition is itself unhealthy and increases the harm to users. Criminalization causes those who are determined to use illicit substances to do so in an illegal and dangerous market where information does not circulate freely, product safety cannot be assured, and disputes cannot be resolved peacefully. Indeed, four-fifths of the roughly 5,000 deaths attributed to illegal drugs can be traced to the effects of prohibition—such as ingesting varying quantities of impure substances—rather than the drugs themselves. (This phenomenon also occurred when the U.S banned the sale of alcohol earlier this century: some drinkers turned to methyl alcohol and adulterated "ginger jake," both of which sometimes proved fatal.)

Another important impact of turning drug users into criminals is to inhibit the flow of information about the dangers of their favored substances. The U.S. government admits that knowledge about drugs is important. Observed the American Justice Department in 1988: "Interest in a given illegal substance often begins first among a particular—usually elite—segment of the population. It is next picked up and spread more broadly through so-called 'casual use' in the mainstream middle class. After a time, the drug's dangers are widely known through public health advisories or painful personal experience, and mainstream use then drops sharply."

In fact, education may be the most important single factor in determining drug consumption. In the 1920s, argues David Musto, a professor at Yale University Medical School, "Interdiction, crop substitution and so forth were ultimately minor factors in the practical disappearance of cocaine; what appeared to matter most was disillusionment with the initial claims for a new drug and shock at its effect on the lives of individuals and their families."

A similar phenomenon occurred in recent years. Marijuana use peaked in 1979, before the onset of the Reagan and Bush "wars" on drugs. Cocaine use began to decline in 1986, before the appointment of a "drug czar" and ever tighter enforcement efforts. Dr. Lloyd Johnston of the University of Michigan suggests that crack use fell significantly because of a greater awareness of its dangers. A number of drug policy analysts believe that education has helped bring down consumption of a variety of drugs by kids: "Obviously, drug education and drug prevention has increased. There's been increased attention in the media to the harmfulness of drugs. Parents and communities have come together to fight the problem," observes one. For instance, Johnston and fellow researchers Jerald Bachman and Patrick O'Malley point out that cocaine use not only fell even as the drug became more available, but dropped by 40 percent among high school seniors, largely because of a more realistic assessment of the risks involved (highlighted so dramatically by the death of collegian basketball player Len Bias). A 1992 University of Michigan study attributed a similar recognition of the risks of drug use to the fact that two new drugs, "ecstasy" and "ice," which once seemed poised to spread rapidly, never caught on with high school students. The latter's "similarity to crack very likely deterred use among the great majority [of young people], who already recognize crack as dangerous," explained Dr. Johnston.

Thus, there may be nothing more important for reducing drug consumption than promoting honest drug education. While the government does conduct educational campaigns as part of its enforcement activities, its efforts often come off as unreliable propaganda. Not only are many public officials biased and likely to cite as fact what may only be conjecture, they also have lied in the past. The long-time head of the Federal Narcotics Bureau, Harry Anslinger, once testified before Congress that one joint could turn the user into a homicidal maniac; the movie "Reefer Madness" presented a similarly false picture of the dangers of marijuana. Equally ludicrous were earlier claims that cocaine use would allow rampaging blacks to survive otherwise fatal wounds and that most attacks on southern white women were "the direct result of a coke-crazed negro brain."

The military atmosphere of drug prohibition also inhibits circulation by others of honest information on the impact of drug use. To simply acknowledge the fact that some people will use drugs is to risk serious censure. Yet lives are lost because users receive no practical advice on how to minimize the risks of consuming illicit substances. Observes Steven Wisotsky, a law professor at Nova University Law Center, "No one at the DEA [Drug Enforcement Agency] or NIDA [National Institute on Drug Abuse] has tried to save the lives of crack smokers by warning them that smoking x number of pellets in y number of hours will put them in the danger zone; nor have they publicized antidotes or emergency treatment procedures."

Nevertheless, James Jacobs of New York University Law School complains that with legalization "we can certainly anticipate the proliferation of consumer-oriented drug magazines like *High Times* to advise consumers on the properties and effects of old and new psychoactive drugs, ideas for mixing drugs, and on the best places for purchasing and consuming different types of drugs." But this phenomenon would both reduce the adverse health consequences of drug use, by warning consumers about the dangers of using high dosages and mixing substances, and would contribute to the socialization process that would promote responsible consumption, just as patterns of responsible alcohol consumption developed over time.

Drug prohibition also inevitably makes drugs more dangerous. In what has been called the Iron Law of Prohibition, tighter law enforcement tends to result in the production of more potent substances. This phenomenon is not hard to understand—if you face prison for producing, transporting, and selling a drug, you want to reduce the likelihood of detection. Traffickers therefore prefer to handle substances that are more concentrated, making them easier to hide and yielding more revenue per volume, and consumers will switch between drugs, using whatever is convenient and available. During America's alcohol "Prohibition" bootleggers concentrated on hard liquors rather than beer and wine. Today, when legal drugs are becoming weaker—wine coolers and low-tar cigarettes have taken increasing market shares of the shrinking alcohol and tobacco markets in the U.S.—we see the same phenomenon evident with drugs. Today, observes Ethan Nadelmann of Princeton University, "you have a shift from lower potency pot to higher potency pot, and you have this shift from marijuana to cocaine and heroin."

For instance, improved detection of foreign marijuana shipments has encouraged greater cultivation in the U.S., where land is more expensive. To improve profitability, producers have planted pot with a greater THC content. As a result, between 1973 and 1984 marijuana became eight times as powerful. In recent years, however, federal authorities have had greater success in eradicating outdoor pot cultivation—causing growers to shift indoors, resulting in an even more potent drug as a result of hydroponic production. Similarly, crack, essentially a more potent form of cocaine, might not have been developed had there been a legal drug market. Interdiction has also spurred chemists to create a variety of synthetic drugs, particularly of heroin; one briefcase of these new substances could supply the needs of all of New York City's addicts for a year. Explains New York City Assistant Police Chief Francis Hall:

> Synthetic drugs are a potential threat beyond most people's imagination. They're cheaper to make than botanical drugs, and more potent.... [A]mateur chemists can duplicate the properties of most drugs in labs at home.... That's one of the reasons I've never been a big fan of interdiction. Let's imagine for a minute that we could stop all drugs coming into the United States—all heroin, all cocaine. Synthetic drugs would take over within two months.

This process is exacerbated by enforcement practices that tend to work most effectively against bulkier products like marijuana. Two decades ago the Nixon administration intensified interdiction efforts against pot, causing some casual users to shift to LSD. Reported a Canadian study commission in 1970: "We have been told repeatedly that LSD use increased rapidly during periods when cannabis was in short supply. Drug users and non-users alike have suggested that the effectiveness of Operation Intercept in the United States [in September 1969] in reducing the supply of marijuana available in Canada was a major cause of the increase in the demand for 'acid'." Cocaine is the most likely illicit substitute for marijuana today. One narcotics officer complained to *The New York Times*: "I hate to say it, but we, law enforcement, may be driving people into the arms of the coke dealers by taking away their grass. But we have got to enforce the law."

Moreover, even law enforcement officials acknowledge that the campaign against cocaine may encourage some drug consumers to turn to ice, a powered form of the stimulant methamphetamine, as well as heroin. As a result of intensified cocaine enforcement efforts, observed Attorney General Richard Thornburg in 1990, "the drug of choice, particularly in smokable form, which is now available, may become heroin." In fact, heroin use has been rising, going against general drug consumption trends. And, law enforcement officials say, the heroin for sale is more potent and purer than ever, apparently the reason that emergency room admissions for drug problems rose so much in 1992.

The ban on drug use also prevents the development of safer substitutes. William Bennett was addicted to nicotine but was able to shift from cigarettes, a relatively high-risk activity, to nicotine gum. Cocaine gum, which has been tested on animals, would be far safer than the illegal cocaine products now consumed by millions of Americans. Indeed, in Liverpool, England, where drugs are available through physicians, doctors distribute heroin cigarettes, which avoid the many problems of needle use.

Further, drug prohibition is largely to blame for the spread of AIDS through the addict population. Roughly one-fourth of AIDS cases in America have resulted, directly or indirectly, from intravenous (IV) drug use and account for the great majority of all heterosexuals testing HIV positive. Another six percent of those with AIDS were both homosexuals and IV drug users. The problem is two-fold. Addicts tend to share needles, which cannot be legally obtained in most states; moreover, social outcasts taking illicit substances are less likely to be influenced by their neighbors and co-workers and to engage in more responsible behavior. Not surprisingly, then, HIV infection rates are dramatically lower in Great Britain and the Netherlands, which allow some legal drug use.

In any case, there is something perverse about jailing people—and putting them in with violent criminals—to "protect" them. The government's "protective" role has become even more twisted with the expansion of mandatory minimum sentences, which result in drug dealers serving more time than murderers and rapists. The desire to deter others from using drugs has resulted in punishments all out of proportion to the "crimes" committed.

In sum, drug prohibition has not prevented tens of millions of people from using drugs; at the same time, the law has made drug use more dangerous while ignoring other, more dangerous drugs. Enforcement of the criminal law has also harmed more people more seriously than has drug use. Protection of potential drug consumers is not a satisfactory reason for banning illicit substances. What of the other justifications?

*To Protect Children*

There is probably no more emotional issue than drug use by kids. It is therefore natural that many supporters of drug prohibition cite protecting children as the main justification for banning drug use by everyone.

Alas, the criminal law has done little more to protect children than adults. In 1991 44 percent of high school seniors admitted to having tried illicit drugs; 39 percent used drugs more than once. Some 51 percent said that it was fairly easy or very easy to obtain cocaine, up from 45 percent in 1984, *despite seven years of an ever-escalating drug war.* The respective figures for marijuana, amphetamines, and heroin were 83 percent, 57 percent, and 31 percent. The number of juveniles arrested for substance abuse has jumped 150 percent since 1985, and many more young drug users obviously go unpunished. Moreover, despite recent progress in reducing juvenile drug use, in October 1992 the National Parents' Resource Institute for Drug Education warned that "in a dramatic reversal of a three-year trend, tobacco, alcohol and other drug use began to rise again during the 1991–92 school year, according to a study of 212,802 students in 1,588 schools in 34 states." Most drugs, students say, are either "fairly easy" or "very easy" to obtain. So pervasive has the drug culture become that in 1990 a seven-year-old boy and nine-year-old girl were found playing drug dealers, using grass for marijuana and sugar for cocaine.

Still, there are presumably some number of children who don't use drugs because of the law. But many others are likely dragged into the drug culture because of the law—that is, on net more kids may use drugs today than would if the substances were legal for adults. Perhaps the most serious problem is the fact that the drug laws have created immensely profitable criminal empires that are prepared, unlike established tobacco and alcohol manufacturers (in contrast to some retail outlets), to sell to the young. Thus, we see pushers on playgrounds and, even more ominously, students as dealers—one student survey in the fall of 1992 found that ten percent of children in grades five through eight in America's capital, Washington, D.C., were helping to sell drugs.

An 18-year-old ex-dealer testified before Congress three years before that traffickers recruit athletes and student leaders because "they know if a person is popular, everybody else will do what they are doing." Many of these young dealers also become users. Says Princeton's Nadelmann, "Where once children started dealing drugs only after they had been using them for a few years, today the sequence is often reversed. Many children start to use illegal drugs only after they have worked for older drug dealers for a while."

And the law makes the employment of children particularly attractive since minors are relatively immune from criminal sanctions. Explains Washington, D.C. City Council member Harry Thomas, "the guys are giving the young kids the drugs because they know they won't get as much [jail] time." Thus, children not only often deal, but also transport drugs and help sellers in other ways. The government's response? To propose higher penalties for both adults and children.

Unfortunately, all of the efforts of law enforcement officials, prosecutors, and judges in the drug war have proved powerless to prevent the reruitment of children. In fact, as the government has intensified enforcement efforts more kids have become dealers. Observes one Chicago cop: "I'll tell you what the biggest change in the last four or five years has been. It's the drug dealers themselves. Now we have 13-year-old dealers who make more than me."

In Washington, D.C., the police arrested 1,478 juveniles on drug charges in 1988, a 23 percent increase over 1984. More telling, however, was the fact that the percentage of juvenile drug arrests for *dealing* jumped from 29 percent to 87 percent of the total. Although the overall number of arrests has since dropped, the share brought in for dealing exceeded 90 percent in 1992. Similar trends are evident in other major American cities. In Baltimore, for instance, in 1981 only 91 juveniles were arrested for the manufacture or sale of drugs; a decade later 1,317 were arrested for the same offense. Among all juvenile criminal suspects positive urine tests rose from 11 percent to 38 percent.

There are several other problems with the assumption that drug prohibition helps protect kids. Current law makes drugs a "forbidden fruit," something curious students want to try precisely because its illegality makes it seem alluring. In contrast, de facto legalization in the Netherlands appears to have reduced the appeal of pot to younger people. Prohibition also makes it less likely that children will discuss the possibility of using drugs with their parents or other adults: the stigma attached to the use of drugs is different than that of the underage use of alcohol, and therefore is more likely to drive the activity underground. The fact that drugs are available only from criminal sources makes it more likely that suppliers will encourage kids to use more drugs more often and to use more potent substances. In short, to the extent that marijuana is a "gateway" drug to more dangerous substances, it is so *only* because they are illegal.

Moreover, the emphasis on illicit drugs has caused many parents and school administrators to treat the use of alcohol almost with relief. Worries Abby Hirsch, a guidance counselor at a New York high school and an adviser to the school's Students Against Driving Drunk chapter, "it's unfortunate, but to some extent we have, as a society, given up the battle to get students not to drink."

Although the ban on drug use is not an effective shield for children, advocates of drug prohibition argue that the law can serve other goals.

## To Prevent Users from Becoming Addicted

Some observers have likened addiction to slavery; the war on drugs is therefore necessary, in their view, to "free" the slaves. Yet addiction is not a unique phenomenon associated only with illicit drugs. Cigarette smoking, for instance, has been called "the most widespread example of drug dependence in the United States." Former Surgeon General C. Everett Koop compared the addictiveness of nicotine with that of illicit drugs: "the pharmacological and behavioral processes that determine tobacco addiction are similar to that that determine addiction to drugs such as heroin and cocaine." Not only is the number of repeat users of tobacco far above the 24 percent for cocaine, but a typical cigarette addict may hit up every hour, a far more frequent pace than most illicit drug users. One study of drug consumers who smoked found that one-half said cigarettes were harder to give up than their other pleasures; one-third said tobacco was much harder to abandon.

Alcohol addiction is also widespread. Roughly ten percent of America's 150 million drinkers are considered to be alcoholics and consume half of all alcohol used in the U.S.

What is the chance that a first time user will become addicted to various substances? According to Dr. Jack Henningfield, chief of the clinical pharmacology branch at Baltimore's Addiction Research Center, the numbers are one in ten for alcohol, one in six for cocaine, and nine in ten for cigarettes. What percentage of those tried to quit but couldn't? Just 3.8 percent for cocaine, seven percent for marijuana, and 18 percent for cigarettes.

Moreover, many users stop consuming for varying periods of time. Heroin may have the worst reputation, but addicts tend to abandon their habit for extended periods of time. In Liverpool one doctor who prescribes heroin states that many older patients quit, and that he views his role as keeping people alive until they get off. In fact, much drug abuse is situational. During the Vietnam War many American soldiers turned to heroin and other drugs. But use was lower in Thailand, where there was no combat, and 92 percent of soldier-"addicts" stopped using when they returned to the U.S.

Cocaine has gained perhaps an even more fearsome reputation of late. Yet a study of addicts at the Addiction Research Center found that most considered heroin to be the most difficult to quit, *followed by cigarettes and alcohol*. Cocaine was fourth. Moreover, in one famous study, often cited by supporters of drug prohibition, monkey would constantly press a lever for cocaine, dying rather than stopping to eat. However, the monkeys behaved the same for nicotine. Their desire for heroin and alcohol was much less.

What of crack, which some people have talked about as if it was instantaneously addictive? Reported *The New York Times* in 1989: "Drug experts now believe that the extreme difficulties they face in treating crack addiction stem far more from the setting and circumstances of the users than the biochemical reaction the drug produces." In short, the problem is that crack is predominantly used by people in depressing circumstances who have little hope for the future. "If crack were a drug of the middle or upper classes, we would not be saying it is so impossible to treat," says Dr. Frank Gawin, director of the Substance Abuse Research Unit at Yale University.

The U.S. government's own figures demonstrate that crack is not uniquely addictive. According to the National Institute on Drug Abuse, 23.7 million Americans have tried cocaine but in 1991 only 6.4 million were considered to be "current users," having consumed the drug in the previous month. Four million people have tried crack, of whom one million used crack in 1991. Less than one-half of them, 479,000, had used crack during the previous month. The last year for which weekly figures are available, 1988, found that little more than ten percent of annual users consumed crack at least once a week, and less than four percent used it every day. While there is reason to be concerned about anyone who is using crack, much of the hype over the drug appears to be the result of inaccurate and politically-generated hysteria.

In any case, criminalization of addictive behavior only drives it underground. First, those most determined to acquire illicit substances do so already. The law is most effective at detering casual use—which poses the least threat to user or society. Second, while the shock of arrest may cause some people to seek help, almost all consumers will be more secretive in an attempt to avoid arrest. It is hard enough for an alcoholic to admit that he has a problem; a crack addict must also admit that he is a criminal. One lawyer-addict at a major law firm said that "the stigma of it being illegal makes people like me afraid to seek help. There was a time when a partner asked be what was wrong with me and I so wanted to tell him, but was afraid because I was breaking the law."

Drug prohibition may do a poor job of protecting users but, many advocates of current policy proclaim, it helps other members of society.

## To Protect Residents of Inner-Cities

Given the prevalence of the crack trade in inner cities, the ban on drug use has been justified by Rep. Charles Rangel (D-N.Y.), among others, as necessary to protect city-dwellers from the depradations of drug dealers and save the underclass from destruction. One of the most extreme expressions of this view comes from James Inciardi and Duane McBride: "The legalization of drugs would be an elitist and racist policy supporting the neocolonialist views of underclass population control." Yet the resort to law enforcement does nothing to solve the underlying causes of drug abuse. As noted earlier, drug experts now say that crack addiction is treatable, though it is important to address users' circumstances. The real problem is not that people use drugs, but that they have so little hope and sense of self-worth that they use drugs. If all the drug war does is move a few would-be crack users to alcohol, then no one is better off.

In the meantime drug prohibition has backfired badly. Argues Sam Staley, President of the Urban Policy Research Institute:

> Rather than alleviate the consequences of drug abuse, current policy has encouraged the spread of drug-related crime. Current policy has made drug use a criminal problem rather than a health problem. By focusing on a supply-side enforcement strategy that maintains extraordinarily high profit margins for drug traffickers, the negative attributes of the underworld now pervade the economic and social systems of the American cities.

It would, in fact, be hard to imagine a more perverse policy. The government's efforts have created a profitable alternative to legal employment, made positive role models of thugs, produced well-funded criminal gangs, and turned inner-city streets into battlegrounds. The result is simultaneously a steady deterioration of the lives of those trapped in urban America and a tinderbox ready to fire into violent outbursts, as in Los Angeles in 1992.

The lack of employment opportunities for inner-city youth, in particular, is obvious. Disadvantaged teens are likely to lack good educations and work experience; regulations like the minimum wage price the least qualified workers out of the market. With legitimate businesses reluctant to move into the city core and hire local people, the multibillion dollar drug business beckons warmly to residents. Most dealers make more than they would in honest work, if they could find it. And some entrepreneurial souls do very well—teenage dealers in such midwestern communities as Topeka, Kansas are known to make between $500 and $1000 a week, tax-free. Complained one anonymous Chicago policeman, "How are you going to convince the kids to get back in school so that they can be a factory worker, or get a low paying job in a fast food place, or be unemployed when they can sell drugs for big money."

The lure of the drug trade is heightened by two other factors. The first is the absence of positive male role models for so many young black boys. Today more than half of inner-city births are illegitimate, compared to less than one-fifth in just 1970. In fact, in the urban core female-headed households outnumber two-parent households three to one. Thus, in the absence of fathers and such community leaders as legitimate businessmen, who are the success stories that many young males look up to? Athletes and, unfortunately, drug dealers, who make up most of the community's financial elite. Explains a teacher and coach at Washington, D.C.'s Cardozo High School, "Nowadays, drugs rival athletics as the way to get out. The thinking is, 'If you can't be an athlete be a drug dealer.' You get big-time respect as a drug dealer. It's horrible, but it's reality."

Second, the drug business has proved to be a major boost for inner-city gangs, just as alcohol prohibition funded the more traditional mob. The number of gangs in Los Angeles doubled, from 400 to 800, between 1985 and 1990, and now boast an estimated 90,000 members. Perhaps the two most notorious urban gangs, the Crips and the Bloods, were active during the Los Angeles riots, committing much of the mayhem—including the televised beating of a white truck driver. Moreover, such organizations are engaged in a wide range of illegal activities, making it hard for any young black male to avoid the lure of a criminal life. Although black Americans only make up between 12 percent and 15 percent of drug users, they account for an estimated 41 percent of drug arrestees. By the early 1990s 42 percent of young black males in Washington, D.C. and an incredible 56 percent in Baltimore, Maryland are enmeshed in the criminal justice system—in prison or jail, on probation or parole, or being sought on an arrest warrant.

And drug-funded gangs have spread to most large cities—during the 1980s the number of urban areas hosting well-organized gangs doubled to nearly 200, including such seemingly improbable cities as Topeka, Kansas, in the conservative Mid-West. Much of the spread reflect a concerted effort by drug dealers to find new markets. About a dozen Crips moved from Los Angeles to Topeka to develop their trade; gang members "look at the town," says Odell Jones, the father of a former gang member, "whether it has a good drug trade and naive police department."

The result is not just more drug trafficking and crime, but also endless shoot-outs between competitors who cannot settle disputes legally. In fact, virtually all drug-related murders are related to drug *prohibition*, not drug use. The carnage, several thousand deaths annually, is truly incredible. From 1984 to 1987 the homicide rate for young black males jumped 40 percent. In the latter year shootings accounted for an astonishing 42 percent of the deaths of black men in their late teens and early 20s. Reports the Centers for Disease Control, a young black is more likely to die in the inner-city today than he was serving in the U.S. army while it was fighting a war in Vietnam. Indeed, the army uses urban hospitals to train its surgeons; explains Dr. John McPhail, chief of surgery at the William Beaumont Army Medical Center in El Paso, Texas, "At King [hospital in Los Angeles], we see the kind of penetrating trauma that we just don't see at other hospitals. It's a place where the residents will have to treat a large volume of high-velocity wounds, the kind we would see in war."

But then, many American cities are engulfed in war, only the adversaries are drug gangs struggling over turf rather than foreign invaders seeking conquest. Drug prohibition surely is not protecting residents of these neighborhoods. Does anyone else benefit?

## To Protect Other Non-users

Lastly, the drug laws are intended to protect society as a whole from the effects of more widespread drug use. Although drug prohibition presumably restrains some people from using drugs, that benefit must be balanced against the many costs of prohibition. In the end, the ban on drugs does more to threaten than protect society.

Perhaps the most fundamental problem in America today is crime. Roughly one-half of all crimes in the country are drug-related, according to the American Correctional Association. At the current rate, predicts the U.S. Sentencing Commission, by the turn of the century half of all federal prisoners will be serving time for drug offenses. Most of these crimes are not the product of drug use but of the drug laws—just as the temporary upsurge in homicides and other crimes during Prohibition was a result not of alcohol use but the ban on alcohol use.

One form of crime generated by the drug laws involves actions that would not otherwise constitute crimes. That is, a willing buyer exchanges money for drugs with a willing seller and they are arrested. This form of crime doesn't directly threaten other people, but these arrests, prosecutions, and imprisonments, which now account more than one-fourth of all federal cases, draw resources away from combatting such crimes as murder, rape, and theft, which do cause grievous harm to others. Complained then-Washington, D.C. Police Chief Maurice Turner in 1989, "All we do is meet about the drug problem. It's driving the resources of the metropolitan police department." There are then fewer police available to deter and investigate other crimes; fewer prosecutors and courts to handle criminals who are caught; and fewer cells in which to imprison them. As a result, says James Ostrowski, who served as vice chairman of the New York County Lawyers Association Committee on Law Reform, "in a world of scarce prison resources, sending a drug offender to prison for one year is equivalent to freeing a violent criminal to commit 40 robberies, seven assaults, 110 burglaries, and 25 auto thefts."

Similarly, punishing casual users of less dangerous substances, such as marijuana, also draws resources away from the campaign to suppress more harmful drugs. In 1989 legislators in the state of Oregon abandoned a move to recriminalize marijuana after opponents pointed out that the lack of adequate prison space would likely result in the freeing of crack dealers to make room for marijuana consumers.

Moreover, the enormous profitability of drug crime—as little as $230 worth of opium can produce $800,000 and more worth of heroin, while $30 of raw coca yields as much as $180,000 worth of cocaine on the street—provides an enormous cash infusion into criminal gangs and organizations that may commit other, non-drug crimes. Drug trafficking has also helped finance the operations of terrorist and guerrilla forces abroad, resulting in violence against foreign citizens. In Peru peasant drug producers have allied themselves with Marxist guerrillas, the so-called Shining Path, threatening the government.

Alas, drug prohibition does more than just squander scarce law enforcement and prison resources and empower criminals to commit other crimes. Current policy fosters other forms of crime as well. First, the drug laws have encouraged a wave of street crime by holding up drug prices, causing addicts to steal, and steal more. Ostrowski reports that roughly 40 percent of all property crime in the U.S. is committed by drug users—roughly four million crimes and $7.5 billion in stolen goods. The relationship has been particularly well established with respect to heroin addicts. According to former D.C. police chief Turner: "If you see an addict going through withdrawal, he's in some kind of damn pain. When they get pretty well strung out, they have about a $100 to $120-a-day habit. When they get that type of habit, they're going to have to steal approximately six times that much to sell on the open market. They're going to have to steal about $600 [worth of fenceable goods] to support a $100-a-day habit."

Formal studies back up his rough estimates. The DEA found that heroin addicts committed roughly $3.9 billion in crime in 1974, almost one-fifth of all property crime. A study funded by NIDA found that 243 addicts committed some 474,000 crimes over an eleven-year period; other researchers have reported that addicts commit crimes on a daily basis, some averaging as many as 22-a-day. Their criminal activity fell sharply, however, when they were off of heroin (as the 243 subjects were one-third of the time) or when they could acquire the drug more cheaply. Detroit police have observed that property crime rates rose when more effective enforcement practices pushed up prices.

More deadly is the crime committed by drug traffickers. During one three-year period during America's experiment with alcohol prohibition gang fights over territory cost 1,000 people in New York City and 400 in Chicago their lives, for instance. We are seeing the same sort of behavior today. Reported *The Washington Times* in 1989: "The shootouts among drug dealers in D.C. and other major cities are reminiscent of the brutal tactics used by Chicago gangsters in the 1920s and '30s, in the view of many law enforcement investigators and analysts." In fact, American rates of murder and assaults with a firearm rose during alcohol Prohibition and fell for a decade afterwards.

The violence is even worse today, however, as the market has grown more fractured: crack is easily manufactured and therefore can be marketed by small groups as well as national gangs. Baltimore, Los Angeles, New York, and Washington, D.C. all set murder records during the late 1980s and early 1990s. While the number of murders fell slightly last year in the latter two cities, it rose in Chicago and Detroit as well as Los Angeles, and set records in Fresno and Oakland, both in California, Little Rock, Arkansas, and both Kansas Cities, in Kansas and Missouri. Of the 24,700 murders nationwide in 1991, between 5,000 and 6,000 were thought to be drug war-related. A frustrated Chief Turner said in 1989 that the city could only wait for the dealers to conclude their turf wars: "We arrested 43,000 people last year. What the hell is the police department going to do?"

Many more shootings were designed to maim and the perpetrators are rarely prosecuted by the victims. In some neighborhoods in America's capital, reports *The Washington Post*, "gunfire has become so commonplace as to scarcely disrupt people's daily routine." Although shooting victims are usually customers or dealers, innocent bystanders have also been hit and killed by stray bullets from warring gangs.

Dealers often also target witnesses in criminal trials and neighborhood activists who've opposed drug activity. More dramatic is the violence in countries pressured by the U.S. to crack down on drug traffickers. In Columbia, for instance, cocaine gangs have engaged in an orgy of assassinations and bombings in retaliation for government drug enforcement. (The first harbinger of similar violence in America came with the 1990 firebombing of a DEA office in the state of Florida.) Yet the Senate Judiciary Committee seemed almost irritated when it observed that: "Despite the public rhetoric, the commitment of the Andean countries to the drug war—at least on U.S. terms—may be waning. For instance, Colombia has sought to end the terror wreaked by the drug lords, but appears less committed to stopping drug trafficking *per se*." Who can blame the Colombians for desiring to curb the violence that stems directly from the drug war, however? And should anyone be surprised that anti-American feelings are rising in these countries?

All of the foregoing crimes result from drug prohibition rather than drug use. And many government officials admit that stricter enforcement efforts make the problem worse. States a recent Senate report: "As former drug director Bennett, Judiciary Committee Chairman Biden, and others have pointed out, lower supplies of cocaine will mean more violence—as hard-core addicts and cocaine dealers fight over fewer drugs and less turf."

In contrast, the form of crime that most people imagine to be drug-related, crimes committed while under the influence of illicit drugs, is not, in fact, common. Dr. Michael Gazzaniga, a psychiatrist specializing in neuroscience, states categorically that "no one has ever maintained that [amphetamines, cocaine, and crack] are 'crimogenic'." Physiologically substances such as heroin and pot do not encourage violence. Even few crack users commit crimes because of their use of crack. A study of New York drug-related homicides found that three-fourths were turf-related; many others resulted from contractual disputes that obviously cannot be settled legally in government courts. Only 7.5 percent were related to the effects of the drug, and two-thirds of those involved alcohol. In fact, "no illicit drug," observes Ethan Nadelmann, "is as strongly associated with violent behavior as is alcohol." More than half of all prison inmates jailed for violent crimes in 1983 used alcohol before their offense; a 1986 survey of state prisoners found that they were far more likely to have consumed alcohol, or alcohol in combination with illegal drugs, than illicit substances alone. Thus, to the extent that drug prohibition shifts users from marijuana to alcohol, it probably *increases* drug-induced violence.

Moreover, drug prohibition foments crime in a more indirect way. For many users an arrest for drug use or sale is their first contact with the criminal justice system; a conviction stamps them with the scarlet letter "criminal" and makes it more difficult for them to procure legal jobs in the future. The problem has become particularly acute in inner cities where legitimate employment opportunities are so few and drug arrestees so many.

A second problem for society, as mentioned earlier, is AIDS. Nearly one-third of all those with AIDS are intravenous (IV) drug users, and they constitute the fastest growing category of people with AIDS. Half of HIV-infected heterosexuals contracted the virus through sexual contact with IV drug users. Two-thirds of perinatal AIDS cases involve children of IV drug users or women who have had sex with IV drug users. The social cost of these protracted illnesses and deaths is enormous and largely results from drug prohibition.

Of course, the ban on drugs is defended as reducing the social loss in productivity and from increased health care costs due to drug use, now estimated at some $50 billion annually. Yet that number itself is inflated by drug prohibition, which has made drugs more dangerous and more potent. Anyway, balanced against this must be the social cost of prohibition, particularly the additional crime, and other harms, such as the limitation on medical uses of marijuana to, for instance, relieve the nausea caused by chemotherapy and AZT and to prevent blindness from glaucoma. In the latter cases the government is denying access to a product that would ease the pain of dying for some and help others fight and live.

Finally, every American citizen loses as civil liberties are increasingly sacrificed in the so-called drug war. Travelers are searched on the basis of nothing more than a secret profile of drug couriers. Bus riders heading north from Florida have been pressured to allow police to search their belongings simply because they are traveling in that particular direction. Suspects are stripped of their property in advance of trial; families lose their homes because of the activities of a child. Employment is tied to a willingness to take random drug tests, irrespective of cause. Apartment owners are ordered to install multi-million dollar security systems to thwart drug dealers or forfeit their property. Innocent homeowners have literally had their doors beaten down by the police; some have been mistakenly shot. The government has browbeaten companies to sell potentially dangerous herbicides for use on Peruvian peasants. And increasing numbers of casual users are being imprisoned for an action that is morally no different than consuming such legal drugs as alcohol and tobacco.

Ultimately the American people need to ask, does freedom matter? Contrast the attitudes of two different men responsible for the administration of U.S. law. At his 1989 confirmation hearings as "drug czar" William Bennett formally promised to defend civil liberties, but announced that "this war is not for delicate sensibilities. This is tough stuff." A year later, federal District Court Judge William Schwarzer had to sentence a small-time dealer to the mandatory ten years in prison. He observed that "It behooves us to think that it may profit us very little to win the war on drugs if in the process we lose our soul."

## Where Does America Go from Here?

The desire of proponents of drug prohibition in America and other countries for a better society is understandable. But their naivete in thinking that drug prohibition can bring about that better society matches the unrealistic hopes of the promoters of alcohol Prohibition in the U.S. earlier this century. Said evangelist Billy Sunday in 1920: "The reign of tears is over. The slums will soon be only a memory. We will turn our prisons into factories and our jails into storehouses and corncribs. Men will walk upright now, women will smile, and the children will laugh. Hell will be forever for rent."

A more accurate analogy for the drug war is America's involvement in Vietnam—"a limited war, fought on the cheap, and destined for stalemate and human tragedy," in the words of Sen. Joseph Biden, chairman of the U.S. Senate Judiciary Committee. Proposals for ever-increasing escalation, one possible strategy, also resemble that conflict. Observed Francis Hall, one-time commander of the New York City police department's narcotics division: "Drug enforcement is like the Vietnam War. In Vietnam, we underestimated the number of Vietcong and their will to fight. We appear to be doing the same thing with street-level drug traffickers." Between 1985 and 1989 his narcotics division increased from 525 to 2000 but, he said, "It's like Westmoreland asking Washington for two more divisions. We lost the Vietnam War with a half-million men. We're doing the same thing with drugs." In 1990 the city quietly downgraded its special Tactical Narcotics Squads, reducing total arrests by 26 percent.

Nevertheless, politicians unwilling to admit the foolishness of their policies naturally advocate increased enforcement efforts. In 1971 President Richard Nixon termed drug abuse "a national emergency" and called for "a total offensive." Around the same time New York State, at the behest of then Gov. Nelson Rockefeller, adopted a set of draconian laws mandating life imprisonment for possession of a pound of cocaine or heroin and a minimum of 15 years for possession of two ounces of drugs, for instance. In recent years a majority of Americans polled say that they favor giving up "a few of the freedoms we have in this country" in an attempt to reduce drug use.

And many of America's most important leaders have proved all too willing to oblige. Former President George Bush, for instance, wanted to execute drug "kingpins"; drug czar William Bennett proposed killing major money launderers. Several state legislators urged executing dealers who sold to kids. Authorities in Washington now claim the right, without the consent of foreign governments, to arrest foreign nationals for activities conducted on foreign soil. The U.S. Senate voted to shoot down unidentified planes entering the country (later reversed by a four-vote margin). Republican Sen. Orrin Hatch proposed further gutting Fourth Amendment protections against unreasonable government searches. Other steps proposed include:

- revoking users' drivers' licenses;
- banning juveniles from renting beepers;
- withholding federal benefits from drug consumers;
- issuing drug war bonds and imposing an income surtax for drug enforcement;
- punishing parents of child drug users;
- eliminating parole for prisoners;
- establishing widespread police roadblocks and randomly searching autos;
- imposing mandatory drug testing for high school and college students, teachers, and professors, policemen, public housing residents, and public and private employees;
- publishing the names and photos of drug offenders;
- calling in all $50 and $100 bills to flush out drug dealers;
- placing policemen on every street corner;
- revoking business and professional licenses of users;
- exiling dealers;
- building numerous new prisons, including "boot camps" for casual users and Arctic and desert camps for dealers;
- strip-searching visitors to the U.S.;
- invading Columbia and other drug-producing countries;
- creating a multinational paramilitary force;
- using the military against domestic drug traffickers;
- calling out the National Guard, a reserve military force, in major cities;
- flogging drug dealers and cutting off a finger per offense;
- sinking drug runners' boats and machine-gunning the crews;
- seizing the property of drug *suspects* even if not related to the drug offense;
- establishing "drumhead" courts in the field;
- declaring a national emergency or martial law; and
- giving individual police officers a share of the assets they seize from drug offenders.

Indeed, consider the scenario advanced by conservative columnist and 1992 presidential contender Patrick Buchanan:

It we truly believed our rhetoric about a "war on drugs," we could win in 60 days: Suspend civil liberties, declare a state of siege, impose martial law, authorize police to capture drug dealers, haul them before military tribunals, to be executed at dawn if convicted. No appeals. If they resist arrest, shoot them as enemy soldiers trying to escape. Buyers who cooperated with police would be sent to POW camps for the 60-day duration, as would drug runners and small dealers who provided evidence on higher-ups, until every narcotics kingpin had been put to death as a war criminal for poisoning America's children and sabotaging our society.

In short, turn America into a police state. Whether such a strategy would actually "work," that is, end the drug trade, is hard to know. Malaysia freely uses both the death penalty and pretrial detention but is still suffering from a steadily growing number of its citizens using drugs. In any case, even Buchanan pulled back from his proposal, declaring that the American people were not ready for such a policy. However, liberal Steven Brill, publisher and editor in chief of *The American Lawyer*, is willing to call for "cops on half the street corners of America" for a year or two.

## The Legalization Option

The other option is to deescalate the drug war and legalize adult drug use. Advocates of legalization have pressed their views for decades, but only recently has this approach entered the mainstream political debate. And even then, during the worst hysteria fomented by the Bush administration, drug legalization only occasionally received a serious hearing. But the political atmosphere is changing: in 1989 64 percent of Americans declared drugs to be the nation's most important problem; only two percent said the same in 1991. Even as the debate has become more reasoned, some advocates of current policy have curiously complained that legalization proponents have an easy time. Argues New York University's Jacobs, "The lack of a fleshed-out legalization proposal makes it extremely difficult to assess or to criticize the legalization position. Skeptics vainly try to fix their sights on a moving target." Yet one need not know the exact contours of a legal drug market to decide that the criminal law is not the most efficacious means of dealing with the problem of drug use. One could simply begin by deescalating enforcement efforts and viewing the drug issue primarily as one of health and social policy.

Nevertheless, the question of what follows the end of drug prohibition is important. Contrary to the apparent assumption of some legalization opponents, however, dropping the ban on drug use would not be a jump into the unknown. The question of how to legalize, observed David Boaz, vice president of the Washington-based Cato Institute, "doesn't strike me as particularly difficult. Our society has had a lot of experience with legal dangerous drugs, particularly alcohol and tobacco, and we can draw on that experience." Indeed, America's experience includes more than a century of time when cocaine, marijuana, and opium were legal. Moreover, there are numerous examples of other nations, such as the Netherlands and Great Britain, that eschew America's draconian prohibitionist policies. Marijuana is essentially legal in the former, while in the latter doctors are able to prescribe not only heroin but, in an experimental program in Liverpool, also cocaine.

Virtually no legalization advocate would have no controls on drug user, and there are a number of strategies for creating a legal market. As Princeton's Ethan Nadelmann has observed,

> the distinction between prohibition and legalization is thus less one of government control of drug distribution than one of emphasis: the drug- prohibition approach is one that relies primarily on criminal sanctions to control drug abuse; the legalization approach, one that relies primarily on public health approaches, non-governmental controls, and the private decisions of citizens.

There are six major legalization options: legalize the least dangerous drugs; decriminalize, rather than fully legalize, drugs; require use through a doctor; sell drugs in government stores, as alcohol is done in some U.S. states; allow the sale of drugs in private establishments, with some restrictions (such as a ban on sales to minors and the use of vending machines), as is done with cigarettes; and permit unrestricted sales.

### Legalize the Least Dangerous Drugs

Even some advocates of prohibition agree that some substances should be exempted from the ban. For instance, Mark Kleiman of the John F. Kennedy School of Government at Harvard would legalize marijuana while preserving the prohibition on cocaine use. Some analysts would also legalize heroin. Businessman Richard Dennis would end the ban on most drugs except for crack. Proponents of this approach generally have been less interested in who would sell drugs than which drugs could be sold. An exception is Australian sociologist Stephen Mugford, who has suggested making cannabis available commercially while establishing a licensing system for cocaine and heroin.

Partial legalization would eliminate some of the worst features of prohibition by dropping sanctions from the most widely used illicit substance or substances. Legalizing marijuana alone would end nearly one-third of all American drug arrests (through 1983 arrests for marijuana possession alone accounted for more than half of all drug arrests) and would eliminate an important profit center for criminal dealers. Moreover, allowing the legal use of pot would help provide a firebreak between the use of the most acceptable illegal drug and use of other, "harder" drugs. In contrast to today, marijuana dealers would have no incentive to move customers on to cocaine and other substances. Moreover, partial legalization would separate the drug scenes. Observes Dr. Giel van Brussel, head of the Narcotics Office of Amsterdam's Department of Health, young people can buy marijuana "in the coffee shops and see that it's relatively harmless. They can also see that hard-drug users suffer from physical deterioration."

This approach would also offer the opportunity to expand the policy after further study. Nadelmann, for instance, suggests a gradual "shift toward legalization" beginning with marijuana, that would provide "ample opportunity to halt, reevaluate, and redirect drug policies that begin to prove too costly or counterproductive."

Nevertheless, maintaining the drug war, even while reducing its scope, would leave in place many of the problems still facing us. If heroin remained illegal, property crime would remain high as addicts continued to steal to finance their habits. Keeping crack illegal would ensure continued gang warfare as dealers fought over territory and resolved disputes violently. Even if the government concentrated on controlling these substances, it would not be able to eradicate their sale, at least not at an acceptable cost. Nor would partial legalization free foreign nations from the violence and terror stemming from their attempts to eliminate the production of cocaine and heroin.

Partial legalization would also maintain a questionable moral policy of imprisoning people who do no direct harm to others. It would continue to drive what is primarily a health and social problem underground, creating a stigma that makes it difficult for some people to get help. And it would discourage medical research and information dissemination about the dangers of drug use.

### Decriminalize, Rather than Fully Legalize, Drugs

The U.S. government could follow Italy's lead in substituting civil for criminal sanctions against drug use, punishing users with a fine rather than prison. The authorities would, however, maintain criminal penalities against sellers, as did the 11 states in the U.S. that decriminalized mari-juana use in the 1970s. This was also the law during America's alcohol Prohibition.

Decriminalization would preserve legal disapproval of drug use, thereby presumably discouraging demand to some degree, without jail-ing people for harming themselves. Enforcement efforts could be re-laxed and prison resources reduced.

Still, decriminalization would not fully address the problems that make legalization the best option. While users would not go to jail, those who were caught would be punished for committing an act not unlike light-ing a cigarette or pouring a drink. Moreover, the government would still arrest and imprison those who supplied substances to willing buyers.

As a result, the black market would remain a profitable field for crimi-nals, leaving largely unchanged the problems of corruption, crime, and violence that exist today. And by keeping drug use illicit if not criminal, this policy would still discourage drug research and information-shar-ing, prevent any quality control or dosage standardization, and leave kids vulnerable to the lure of the drug trade.

*Require Use through a Doctor*

Another alternative would be to adopt an analogue of the British sys-tem. Drug use would be legal, but drugs would be available only through a doctor, who would either provide a prescription or actually dispense the drugs. In 1989, for instance, legislation was introduced in the New York state senate to allow licensed doctors and pharmacists to sell drugs. A related approach would be to limit the availability of drugs to recog-nized addicts through special clinics. Another restrictive proposal, from Harvard's Kleiman, is to create a "drinking license" for alcohol that could be revoked if abused.

The advantage of these sort of systems is that they would retain some control over use even after prohibition was eliminated. Users would have to sit through a lecture on the health effects of their preferred drug to receive a prescription or a license; doctors could better monitor health problems if they knew the users; the system would preserve some stigma for users, discouraging demand.

Unfortunately, the very benefits of the system would also cause its biggest drawbacks. By placing users under the control of doctors, the system would degrade consumers. Such a process seems unfair—why pot smokers but not cigarette smokers? Also, the more stringent the system, the more likely that an illicit market would continue. If only addicts could receive drugs, there would still be widespread demand for black market supplies. Moreover, some people would attempt to be recognized as addicts simply to become eligible to receive drugs; addiction would actually become a legal privilege.

Great Britain's experience demonstrates the problem of restricting use in this way. A small number of doctors with a special license may prescribe cocaine, dipipanone (a powerful narcotic), and heroin. They may also determine how the addict satisfies his desire—with oral doses of methadone, for instance, rather than injections. The stringency of the system, especially after the government tightened its rules in 1968, sharply limits users' legal access to drugs. As a result, the country found itself the victim of increasing crime levels as more users attempted to circumvent what they considered to be a humiliating rule. Observes Arnold Trebach of American University, "the rise in addict crime and the drug black market took place in the wake of a tougher prescribing policy toward addicts regarding heroin and all narcotics." (Lest there be any doubt as to the British government's attitude, one need only review its official publications that emphasize the restrictiveness of its laws.)

Nevertheless, the resulting black market is not nearly so severe as in the U.S., with far less crime, for instance, as well as fewer deaths from AIDS passed among IV drug users. However, only about 7,000 of an estimated 30,000 to 35,000 heroin addicts were purchasing drugs legally in 1985. Leaving a similar 80 percent of cocaine, crack, heroin, and marijuana users outside of the legal market in the U.S. would ensure the continued existence of a huge, violent, criminal underground.

Particularly successful is the Liverpool experiment, in which doctors prescribe not only heroin but also heroin cigarettes, along with cocaine, crack, and crack cigarettes. The share of heroin addicts infected with the HIV virus is less then one percent, compared to an estimated 50 percent in New York City. Drug users hold jobs, marry, and raise families, and many eventually drop their habits: "fifty-fifty after ten years are off. They seem to mature out of addiction regardless of any intervention in the interim. But you can keep them alive and healthy and legal during that ten years if you wish to," explains Dr. John Marks, who runs an addiction clinic in Liverpool. Not only is violent crime down, but so is dealing, since addicts no longer have to support their habits in that way. "So if you want to get rid of your drug problem, which presumably all societies do, there are ways of doing it, but you have to counter your own moral and political prejudice," explains Allan Parry, a former British Drug Information Officer.

Even a system allowing most anyone to use drugs but only at a clinic would not eliminate the black market entirely. Such a system, observes attorney and doctor Nancy Lord, would "not be attractive to addicts who use drugs in a home environment, with their choice of friends, music, and food. The prospect of restricting their drug use to a clinical or governmental setting would probably be so unattractive to them that the demand for black market drugs would undoubtedly continue."

Lastly, such a system would place an inappropriate burden on doctors. Many, who view their job as healing the sick, would be uncomfortable dispensing potentially dangerous drugs, even to willing users. This approach would also impose a serious new burden on a health care system that is not perceived to be functioning as well as it should.

## Sell Drugs in Government Stores, as Alcohol is Done in Some States

When alcohol Prohibition was ended by the 21st Amendment to the American Constitution, the law did more than just return to the status quo. Instead, the 21st Amendment both repealed the 18th Amendment, which had made the manufacture, sale, and transportation of alcohol illegal, and gave individual states almost absolute power over the alcohol business within their borders. Thus, alcohol regulation across the United States is a patchwork. Most states allow sales of beer and wine in private stores, but some limit hard liquor sales to state "ABC" stores. Some give counties authority to ban sales by the drink in bars (rules which are often circumvented by bars operating as "clubs" or offering food priced at whatever the law requires for the sale of alcohol). The drinking age in many states was once 18, but federal pressure—including the threat to cut off highway funds—has caused every state to increase the age to 21. Advertising for beer and wine is common in the electronic media, and magazines and newspapers run ads for hard liquor as well, though state stores do not push their wares.

One option for legalizing drugs, then, would be to make currently illicit substances available to adults (the line probably being set at between 18 and

21 years, though some states allow younger people to purchase cigarettes) in state stores. The government would merely be in charge of selling, not growing or making the substances, which could come from domestic or foreign sources. There would presumably be no advertising and prices would reflect a component to help pay for the social cost of drug use.

This approach would be a dramatic improvement over drug prohibition, eliminating the black market and the vast profits made by criminal enterprises. A grey market serving the young would still exist, but such "leakage" would pose less of a problem than we have today. First, illegal sales would largely disappear, as only seven percent of cocaine is currently estimated to be consumed by those under 18, for instance. Users between 18 and 20 account for only 16 percent of consumption, and these figures probably overstate their use because older users have greater purchasing power. Second, the harm from these sales to juveniles would be less since the products would at least go through the normal quality control process of a legal market. Moreover, legal enterprises would be much less likely to recruit kids as dealers—no high school students wear beepers to market cigarettes, as they do marijuana today, despite leakage in the former case.

However, having the government provide and profit from drug sales may appear to some to sanction drug use. A separate concern is that putting drug sales in the hands of a government monopoly would eliminate the traditional benefits of competition for users. Prices would likely be higher, access more restricted, and service poorer in a government controlled system. Of course, since even most advocates of legalization want to restrain drug use, just without resort to the criminal law, such inefficiency might be considered a benefit—unless it was so great as to make a black market a profitable option. However, restraints on demand could be better achieved through taxes on private sales rather than a system of government stores. It would also be easier to adjust the tax to ensure that no black market survives.

*Allow the Sale of Drugs in Private Establishments, with*
*Some Restrictions (Such as a Ban on Sales to Minors and*
*the Use of Vending Machines), as Is Done With Cigarettes*

Tobacco is widely sold by private firms, including grocery stores, service stations, and almost any business with a vending machine. Sales to minors and television advertising are generally prohibited.

The most obvious benefit of following a cigarette-like drug policy would be to eliminate the primary costs of drug prohibition: more than one million arrests annually, rampant crime, pervasive corruption, violent criminal undergrounds, and foreign terrorism. The substances sold would themselves be safer, since quality and quantity would be standardized, manufacturers would be liable for impurities, and information about the health effects of different dosages of substances would be widely available. This approach would also be more appropriate for any society that calls itself free, more closely matching the way most goods and services are provided, with a minimum of government control.

The major draw-backs with this approach would be two-fold. The first is that demand would probably increase to some degree. There are a number of reasons to believe that allowing the private sale of drugs would not turn the U.S. and other nations into lands full of druggies. For instance, America appeared to have no more opium addicts per capita when use of that product was legal than it has heroin addicts per capita today. (Earlier this century the U.S. averaged between 110,000 and 150,000 opium addicts; that number is thought to have peaked at about 264,000 in 1900, after which it declined, *before* passage in 1914 of the Harrison Act which outlawed the drug.) Moreover, drug use responds to many factors, as does consumption of such substances as alcohol and tobacco, the use of which has been falling in America even though they are relatively cheap and legal.

Nevertheless, the government could take steps to temper demand without being so draconian as to recreate a black market. Taxes could be imposed to collect a significant amount of revenue to help meet the cost imposed by drug users on society. All advertising, including sponsorship of sporting events, vehicular logos, and newspaper circulars, could be banned, just as U.S. law currently forbids TV ads for cigarettes and distilled spirits. It has also been suggested that drugs be sold generically, without any brand-name competition.

The second major problem would involve young people, who would undoubtedly gain access to drugs just as they are able to acquire cigarettes and liquor today. No system can be foolproof; indeed, despite years of "war" the U.S. government has been unable to prevent as many as one-in-three teenagers from trying illegal substances. And the number of children using drugs started falling in 1979, before the most draconian enforcement efforts undertaken by the Reagan and Bush administrations.

At least enforcement could be focused on the youth market if drug use were legal. And more children might become acculturated to drug use in a home environment, helping to limit their abuse of the products.

## Permit Unrestricted Sales

All regulations, other than tort liability for adulterated products, on currently illicit drugs could be lifted. Advocates of this position are few but include America's 1988 Libertarian Party candidate, Ron Paul, who has proposed: "Drugs could be distributed by any adult to other adults. There should be no controls on production, supply, or purchase (for adults)." He is joined by psychiatrist Thomas Szasz, who sharply denounces the so-called "legalizers" for supporting some government controls and calls for a "free market" in drugs. Drugs would be treated like aspirin or products containing caffeine, with virtually no sales restrictions. Use by children would probably, though not necessarily, be limited; five American states do not prohibit cigarette sales to minors. People using drugs would be held legally responsible for their actions, as are drunk drivers today.

The main practical benefit of such an approach is that it would eliminate the evils of prohibition. Compared to more regulated regimes it would avoid the costs and inefficiencies of government control and would not encourage the existence of any black and perhaps even grey markets. Finally, this strategy would maximize the freedom of individuals, an important consideration usually overlooked in debates on drug policy.

Nevertheless, the costs of this strategy might be significant. Children would certainly have greater access to drugs, yet the interest in protecting them until they are considered to be legally competent to decide to use dangerous substances is substantial. Moreover, drug use would likely increase more sharply than under other systems. Not that serious problems would inevitably result. Cocaine use was legal in the 1800s and earlier this century and there was no crisis. Writes attorney James Ostrowski, "A search through the *New York Times Index* for 1895–1904— years of peak drug use and minimum legal control—for articles about the negative effects of cocaine use found none. In contrast, there were 1,657 articles about the cocaine problem during the peak years of the drug war—1979–1988." Nevertheless, given the risks posed by widespread drug use, it would be reasonable to design a system that would mildly discourage drug use and collect revenue from users to help cover the costs that will likely result from their behavior.

## A Tentative Proposal

If citizens choose to adopt the legalization rather than the enforcement path, they would be right to remain concerned about drug use. Thus, some restrictions on the use of such substances is legitimate. Argues Harvard's Kleiman: "Our central concern should thus be with classes of users for whom the damage done by the drug is disproportionately higher: the young, the poor, and the heaviest users, and with the illicit market whose corruption, crime, violence and criminal income cause widespread damage." What, then, should a legal market in America look like?

Use by adults should be legal; criminal penalties should apply only to those who sell to youngsters. The national Drug Enforcement Agency should be disbanded, with enforcement entrusted to local police, since sale to minors, rather than production or smuggling, would be the primary drug crime. Public pressure, too, could be brought to bear on firms to combat youth drug use; in late 1990 the U.S. tobacco industry announced a campaign to curb smoking by minors.

The federal government should prohibit advertising in any national or interstate medium and ban interstate sales by mail.

All federal laws controlling distribution and sale should be repealed, however, leaving the issue up to the individual states. Thus, local and state governments would experiment with the type of system that best serves their citizens' interests.

That best system would probably be a modified cigarette model. States would legalize the sale of all illicit substances. As Ostrowski has observed, "We cringe at making some drugs legal, but these are the very same drugs that the public would cringe at using if they were legal." Especially if a wide range of less dangerous drugs were available. The only exception to legalization should be substances shown to cause a very high percentage of users to commit violent acts against others— perhaps PCP. However, users of newly legalized drugs would be civilly and criminally liable for actions that they committed while under the influence.

Private firms would be allowed to sell formerly illicit drugs, but such establishments would have to be specially licensed and regulated to limit

leakage to children. Moreover, use of vending machines would be prohibited. As Princeton's Nadelmann has noted: "It is important to realize
that legalization does not have to mean following in the same stupid
footsteps traced by our alcohol and tobacco policies. We do not have to
make potentially dangerous substances available in vending machines
at seven cents a piece in packages of 20. Nor do we have to subsidize
growers or provide the substances at subsidized rates to our military
personnel." For the same reason, advertising would be banned; warnings would be included on packages and health information would be
made available in stores.

Manufacturers and sellers would bear normal tort liability for contaminated or mislabeled products, but users would assume the overall
risk of using the drugs. Developers of new drugs, however, might be
held normally liable for any ill effects of their products. This would help
discourage the development of new substances. Such drugs could appear on the black market, but consumers are unlikely to prefer products
which are more likely to cause uncompensated harm over those already
legally available. Even in today's illegal market most users have proved
to be rational, sharply reducing their use of LSD, PCP, and even crack
once the substances' dangers were apparent. Retail outlets would face
liability for selling to intoxicated patrons (as do many bars under
America's so-called "dram shop" laws, for instance) and could be closed
as public nuisances if they created unreasonable disturbances in a
neighborhood.

States could levy a tax on drugs to finance an advertising and educational campaign on the substances' dangers, fund health care and addiction treatment programs for indigent users, and provide social services
for the families of users who are harmed (just as some families fall into
poverty because of irresponsible alcoholics or gamblers). Special consideration should be given to the use of drugs by pregnant women. Perhaps sales to anyone who is obviously pregnant should be banned; perhaps
putative mothers who used drugs, including alcohol and tobacco, should
face charges of child abuse.

All told, then, it makes sense for the government to treat drugs with
what Kleiman calls "grudging toleration." Even more grudging and less
tolerant should be the reaction of private individuals and institutions to
drug use. Indeed, government officials should emphasize the role of the
family, church, community, and business in restraining otherwise destructive behavior, and helping users and their families. Social pressure

has helped reduce the appeal of alcohol and cigarettes; a growing majority of Americans support discouraging tobacco use in public places. Even illicit drug users today respond to various forms of social pressure; for instance, in Australia Stephen Mugford found that a group of cocaine users "limited their use, and did so because of the wider web of social ties into which they were embedded." Churches, in particular, can speak to some of the more fundamental needs that lead people to seek solace in drugs, while private firms can limit drug use when it adversely affects productivity and safety. This multi-faceted approach can best meet a problem that is primarily a health and social concern rather than a criminal one.

## But It Would Be Wrong

The debate over drug legalization is an emotional one. James Jacobs of New York University, for one, argues that "Perhaps the most negative effect of [the legalization] debate is that it is diverting time, resources, and attention from the more pressing question of how to reform the war on drugs so as to reduce drug use more effectively, and to minimize social and economic costs while preserving civil liberties." Yet that is precisely what the argument over legalization is about—moving to a strategy to better restrain drug use at far less social cost. The burden of justifying continuance of drug prohibition—a policy that, in America, at least, is imprisoning an entire generation of young people, violating the civil liberties of the law-abiding, creating shoot-outs in major cities, threatening to topple foreign governments, making drug use more dangerous, and sucking kids into a criminal underground, all the while permitting tens of millions of people to continue to use drugs—is a heavy one.

To justify maintaining, let alone intensifying, the drug war, proponents of current policy have a serious burden of proof to meet. They need to demonstrate that the war on drugs is moral and that it can stem drug use. They also need to show that ending drug prohibition would likely result in a huge increase in drug use and that such an increase would not be significantly offset by a decrease in dangerousness of today's illicit substances as well as the consumption of dangerous but already legal substances. Finally, they need to show that the costs of increased consumption would not be counterbalanced by legalization's reduction in crime, corruption, and foreign instability. In short, they need to demonstrate, as opposed to merely assert, that the benefits of drug prohibition exceed the costs.

## The Moral Basis of the War

When a telephone questioner proposed beheading drug dealers to drug czar William Bennett, he replied that "morally, I don't have any problem with it." He later wanted to include major drug money launderers to his death list.

However, what makes it just to kill someone for providing a product to a willing buyer, one who might not be punished at all? And what makes death, or any severe punishment, appropriate when individuals are growing rich selling other, even more dangerous and addictive, yet legal, products? Moreover, what warrants punishing dealers more seriously than *murderers, rapists, and other violent criminals who have harmed unwilling victims?*

Further, what is the moral basis for jailing casual users, as the U.S. has been increasingly doing? There are powerful grounds for arguing that individuals have a moral right to determine what they put into their own bodies; psychiatrist Thomas Szasz grounds this right in the right to property ownership and contends that "the right to chew or smoke a plant that grows wild in nature, such as hemp (marijuana), is anterior to and more basic than the right to vote." Todd Austin Brenner speaks of "the right to personal autonomy" and the "right to privacy," both of which suggest leaving decisions over drug use to individual consumers, so long as others are not directly harmed.

Even if that seems to be going too far, proponents of drug prohibition have yet to articulate an adequate justification for punishing so heavily someone who uses marijuana in his home while leaving cigarette smokers alone. Does a health danger give the government the right to imprison someone to "protect" him? And to imprison him or her for longer than the average murderer? The Washington, D.C.-based Families Against Mandatory Minimums cites a number of horrendous cases: 23-year-old student Terry McCabe sentenced to 46 months in prison for selling $150 worth of LSD, one-time teacher Jacqueline Hendricks sentenced to eight years for carrying 4.4 pounds of cocaine from Los Angeles to Seattle; Richard Anderson receiving ten years for driving a car in which 3.7

ounces of crack was exchanged; and Jeff Stewart getting a five-year sentence for growing marijuana in his home.

Former President George Bush came up with another argument, blaming the gang warfare in the U.S. and the terrorism in other nations on the demand for drugs reflecting recreational use: "casual drug use is responsible for the casualties of the drug war. From the city streets of America to the street bombings of Columbia, even dabblers in drugs bear responsibility for the blood being spilled." But these crimes are the result of drug prohibition, not drug use. It is legislators who enact draconian drug laws who bear the primary moral responsibility for creating an environment in which such crimes occur.

The important moral point is that crimes like murder require punishment because they involve violations of *inter*-personal morality, that is, they harm unwilling victims. Simple drug sales, purchases, and use, in contrast, involve *intra*-personal morality and hurt only willing victims. Self-victim crimes such as these should fall outside the scope of government since its primary task is to create a framework for the interaction of individuals with one another; moreover, self-victim crimes are much more difficult to prosecute, and thus require much more intrusive enforcement practices, because of the lack of a complaining witness.

Distinguishing between inter- and intra-personal morality is particularly appropriate in the drug debate because there is nothing intrinsic to the act of injecting heroin or smoking pot that distinguishes it from using dangerous but legal substances like cigarettes or engaging in potentially fatal activities such as hang-gliding and mountain-climbing. All impose general social costs, but none directly victimize third parties in the same sense as does murder. Something more than concern over lost economic productivity is needed to justify a policy to execute dealers, imprison users, and foster violence here and abroad.

*Can Prohibition Work?*

Four months after President Bush unveiled his new drug initiative, "drug czar" William Bennett acknowledged that "Drug markets have shown a flexibility and endurance in the face of pressure." That has proved to be perhaps the understatement of the decade. Steadily tougher enforcement policies in the U.S. have not been able to prevent an upsurge in heroin addiction and increased emergency room admissions for cocaine. Casual use of the latter has been falling, but so, too, has consumption of alcohol and tobacco, both of which are legal. In short, those Bennett denounced as "cynics and defeatists" were right: the enforcement strategy is bankrupt.

First, Washington can't stop drugs from being produced. Sustained pressure on South American governments was not able to prevent cocaine production from hitting a new high in 1991, for instance, 44 metric tons higher than in 1988. Nor can the U.S. government stop drugs from entering the U.S.—as little as one-twentieth of foreign shipments are seized, and domestic chemists have proved able to make synthetic versions of most drugs. Even the Bush White House admitted that "heroin may prove even more difficult to control than cocaine...opium and heroin production, distribution and consumption patterns show an alarming persistence and resistance to control."

Once drugs are in the country the government has been shown to be powerless to stop their sale. Despite more than one million arrests annually, bulging prisons, unreasonable mandatory minimum sentences, ad infinitum, new dealers always appear to replace the old ones. "They're not winning the drug war," one St. Louis cocaine dealer told the *New York Times*. "There's never a shortage of cocaine in this city. They could lock up a thousand brothers, even 10,000 brothers. There's always going to be someone new out here selling."

Even several thousand drug trade murders don't seem to have much impact. Explained one 19-year-old crack dealer in Washington, D.C.: "dying is the risk you take." Once they are offered for sale they are purchased and used—despite the drug war casual use of cocaine climbed by 14 percent over 1991 to 1992. Heroin use rose as well, while marijuana consumption remained roughly constant. Short of turning countries into prisons, it would seem, governments have no hope of staunching the flow of drugs.

## The Effect of Legalization on Drug Use

Around the turn of the century, notes psychiatrist David Musto, "Chicago's poor neighborhoods did not differ much from the worst inner-city areas of today. One observer called Chicago 'first in violence, deepest in dirt; loud, lawless, unlovely, ill-smelling, new...' Cocaine was everywhere, from soda pop to sniffing powders." Today, cocaine is...everywhere, from powder to crack. The beneficial effects of the drug war, it would seem, are hard to see. Yet if drug prohibition is not actually limiting total drug use, it makes no sense at all.

Supporters of current policies therefore argue that legalizing drugs would lead to much higher use and a social disaster. However, while one would expect increased usage once a product was made legal and its price fell, the effect might not be great. First, availability would change little—most people who want drugs today can obtain them if they desire. Even high school students say that drugs are readily accessible (and more say they are available than use them). The sad reality is that prohibition doesn't work, something government officials will occasionally admit in moments of unusual candor. Assistant Secretary of the Treasury Francis Keating was asked in hearings before Congress: "as a result of all these efforts in the increase of expertise, technology, and efforts put into this area, are you suggesting that there might be one ounce less of heroin, opium, cocaine, or marijuana on the street as a result of that?" His answer: "No."

Second, drug use responds to many factors, of which legality and price may not be the most important. As law professor Steven Wisotsky has argued, "The demand for any product at a given price has a natural market size. People do not want unlimited supplies of anything. With marijuana, something approaching full market penetration had already occurred before the law changed in the 1970s." A recent Rand Corporation study found that a drug education program which related the problems of drug use to students' daily lives reduced use of marijuana and tobacco. Consumption levels for alcohol and tobacco are also falling and they are legal; social pressure and a recognition of their dangers operate independently of the law. Indeed, enforcement efforts appear to have little direct impact on drug use, as availability has at times proved to be *inversely* related to consumption. Wrote three University of Michigan researchers in 1990: "Although the declines in rates of use for marijuana and for cocaine began at different points in time, they have two important features in common: 1) each was accompanied by a sharp shift in attitudes about the drug and 2) in each case the decline in use was *not* accompanied by any decline in perceived availability of the drug."

Moreover, the threat of arrest is smaller than enforcement addicts might believe. More important, the perceived likelihood of arrest by users is even less. Observes author Richard Lawrence Miller: "Such results are hardly surprising; people who live for the moment are undeterred by future consequences; most criminals do not expect to be caught, and indeed most are not."

Of course, legalization would lower prices. Still, Harvard's Kleiman, who fears a sharp upsurge in cocaine use from legalization, admits that "cocaine is less widely used than alcohol for many reasons, including tradition and reputation." Moreover, research suggests that increased consumption would be concentrated among compulsive rather than controlled users, the 25 percent who currently consume three-quarters of all drugs. These are, after all, the people who have proved particularly resistant to today's anti-drug efforts. Admitted the White House in 1992, "Even though casual use, especially among younger people, continues to decline significantly, the problem of hard-core use will improve slowly." Most nonusers are likely to have little interest in taking drugs, just like most nonsmokers are not interested in using cigarettes. After all, writes Miller, "most abstainers are repelled by the drugs rather than the law." It is presumably for this reason that a 1990 survey of non-drug-using adults found only 1.7 percent to be interested in using cocaine if it was legal.

There are no controlled experiments as to the impact of legalization on drug use, but the experience of a number of nations suggests that the result would not be disaster—the sort of widespread opium use seen in China in the 19th Century, for instance. As noted earlier, the U.S. had fewer opium addicts per capita at the turn of the century than the number of heroin addicts per capita today. Just as opium use is thought to have peaked before it was banned, so, too, did consumption of cocaine, which is believed to have started falling in 1907.

More recently, education and social pressure appears to have had a significant impact on drug use. Substances such as LSD and PCP have gained bad reputations and fallen from favor. Similarly, a recent University of Michigan study attributes the failure of Ice and Ecstacy to catch on among the young to greater awareness of the dangers. Marijuana use peaked in 1979, before Ronald Reagan's election, let alone the inauguration of his celebrated drug war. Cocaine use peaked in 1985, before the creation of a "drug czar" and the dramatic increase in enforcement spending during the Bush administration.

State laws may have a more important impact on consumption, since most drug prosecutions occur at that level. Yet the legalization of marijuana for personal use in Alaska (narrowly overturned by voters in 1990) had little apparent impact on consumption: fewer high school students appeared to consume pot afterwards than before. Ten other states decriminalized marijuana use during the 1970s, substituting civil for criminal penalties. Surveys of California and Oregon found only slight increases in consumption, matching the rise in states where such behavior remained a crime. And soon after the minor decriminalization wave marijuana use nationally *fell.*

Another argument, offered by sociologist James Q. Wilson, is that only the law prevented an exponential growth of heroin addiction with the return of Vietnam veterans to the U.S. However, this argument ignores the circumstances that faced soldiers and which would likely be a far more important determinant of heroin use: quite simply, an unhappy draftee in a bloody foreign war is more likely to shoot up than a soldier who has returned safely to the U.S. And, in fact, follow-up studies of heroin users from Vietnam found no difference between addiction rates among those who lived in low-income urban areas, where heroin was readily available, and those who lived in rural or suburban areas. Equally significant is the fact that heroin use by soldiers in nearby Thailand, where the drug was equally available but dangers were significantly less, was lower than in Vietnam.

Finally, the Netherlands has legalized marijuana and substance abuse has actually fallen. Use by teens has dropped by one-third since 1976, for instance. As of 1985 just .5 percent of Dutch high school seniors used marijuana daily, compared to 5.5 percent in the U.S. In December 1989 1.8 percent of Dutch 10- to 18-year-olds said they'd used pot the previous month, far below the corresponding number of American teens, 9.1 percent. A 1987 household survey in Amsterdam found that only six percent of respondents used pot and barely more than one percent used heroin (in contrast, nearly three-quarters used alcohol). The country is also thought to have the lowest number of addicts in Western Europe and the lowest proportion of AIDS patients who are IV drug users (three percent). The Dutch tend to complain about drug-using tourists who don't wash rather than gangsters who shoot their competitors.

In Britain, where heroin is available through doctors, the number of heroin addicts has increased sharply since the 1960s, but the rate of addiction, roughly 62 per 100,000, remains about one-third the level in the U.S. Moreover, observes James Ostrowski, "To argue that the system *caused* the increased use of heroin in England in the sixties is to confuse correlation with causation. If the system caused increased drug use in the sixties, why did it not do the same during the preceding four decades it was in effect?" The sizable black market developed *only after* the government moved towards the prohibitionist model. Reported one British publication in 1985, "the evidence suggests that the illicit market in heroin and the involvement of criminal syndicates, increased in direct relationship to the policy of the clinics in rapidly cutting heroin prescribing." Moreover, drug-related crime is still virtually absent, in striking contrast to American cities. And the less restrictive experiment in Liverpool is proving to be a success, with neither the crime nor the harm to the users—with one-fiftieth the rate of HIV infection, for instance.

## The Phenomenon of Drug-Switching

People looking for pleasure or seeking escape can choose from a number of different substances. Many of these products compete with one another. For instance, consumption of marijuana first became popular during alcohol Prohibition because it was then a legal substitute. Today, surveys suggest, pot users consume less alcohol than they otherwise would. Thus, if marijuana and other illicit substances were legalized, there would likely be a shift away from alcohol and tobacco. This would moderate the net increase in drug use and, because marijuana is implicated in far fewer deaths than alcohol, likely reduce the number of deaths and injuries caused by drug use.

## The Impact of Legalization on Crime

As discussed earlier, it is drug prohibition, not drug use, that has created a literal war in American urban areas and foreign nations. It is the drug war that has fostered a wave of property crimes and murders that terrorize the innocent; it is the punishment of willing drug buyers and sellers that has eroded civil liberties in America and clogged its courts. It is the incredible profitability of drug enterprises that has captivated ghetto youth, drawn dealers into schools, and created transnational criminal empires.

Although some drug users and dealers would undoubtedly commit crimes in the absence of drug prohibition, legalization would eliminate the most profitable and violent activity now available to them. The end of prohibition would also defund domestic drug gangs and international cartels, reducing their ability to do harm. As prices fell addicts would have to commit fewer thefts to support their habits. In fact, police in Liverpool say that the legalization program has cut crime since users neither have to deal nor steal in order to acquire drugs. Increased drug consumption due to legalization may lead to some rise in low-grade violence between users and family and friends, but, again, drug switching may reduce the problems currently caused by alcohol consumption. Only a policy that was producing enormous benefits—rather than simply believed to be preventing some unspecified amount of drug use—could justify creating so much crime.

### Other Impacts of Drug Prohibition

The drug war has led to serious corruption in the U.S. and foreign nations. Police officers, customs department officials, DEA agents, prosecutors, county commissioners, judges, Coast Guard personnel, prison guards, and even members of the armed services have all accepted cash to facilitate or cover up drug activity. So serious is the problem that the Customs Department has set up its own informer program.

The impact of the war against the drug trade also threatens the stability of foreign governments. Bolivia has suffered at least one successful coup backed by drug interests. Drug money apparently helped Manuel Noriega maintain power in Panama. Leftist guerrillas in Peru have gained support from coca-growing campesinos. Colombia's crackdown on the cocaine cartels has sparked widespread violence and weakened local anti-insurgent activities funded by drug producers. The huge social costs caused by the drug war in these countries has led to significant anger against the U.S., the source of most of the pressure for enhanced enforcment activities.

These very different problems are the result of drug prohibition. While legalization of the drug trade would not end all corruption and violence, it would eliminate the major source of those problems today.

### Conclusion

During the height of the Bush administration's campaign against drug use, Drug Czar William Bennett vilified proponents of drug legalization: the mere idea, he exclaimed, was "morally scandalous." In his first annual report he attacked "the cynics and defeatists" who believed that the war was not being won. Nor was he alone in attacking slackers in the war on drugs. But as one vice cop told columnist Mike Royko, "I keep reading that every poll shows that most people are against any kind of legalizing of drugs. You know what that tells me? It tells me that most people who get polled don't know what the hell is going on out here." Similarly, a crack addict talked with *The New York Times* and said, "This war on drugs, they might as well forget about that. It's a lot worse than they think."

A number of leading Americans have publicly endorsed drug legalization: economist Milton Friedman, columnist William F. Buckley, former Secretary of State George Shulz, Baltimore Mayor Kurt Schmoke, and federal Judge Robert Sweet. A number of conservative as well as liberal congressmen, state attorney generals, and law enforcement officials privately back legalization as well. All of these people are aware of the problems associated with drug use. But all have decided that such social problems, just like those associated with alcohol—addiction, lost productivity, babies born with Fetal Alcohol Syndrome, health difficulties, indirect deaths—are best dealt with outside of the criminal law. And even without the supposed "tutelary" fuction of legal prohibition, alcohol policy today is working. Liquor consumption is falling *without* filling the prisons with whiskey runners, turning the inner cities into war zones, and undermining foreign democracies through an alcohol war. In contrast, the drug war has given us the worst of both worlds: widespread drug use *and* ineffective but draconian drug prohibition. Legalization would be risky, but the risks pale compared to the costs of today's deadly yet failed policy.

Charles Colson, former aide to President Richard Nixon convicted for crimes during the Watergate scandal and now head of Prison Fellowship, says that he has yet to visit a prison where drugs are not readily available. "When I was in prison, I went to bed with the smell of marijuana wafting through the dormitory." And the problem has worsened as the drug war has been intensified. "There's been a real explosion in drug use in prison," says Dr. Harry Wexler of Narcotics and Drug Research, Inc. "The explanation is simple: There's been a real explosion of drug users going to prison."

If we can't keep drugs out of prisons, we can't keep them out of the hands of the rest of the population, even if we attempt to turn otherwise free societies into prison camps. And turning all citizens into inmates would be too high a price to pay even if it would wipe out drug abuse. Since escalation is not the answer, we should take the different path of legalization. Of course, legalizing adult drug use will not solve the problem of drug abuse, just as the end of alcohol Prohibition in America did not solve the problem of alcohol abuse. It would, however, turn a disaster into a problem, allowing us to better manage the consequences. It's time to end the drug war—not to "surrender" to evil, but to abandon a costly but ineffectual campaign. Then we can get on with the task of combatting the conditions that give rise to drug abuse and mitigate the impact of all forms of drug use.

March 1993

# VII

# Redistribution without End

# 20

## Still Paying for Government

April 15 is past, but people are still paying for government. In fact, the Tax Foundation estimates that we will continue doing so through May 3, 1993, "Tax Freedom Day," after which we start working for ourselves. That's the same day as last year, and one day later than 1991. But if Bill Clinton has his way, Tax Freedom Day next year will be the latest ever—May 6, increasing to May 8 by 1998.

Moreover, residents of several states today have to wait even longer until they start pocketing their earnings. New Yorkers labor for government until May 22nd. Alaskans work until May 19, residents of Connecticut until May 14, and Hawaiians don't get out on their own until May 11. Even the best states are not very good: residents of South Dakota are liberated on, of all days, April 15, while those in Montana have to work two additional days for the state.

It is easy to underestimate the reality behind these simple statistics. The *least* taxed citizens of America work three and one-half months for the government. Far more people labor four and one-half months for politicians before earning a penny for themselves.

Alas, even these numbers understate the impact of government on taxpayers. The Tax Foundation only looks at tax collections. The federal government, however, relies on deficits to expand its outlays and uses regulation to control even more private activities. Thus, Americans for Tax Reform, a taxpayer advocacy group headed by Grover Norquist, perhaps the nation's leading opponent of a Value-Added Tax—apparently the Clintonistas' next revenue target—estimates that while Americans last year stopped paying taxes on May 3, Spending Freedom Day didn't occur until *May 20*, when people stopped paying for government outlays. And Cost of Government Day, when citizens were finally free

297

of the total expense of government, including regulation, was more than a month later, on June 29.

In short, the average American spends *half* of every year working for government. Feel liberated by the passing of April 15? You shouldn't—you have *two more months* before the money you earn is truly your own.

Thus, President Clinton's attempt to claim the mantle of Thomas Jefferson takes on a different meaning than the President intended. Speaking on the 250th anniversary of Jefferson's birth, Mr. Clinton argued: "I think Thomas Jefferson would tell us that this is one of those times when we need to change." Jefferson would surely agree—but what sort of change would he advocate? That we need *more* spending, *more* taxes, and *more* regulation?

The real Thomas Jefferson helped construct a government of sharply limited power, contending that "The government that governs best governs least." But he knew that faux Jeffersons like Bill Clinton would come along, working overtime to expand state power and circumscribe individual liberty. Jefferson's response? "The tree of liberty must be refreshed from time to time with the blood of patriots and tyrants. It is its natural manure."

Not that Bill Clinton is the only person who doesn't get it. There's also Rep. Tony Hall (D-Ohio), who is in the midst of a hunger strike until Congress restores his Select Committee on Hunger, one of four panels recently eliminated by the House. Congress' vote "has opened my eyes to the profound problems within this institution," he explains.

Obviously Capitol Hill has "profound problems," but undue fiscal frugality is not one of them. Rep. Hall is, by all accounts, one of the more sincere and decent men on Capitol Hill. Yet his committee—a "temporary" body created in 1984 which had no legislative authority—is merely another symptom of a government out of control. If Congress doesn't start cutting committees that serve no practical function, where will it start? Rep. Hall would do more good if he launched a hunger fast until Congress cut back *other* useless committees and subcommittees, reduced the number of staff, and reigned in abuse of the postal frank.

You may have thought you were done paying taxes, but you actually have two more months to work for the government. Don't worry, however. The President knows you want change and is therefore committed to making you pay *more*; he even cites one of America's founding radicals as supporting higher spending and taxing. The President is joined by a leading Congressman, who is fasting in order to get his colleagues to spend more money on more committees to do nothing. And unless you let legislators know that this isn't the sort of "change," that you want, it is almost certainly what you will get. Alas, the real Thomas Jefferson was right when he warned: "The natural progress of things is for liberty to yield and government to gain ground."

April 1993

# 21

# The Decade of Envy

Democrats have long criticized the 1980s as the decade of greed, but it appears that the 1990s may end up as the decade of envy. For President Clinton has used the guise of patriotism to reignite a class war as a means of turning his budget program into law.

Much of his tax program is directed at the "rich." He wants a higher marginal rate for high earners and a surtax on those with the highest incomes. Those who have gained the most, he argues, should be willing to sacrifice the most. "Before I ask working Americans to work harder and pay more," he explains, "I will ask the economic elite who made more money and paid less in taxes to pay their fair share."

And there are Democrats who would push much further. Senate Budget Committee Chairman Jim Sasser would like to reverse the effects of Ronald Reagan's 1981 tax cut which, Sasser claims, "distributed its benefits disproportionately among the rich and the very rich." Sasser goes on to propose raising the top marginal rate still further, lifting the Medicare tax cap, and imposing a surtax on far more people. "All of these are rational, fair and effective alternative revenue sources," he explains.

These proposals are based on simple demagoguery. The Reagan tax break, an across-the-board 25 percent rate reduction, provided more in tax cuts to the rich because *the rich were paying so much more in taxes*. It was simple fairness to provide someone who paid ten times as much in taxes ten times as much in tax relief.

In response, some enthusiasts of the soak-the-rich school argue that the tax code should be more progressive. Why? Ability to pay may be a politically popular criterion for setting tax schedules, but there is nothing particularly fair about it. A flat rate, taking the same proportion of every one's income, seems much more fair. It would also do a better job

301

of making the beneficiaries of government pay for its operation and thereby discourage the notion that government programs are a "free lunch." The more progressive the tax code, the easier for majorities and influential minorities to use the political process to loot wealthier classes.

In short, we live in an age of envy. People don't so much want more money for themselves as they want to take it away from those with more. Greed is bad enough, eating away at a person's soul. But envy is far worse because it destroys not only individuals, but also communities, poisoning relations as everyone attempts to use the state to live off of everyone else. Perhaps Ronald Reagan's greatest accomplishment was to more than halve the top rate from 70 percent in 1980—a confiscatory level representing state-sanctioned theft of private property.

Even today, the much maligned "rich" are paying a huge proportion of their incomes in taxes. Today many people face a marginal rate of 50 percent in federal taxes alone—income, Social Security, and Medicare. Added to that are state and local income taxes, county business licenses, and a host of other levies. By what right should the majority be able to divest one of two-thirds or more of every extra dollar he or she earns?

And not just the rich are subject to such extraordinary levies. The National Taxpayers Union reports that a family earning the median income of $52,895 pays an extraordinary $26,689 in taxes, more than half. Is that fair?

There's another, indirect cost of playing up the politics of envy. Anyone seriously interested in the plight of the poor should be more concerned about expanding the nation's economic pie than stealing additional funds from those who are economically successful. At some point higher marginal rates become clearly self-defeating: people are discouraged from working and investing at all, preferring to consume, often conspicuously; higher earners are also encouraged to spend significant resources in tax avoidance activities, wasting money in order to shelter a little more from the tax man.

Indeed, the Organization for Economic Cooperation and Development, representing European governments that have been nothing close to libertarian in orientation, observed a decade ago that: "The income tax system is certainly a less effective tool for achieving equitable income distribution than are full employment and well-functioning social policies."

Yet the sort of class warfare represented by attempts to "soak the rich" will hinder attempts to achieve full employment in yet another way—by reducing the availability of private investment capital. President Clinton worries about a credit crunch, yet it is the wealthy who provide much of the capital that the business sector uses to employ people and expand. According to a study for the National Center for Policy Analysis, Americans with incomes of over $1 million derive three-fourths of their incomes from investments, while those earning $200,000 a year or more receive sixty percent of their incomes from investments. Such large, investment-based incomes may seem scandalous to the envious, but they help create the jobs that employ low- and middle-income Americans.

If President Clinton really wants the all Americans to work together to solve our economic problems, he should eschew the politics of envy. Demagoguery is no substitute for leadership.

February 1993

# 22

# Not Theirs to Give

Although during the summer of 1993 congressional budget negotiators spent weeks of apparently arduous labor forging a compromise package, the outcome was preordained: the taxpayers would be plucked. The federal government is spending $1.5 trillion in 1993—slated to increase to some $1.8 trillion by 1998 under virtually every "deficit reduction" proposal. Once again, Congress' budgetary debate was primarily smoke and mirrors.

The steady increase in government expenditures is constantly justified on the basis of "compassion." In its recent rush to be compassionate to flood victims Congress simply increased the deficit, preferring not to be bothered by finding counterbalancing cuts elsewhere. Untold billions more are spent annually to demonstrate compassion for the elderly, compassion for the sick, compassion for farmers, and compassion for anyone else lobbying for a place at the federal trough.

Of course, however civic-minded America's legislators, most are at least as interested in winning votes as in exercising compassion, which helps explain why their professed generosity extends to huge aerospace concerns, small liquor stores, yacht owners, labor union executives, and any other interest group with at least three members. Still, the desire to be compassionate undoubtedly affects many votes. It certainly helps explain why congressmen overwhelmingly voted to give away billions of their constituents' money to residents of flood plains who chose not to purchase flood insurance. Even many supposedly sober fiscal conservatives believed that compassion required them to say yes to Uncle Sam as all-around Sugar Daddy.

Compassion is such a powerful motivator because it trumps other arguments. A program may be inefficient and wasteful, create perverse

305

disincentives to self-help and work, reward improvidence and careless-ness, and deprive others of money that they have earned. But who wants to be uncompassionate, let alone look uncompassionate to voters, by saying no?

The problem with compassionate legislating is not that compassion is bad, but that legislative compassion is not compassion. There is, in short, nothing compassionate about giving away other people's money.

The Washington, D.C. City Council recently learned this lesson after it voted to provide $150,000 to Bonita Wilson, widow of late council chairman John Wilson, and to "adjust" his term of service to double the pension benefits that she will receive. Acting Chairman John Ray justi-fied the payments because "Our council chairman died a tragic death."

In fact, Wilson's suicide was tragic. But Washington is a city full of tragedy, largely affecting people with far fewer resources than Bonita Wilson. Nevertheless, she, in contrast to most other residents, had im-portant friends with access to public funds—at a time when the city faced a budget gap of $152 million and was laying off workers.

Particularly perverse was the fact that council members decided to start easing the pain of widows with one who had earned a six-figure salary and whose husband had collected more than $80,000 a year. Ray explained that Wilson had no insurance and heavy debts. A family friend noted that the Wilsons survived paycheck to paycheck, preferring to live well than save—or buy even the low-cost insurance offered by the Council. In short, the Wilsons were improvident, disastrously so. This, however, only made the need for compassion greater in the minds of council members. Observed Ray, "Of course, we were sensitive to the fact that he didn't have insurance." So a "compassionate" city council voted to stick poor residents with the bill.

But none of these concerns, powerful though they were, went to the crux of the issue. Even if the city had been flush with money and Bonita Wilson had been earning poverty wages, the council's action would have been improper. The money was simply not the members' to give.

Tax dollars are collected coercively; they are supposed to be used for public purposes, not private enrichment. After being criticized for the Council vote, Ray asked: "What were we supposed to do—go around and take up a collection?" Yes. Compassion once meant to suffer with the person in need. Over time people have increasingly come to believe that compassion means writing a check. Now legislators—city, state, and national—think compassion is making *other people* write a check.

In the case of D.C., the City Council's decision to turn the public budget into a private charity aroused the voters' wrath and caused Ray and company to drop their $150,000 gift. Congress will curb federal spending only when people send the same message to Capitol Hill: there's nothing compassionate about spending taxpayers' money. In the end, many problems should be met privately by, yes, people voluntarily taking up a collection and sacrificially helping their neighbors.

August 1993

# 23

# Tax Fairness, Clinton-Style

Candidate Bill Clinton campaigned against a hike in the federal gas tax; he rightly called the levy, which, along with state and local taxes now accounts for roughly one-third of gasoline's price at the pump, "back-breaking." Once inaugurated, however, he almost immediately proposed a surreptitious increase by making permanent the "temporary" 2.5 cent hike passed in 1990.

Then far worse, the President decided to push for not just a higher gas tax, but a tax on *all energy sources* based on the heat content measured in British thermal units (Btus). His justification? In his speech of February 17, 1993 the President told that nation that a Btu tax was "the best way to provide us with revenue to lower the deficit, because it also combats pollution, promotes energy efficiency, promotes the independence economically of this country as well as helping to reduce the debt, and because it does not discriminate against any area." It would be fair, his officials argued, in keeping with his campaign against special interests and the way Washington normally does business.

But the President's Btu tax quickly began to look less fair day by day. Tax bills have traditionally provoked an orgy of self-dealing and log-rolling amongst legislators, lobbyists, and interest groups, and the BTU tax proved to be no exception. What is striking is how willing the supposedly change-minded White House was to play the game like everyone else.

Indeed, industry and Capitol Hill sources reported the same story: early on the Treasury Department indicated that business groups which were willing to acquiesce in passage of the tax would receive favored treatment. Those that forthrightly opposed a tax notable for its regressive arbitrariness and economic destructiveness would bear the bulk of the tax burden. It was, observed one business lobbyist, a forthright strategy of divide and conquer.

In practice that's what we are seeing. Because of its early opposition to the tax, the oil industry has been targeted by the administration to pay more tax than anyone else. Virtually every other business, in contrast, is playing the exemption game. Complained Ed Rothschild of Citizen Action, a liberal interest group, "Nearly every major energy using industry is seeking to avoid all or a large portion of the Btu tax." In May 1993 Citizen Action estimated that all of the proposed loopholes—exemptions, rate reductions, and the like—would cut revenue under the tax by $13.4 billion through 1998. And most favor-seekers got their way.

Of course, there is nothing wrong with industries seeking tax breaks, particularly as protection from a levy with such a disproportionate impact on disparate industries and regions. The entire population, however, deserved an exemption for the same reason. The real problem caused by the proliferation of preferences is that if the administration remains committed to raising the same amount of money irrespective of the exclusions given favored interests—revenue needed to finance the President's varied spending *increases*—then it will have to hike still further the rate on other users, particularly the average consumer. In fact, the administration's recognition of precisely this point caused it to hold the line against a few industries. Admitted a spokesman for the American Public Power Association, "if they start slicing off the bottom line, then any change that, for example, helps hydropower is going to have to come out of the hide of somebody else." According to Citizen Action, the raft of preferences would translate into an extra dime a gallon charge on gasoline, or $75 annually, for the average family.

The full tax rate was 59.9 cents per million Btu, about $3.47 for a barrel of crude—roughly one-fifth of the current price. But the oil industry was about the only sector of the economy to pay this "supplemental" rate. Everyone else successfully jockeyed for preferential rates or full exemptions. The result was more than a dozen loopholes, all of which were shrouded with a pretense of intellectual justification while reflecting the influence of one interest group or another.

Natural gas, for instance, was to pay only what was termed the "base" rate of 25.7 cents per million Btu, about 15 percent of current prices. (The industry was undoubtedly not hurt by the fact that Chief of Staff Mack McClarty previously served as CEO of a natural gas pipeline and utility company.) Liquified petroleum gases, such as propane, would also be subject to the lower base rate, along with heating oil, a matter of particular interest to Northeastern legislators like Sen. Majority Leader George Mitchell (D-Maine), Sen. Ted Kennedy (D-Mass.), and Rep. Barbara Kennelly (D-Ct.). Evidence of their prolific clout was the fact that the House Ways and Means Committee voted to apply the exclusion to commercial as well as home use of heating oil.

Coal, with formidable Senate Appropriations Committee Chairman Robert Byrd (D-W.Va.) in its corner, was to pay just the base rate. But not all coal. Coal used to make steel would have been exempt from the tax. So, too, was to be fossil fuels, coal and petroleum alike, used for non-fuel purposes or turned into non-fuel products—feed stocks, plastics, computers, and asphalt, for instance. Also exempt was coal used to make synthetic natural gas and coal-seam methane generated in the coal mining process. Further, coal and natural gas used in enhanced oil recovery (to generate steam that is pumped underground to warm heavier oil to make it flow) would not have been taxed. Finally, Sen. Byrd successfully pressed for tax immunity for exports of fuel, principally coal, and electricity.

A number of other fuels also won full exemptions. For instance, crude oil and natural gas produced and used on site was to be free of the tax. So, too, would have been other non-purchased fuels—for instance, anything given off during the process of "cooking" crude oil and used by the refinery. Other exclusions included jet fuel used on international routes and bunker fuel—low-grade petroleum—used for international transport. Natural gas consumed in natural gas separation plants was not to be taxed. Biomass, municipal solid waste, and tires would have been exempt. So, too, would have been solar, wind, and geothermal power. Imports of non-fossil, non-nuclear, and non-hydro power—environmental favorites such as biomass—also would have avoided the tax. Even more esoteric was the exclusion for hydro-electric power resulting from pump storage, a method used to generate extra power for periods of peak demand. In fact, Sen. Slade Gorton (R-Wash.) proposed exempting all hydro-electric power, but was unsuccessful; the industry's argument, that it provides an environmentally-friendly renewable resource, has been overwhelmed by concern over the revenue that would have been lost.

One of the biggest political battles involved ethanol, methanol, m.t.b.e., and other oxygenated fuels. For a time it looked like these fuels would be fully excluded from the Clinton tax—a matter of some surprise, since its most important beneficiary, Dwayne Andreas, head of Archer-Daniels-Midland (ADM), was a long-time supporter of Senate Minority Leader Robert Dole. The White House was therefore originally inclined to let Andreas' already heavily-subsidized alcohol fuel be treated like any other energy source. But ethanol is made from corn, and therefore has widespread backing in the farm belt. Apparently Senators Paul Wellstone (D-Minn.), Kent Conrad (D-N.D.), Thomas Daschle (D-S.D.), among others, liked alcohol fuels as much as does Dole, and Daschle, in particular, reportedly used his influence with Majority Leader Mitchell to secure White House support for an exemption. However, serious opposition developed in the Senate and the House dropped the exemption in return for applying the lower base rate on fuel used by farmers. But ADM, which retained numerous important political courtiers, never gave up the fight. (Also helpful to ADM's cause was the fact that Andreas, who contributed $400,000 to the Republican Party's President's dinner last year, stiffed the GOP in 1993.)

The tax preference game continued not only for ADM, but also lots of other players. The Btu tax would not have been applied to coal or petroleum that was used to make coke for steel production. The theory in this case, as well as the example of oil being turned into plastic, explains one tax analyst, was that the firms are just "moving molecules around." More cynical observers were inclined to believe that lobbyist pressure, and the administration's desire to defuse business opposition to the tax, offered better explanations.

For instance, among the last Btu tax preference winners before the levy was dropped included the chlor-alkali industry and aluminum makers Alcoha, Kaiser, and Reynolds, which were to escape taxation on roughly half of the energy used in the manufacturing process. Taking a calculated risk, the aluminum industry refused to join in February 1993 with a coalition being led by the National Association of Manufacturers opposing the BTU, thereby theoretically remaining eligible in the President's eyes for special treatment. Nevertheless, the administration strenuously resisted the industry's pitch and distinguished aluminum from other industries benefiting from similar exclusions. Stated Treasury Secretary Lloyd Bentsen: "In making petrochemicals, the atoms of the feedstock hydrocarbons become the atoms of the polymers and other products." With aluminum, in contrast, he explained, "electricity does not contribute net electrons of the reaction; it contributes the energy that causes the chemical reaction to occur."

Unimpressed by Bentsen's chemistry lesson, however, were Northwest legislators. The exemption effort was led by Rep. Jim McDermott (D-Wash.), a member of the Ways and Means Committee, Rep. Mike Kopetski (D-Ore.), and Sen. Max Baucus (D-Mont.). An even more important backer was House Speaker Tom Foley (D-Wash.). Kaiser Aluminum is the largest employer in his district and contributed generously to defeat a statewide initiative that would have enacted strict term limits, threatening Foley's career. It is perhaps no surprise, then, that he pressed for an aluminum exclusion from the Btu levy.

Electrons aside, the industry's primary argument was that it operated in a competitive international market and couldn't afford to pay the extra two to three cents a pound that would be added by the tax. There was, however, nothing intrinsically different about aluminum manufacturers, the steel and plastics makers that also won exemptions, and any other firm trying to operate in the world economy. The Btu tax would have placed the latter, too, at a disadvantage both in selling overseas and in meeting foreign competition in the U.S. Rather, what distinguished the cases was the clout of the industries and quality of lobbyists involved.

And the lobbyists remained busy to the end. The farmers wanted to avoid the BTU tax just like they avoid the gasoline tax on fuel used on the farm. The gave the farmers, at least, half of what they wanted: the lower base rate on natural gas. And the farmers had equally strong supporters in the Senate, which ultimately killed the entire proposal.

Another important issue was where the tax would be paid. The administration initially proposed taxing natural gas as the wellhead and coal at the mine. Under pressure from producers, Clinton agreed to collect the tax after the gas left the pipeline and from the end users of the coal. Moreover, utilities, fearing having to go through new rate proceedings in order to recover the cost of the tax, won House approval to bill consumers separately for the tax.

And advocates of other preferences kept up a constant drumbeat. Mass transit officials, for instance, lobbied for an exemption since, they said, their enterprises were already energy-efficient. Truckers were asking that their diesel fuel escape the tax. Manufacturers of industrial gases—oxygen, nitrogen, and the like—also pressed for special treatment, citing the plight of hospital patients dependent on their products. Sen.

Bennett Johnston (D-La.) argued, unsuccessfully, for exempting rice hulls and sugar cane stalks when burned. So free was the administration with exemptions and preferences that lobbyists joked that any group with the backing of at least a handful of Democrats could get relief.

But as harmful as would have been the Btu tax for businesses, which had been lobbying so hard for exemptions and preferential rates, the measure would have most victimized consumers, who had no one else upon whom to shift the burden. And that, in fact, was the administration's intention, despite its professed concern for the poor and middle-class. Stated Treasury Secretary Lloyd Bentsen, "If the tax is to effectively promote conservation, it must be borne by the ultimate consumer. The administration is continuing to explore methods of assuring that the tax is in fact passed through."

In the end, Congress rightly rejected the Btu tax. President Clinton's tax hike would have fallen on families who were already paying more because of the large tax hikes agreed to in 1990 by his predecessor. Moreover, the Btu tax would have disproportionately burdened the poor as well as energy-intensive firms and states. At the same time, the alleged conservation benefits of the administration proposal were minuscule; indeed, the measure would have punished "environmentally friendly" energy sources like hydro and nuclear power.

But there was another, equally persuasive reason for the American people to demand that their representatives vote down the new Clinton tax. The orgy of favor-seeking and influence-peddling surrounding the bill made a mockery of the President's promises of fairness; in fact, it brought out the worst in both and administration and Congress. Although the levy was ultimately defeated, its sordid though short life demonstrated how quickly the candidate of change had irrevocably turned into the president of the Washington status quo: more spending, more taxes, and more special interest manipulation of the legislative process.

May 1993

# 24

# The New Democrats: Spend and Tax, Rather than Tax and Spend

In February 1993 President Clinton told the nation that "it is time for government to demonstrate...that we can be as frugal as any household in America." Indeed it is. But the President's budget certainly doesn't demonstrate thrift. Despite all of his discussion of cuts, President Clinton wants total federal spending to *increase* from $1.38 trillion in 1992 to $1.78 trillion in 1998, a jump of 29 percent. Domestic spending alone is to rise 5.5 percent a year. The president would pay for this spending splurge by raising taxes and other receipts even more, from $1.09 trillion to $1.53 trillion, a 40 percent hike. So much for his administration being "frugal."

In fact, in the first two months after proclaiming the importance of "tightening the rein on the Democrats as well as the Republicans," the President *further upped* his proposed expenditures. Pressed by a reporter about coming "back with more spending" so soon, Budget Director Leon Panetta responded churlishly: "Give me a break! Out of $1.5 trillion we're doing about $6 billion in targeted spending." After all, what's $6 billion among friendly Democratic interest groups? When the reporter persisted, pointing out that every change made since February was "away from deficit reduction," Panetta explained that "The bottom line here is that we're looking at $514 billion in deficit reduction."

If only that was true. Unfortunately, the word "reduction" doesn't mean the same in Washington as elsewhere. With so much "deficit reduction" you would expect the deficit to shrink dramatically, if not actually disappear. In fact, the administration projects that the deficit will *rise* from $290.4 billion in 1992 to $322.0 billion this year (1993), fall to $211.7 billion in 1996, and then *rise again*, hitting $250.4 billion in

315

1998. In short, $514 billion in "deficit reduction" means that the federal government will accumulate another $1.5 trillion in red ink. The annual deficit will fall by $40 billion over six years. Some achievement.

The basic problem is that in Washington "cuts" are measured not against current expenditures, but against a fantasy "baseline" of what outlays would be if officials spent as much as they wanted. Thus, the administration figures that it is "cutting" $60.4 billion in 1998 *even though it expects total outlays to have risen $400.1 billion from 1992*. It is as if someone spending $40,000 on an income of $30,000 claimed that his decision to spend $45,000 the following year was actually a fiscally responsible "cut" of $5,000 since he had originally intended to spend $50,000.

In any case, the administration's deficit estimates are almost certainly wildly, even hilariously, optimistic. Consider the initial forecasts of other presidents. In April 1981 President Reagan predicted that spending in 1986 would run $912.0 billion and the deficit would be $28.0 billion; the actual numbers were $990.3 billion and $221.2 billion, respectively. In 1990 Bush OMB head Richard Darman projected outlays of $1.48 billion in 1995, along with a *surplus* of $9.38 billion. Now Panetta says that in the latter year, *after* implementation of the Clinton's "deficit reduction" package, spending will run $1.57 trillion and the deficit will hit $246.7 billion!

One reason the administration is likely to end up spending far more is that Clinton's plan is full of the usual smoke and mirrors. For instance, many of the claimed budget cuts are not budget cuts by any definition except that of the Clinton administration. In 1994, for instance, the administration terms $3 billion in tax hikes on Social Security "budget cuts." Another billion dollars in tax increases and user fees—such as charging breweries and slaughterhouses for government inspections and raising patent and trademark fees—are called "budget cuts." The administration also cites $1 billion "saved" by putting hospitals on a calender year and $600 million cut by "streamlining government," something every administration claims to do. Tax increases masquerading as spending cuts total $29 billion from 1994 through 1998. Phantom cuts of "administrative savings" and the like run $55 billion over the same period.

Moreover, even if the President's and Congress' support for budget-cutting today is genuine, their enthusiasm for politically painful reductions is likely to wane once public attention fades and interest groups retake the high ground on Capitol Hill. Today everyone is worrying about the deficit; congressmen will therefore be at least a little skeptical when, say, beneficiaries of the Rural Electrification Administration's subsidies for power and telephones ask that their benefits be preserved. Tomorrow Congress will be election- rather than deficit-minded and thus will be far more receptive when the mohair producers regale legislators with stories about the strategic importance of Angora goats and why it is imperative that ranchers receive up to $340,000 each to increase their herds.

Another problem is that minor economic changes can have a major fiscal impact: a one percent lower rate of growth of the gross domestic product will hike the deficit $5.8 billion this year and $106.4 billion in 1998. A one percent higher interest rate will increase federal red ink by $4 billion now and $42.6 billion five years from now. The president naturally presumes that the economy will boom in response to his program. If it doesn't, the deficit will quickly worsen. And given where the Clinton administration is moving—more draconian environmental regulation, hefty payroll taxes for everything from job training to health care, trade protection, mandated benefits, medical price controls, and as much as $150 billion in new taxes to fund a national health care system—the economy will more likely fall into another recession.

The most fundamental problem, however, is that spending for almost everything continues to rise. Only the departments of defense and labor, along with a couple of agencies, such as the Corps of Engineers, are projected to spend less in 1998 than last year. Three other departments, agriculture, education, and interior, plus some more agencies, all of which received dramatic parting increases from the Bush administration, will see their outlays fall from 1993 to 1998. Spending for everything else is going up, and some of the increases are huge, such as for the Department of Health and Human Services—57.3 percent.

Few Americans are aware of the plethora of activities in which the federal government is engaged. And in most of these areas the Clinton administration will spend more, often dramatically more. Despite the end of the Cold War, for instance, outlays on atomic energy defense programs will rise. There will be more money for foreign aid through the Agency for International Development as well as the so-called multilateral development institutions, like the World Bank. There will be more spending on refugee programs, international organizations, the Peace Corps, State Department overhead, and the United Nations. International communism has waned, but Clinton wants to up spending on the U.S. Information Agency. There will be more cash for the Export-Import Bank, which subsidizes big business. Science research, the National Science Foundation, NASA, energy research, federal conservation activities—outlays on all of these will rise. Expenditures on the Army Corps of Engineers, Forest Service, Bureau of Land Management, mining reclamation, park acquisition and operation, and environmental regulation will grow.

The rural dole will continue, with more money for price supports, farm credit insurance, and agricultural research. There will be more money for rural housing, business research, international trade promotion, highway construction, mass transit, railways, airports, aeronautical research, and marine transportation. A host of "community and regional development" programs—largely politicized subsidies of businesses and local governments—will expand, some significantly. Educational programs, student financial aid, employment training, and a score of social service initiatives are to receive large increases. Spending on Medicaid alone will more than double, and other federal health care expenditures will also grow dramatically. There will be more money for Social Security, low-income housing, federal retirees, Food Stamps, special nutrition programs, veterans' educational and health benefits, and a host of other social programs. Finally, the President wants to spend more on law enforcement, the federal courts, the IRS, Congress, and executive branch.

It is not just standard expenditures that will rise. Federal credit subsidies, too, will also jump dramatically, as well taxpayer losses. Loan disbursements will almost double from 1992 to 1998, while the volume of loans guaranteed will increase by nearly one-quarter. Sadly, in terms of both outlays and loans President Clinton is only building on increases supported by his predecessor: 1993 is proving to be the fifth year of the Bush-Clinton spending boom.

Obviously, serious cuts are hard to make politically: most federal programs benefit someone and a number have a strong sense of "entitlement." But with domestic spending running ahead 5.5 percent annually the administration cannot seriously suggest that there are no further places to cut. Certainly the American people are not receiving $1.5 trillion worth of benefits from the federal government today. The need for real and deep reductions across-the-board becomes even more compelling when one realizes that the President currently plans on adding another $1.4 trillion to the national debt *even after sharply hiking taxes on all Americans.*

Serious alternatives are not hard to come by. The Heritage Foundation, for instance, has suggested holding domestic spending to a two percent annual increase, hardly an unreasonable step when the federal government is consuming one-quarter of the GNP, a peacetime record. This strategy would save $584 billion through 1998—enough to both lower the deficit and deliver middle-class tax relief, as the President once proposed. Another proposal comes from Steve Moore and William Niskanen of the Cato Institute. They would more sharply cut military outlays, given the end of the Cold War; reduce the rate of increase in Social Security benefits for *future* retirees, who will still receive more than they and their employers contributed; freeze domestic spending, which grew at an astonishing rate of 7 percent annually under the supposedly conservative George Bush; reduce outlays on medical care through carefully targeted reforms; and cut or terminate scores of non-essential programs.

The latter is point is critical. Contrary to the President's arguments on behalf of his budget package, there are plenty of programs that could be cut without harming the public weal. Moore and Niskanen point to such bloated subsidy programs as the Commodity Credit Corporation, IMF and World Bank, Small Business Administration, Rural Electrification Administration, and Agency for International Development. Also ripe for reform, they argue, are a range of welfare programs, transportation initiatives, and regulatory policies. Scott Hodge of the Heritage Foundation has compiled a similar list, as has Sen. Hank Brown (R-Co.) and the Congressional Budget Office. The latter, a nonpartisan legislative agency, provided in February 239 suggested reforms to save $450 billion between 1994 and 1998. The administration could even have relied upon an earlier list developed by then Rep. Leon Panetta. Alas, his proposals to, for instance, cancel the super collider and space station, end transportation subsidies, and cut foreign aid did not make it into his current boss' budget.

President Clinton hit the airwaves and road in an attempt to sell his program, but its specifics keep getting in the way. The unfortunate reality is that his administration's supposed deficit reduction program will increase not only taxes but also *outlays*; as a result, its impact on the deficit will be marginal at best. And the President still doesn't get it. "We're slashing subsidies and canceling wasteful projects," he said, even as he proposed spending nearly a third more by 1998. Indeed, for weeks his top priority remained a pork-ridden "stimulus" package that was little more than a political pay-off to urban interests. And after Republicans criticized him for wanting to use federal money to give to localities to spend on swimming pools, his best argument for his spend-and-tax budget was: "The Senate's got a swimming pool, doesn't it? Doesn't it? And it was built with taxpayers' money."

More than anything else, the President's commitment to spending *more* on wasteful pork demonstrates the importance of making the federal government live within its means. "It's the economy, stupid" was an effective campaign slogan; "It's spending, stupid" should be the new governing slogan. If the president attempts to maintain his present spendthrift course it will be up to Congress—led by moderate Democrats, in particular—to impose some fiscal discipline. But legislators are more likely to defy the president if their taxpaying constituents state loudly and clearly that they like the new Democratic president's "spend and tax" policies no more than the old Democratic presidents' "tax and spend" policies. And only if the people makes themselves heard in this way do we have a chance of seeing Bill Clinton's election-winning promise of a new approach to government.

July 1993

# 25

# A Coast-to-Coast Federal Dole

That the federal government is expansive and expensive is evident from the fact that Uncle Sam is spending some $1.5 trillion in 1993 and will become steadily more profligate under President Clinton.

But such numbers give little indication of how intrusive the federal government really is. A far better measure is J. Robert Dumouchel's *Government Assistance Almanac: 1993–94* (Detroit: Omnigraphics, 1993), which, proudly announces the publicity brochure, catalogues all "grants, loans, insurance, personal payments and benefits, subsidies, fellowships, scholarships, traineeships, technical information, advisory services, investigation of complaints, sales and donations of federal property." The result is 850 pages of pork, along with detailed instructions on how to grab a slab or two.

Indeed, if you are a businessman frustrated by international competition, a potential homeowner after a cheap loan, a college student desiring educational assistance, a farmer—especially a farmer—hoping for a little extra cash, or most anyone else looking for a federal handout, the *Almanac* is the book for you. Not only does the volume list 1288 grant programs, but, explains the publisher, it "is bound and conveniently indexed, helping users target their benefit search."

Where to start? If you're hungry, try the Agriculture Department. There is, for instance, the Food Distribution program, by which surplus federal commodities are donated. There are Food Stamps, which most everyone is familiar with, as well as the School Breakfast Program, which underwrites breakfasts for school kids. Similar is the National School Lunch Program, Special Milk Program for Children, and Summer Food Service Program for Children. On top of these are the Special Supplemental Food Program for Women, Infants, and Children; Child and Adult

Care Food Program; Nutrition Education and Training Program; Commodity Supplemental Food Program; Temporary Emergency Food Assistance; and Food Commodities for Soup Kitchens. Special Groups, too, are eligible for Uncle Sam's helping hand through the Nutrition Program for the Elderly, Food Distribution Program on Indian Reservations, and Nutrition Assistance for Puerto Rico.

But USDA does far more than just help people eat. The Foreign Agricultural Market Development and Promotion program pays to advertise farmers' products abroad—grants range from $158,000 to $18.4 million. The Department aids forestry research; one recent project, explains Dumouchel, was an "experimental system for continuous press drying of paper." Grants go to localities and states for roads in counties in which federal forestland and grassland is located. Minnesota has its own special grant program "to share receipts from national forest lands."

The Rural Electrification Administration subsidizes electrical coops and telephone utilities. It also offers Rural Economic Development Loans and Grants to promote business, as well as Distant Learning and Medical Link Grants for educational and medical computer networks. The Soil Conservation Service doles out money and advice; the Agricultural Research Service, not surprisingly, gives grants for research. Then there is the Agricultural Stabilization and Conservation Service, which made 252,000 new loans in 1991. If you want money for cotton, dairy, feed grains, wheat, wool ("National Wool Act Payments"), forestry, rice, or livestock, come on down to USDA! There is even the Grain Reserve Program, which, after you have been paid to grow your crop, will provide "incentives to farmers to place harvests in storage, thus increasing prices of the grains by lowering the marketable supply." Such a deal: paid to grow it and then paid to store it.

But just living near farmers is enough to benefit from Uncle Sam's largesse. Consider the Farmers Home Administration with money for destroyed property, laborer's housing, farm operation, enlarging farms, low-income rural housing, low-income rural housing site improvement, rural recreation facilities, rental property, "very low-income" home repair, rural waste disposal, flood prevention, rural schools, rural businesses, rental payments by low-income senior citizens, low-income rural home rehabilitation, rural foundations, and dispute mediation between rural borrowers and creditors. But wait—there's more: technical assistance, aid for indian tribes, the Intermediary Relending Program, and emergency assistance to comply with the Safe Drinking Water Act.

While farmers have their own department, most other businesses have to line up at the Commerce Department. The Census Bureau provides technical assistance and information; the International Trade Administration, when it isn't busy blocking the entry of inexpensive, quality imports, counsels exporters; and the Export Licensing Service and Information provides "information, training, seminars, and other assistance on export licensing requirements, regulations, and policies." In 1992 alone, reports Dumouchel, the Bureau counseled 309,000 exporters, handled 100,000 phone inquiries, and held 308 export licensing seminars.

But the real money is elsewhere. The Economic Development Administration provides grants—149 in 1991—"for public works and development facilities." There are also guaranteed loans to create jobs through redevelopment projects, as well as grants for renovating public works, planning economic development, and assisting firms hurt by imports. One EDA gem: "Special Economic Development and Adjustment Assistance Program—Sudden and Severe Economic Dislocation and Long-Term Economic Deterioration."

The National Oceanic and Atmospheric Administration provides loads of cash for research, fish conservation, fisherman's compensation, research, fishing ship construction, coastal management, research, climate centers, marine sanctuaries, and research. The National Telecommunications and Information Administration, National Institute of Standards and Technology, and National Technical Information Service all provide information, technical assistance, and money.

The Commerce Department also has a Minority Business Development Agency, which spares no expense to promote minority-owned businesses. There are, for instance, Minority Business Development Centers, Indian Business Development Centers, and Minority Business Resource Development grants "for activities advocating the expansion of opportunities for minority business firms," by, among other things, "decreasing minority dependence on government programs"!

The Defense Department isn't a particularly fruitful goose to be plucked, unless you want money for help in "controlling and eradicating obnoxious plants in rivers, harbors, and allied waters." But the Department of Housing and Urban Development remains a fount of federal subsidies. In fact, there may be no housing *not* backed by HUD. Do you want to rehabilitate run-down property? Get an insured loan under Rehabilitation Mortgage Insurance. Do you want to buy a mobile home?

Get an insured loan under the Manufactured Home Loan Insurance. Want to construct a condominium? Check out the Mortgage Insurance for Construction or Substantial Rehabilitation of Condominum Projects. There's also mortgage insurance to construct facilities for medical group practices; guaranteed mortgages to build one- to four-unit homes. Insured mortgages for homes for disaster victims and low-income families. The government will also guarantee mortages for "homes in urban renewal areas," "housing in older, declining areas," and "nonfarm homes, or new farm homes on at least two and one-half acres adjacent to an all-weather road, in outlying areas."

HUD pours forth guaranteed mortgages for cooperative projects, mobile home parks, hospitals, and nursing homes. People seeking to buy units in condominums, "sales-type cooperative housing units," and leased land can receive federally-backed mortgages. HUD welcomes builders desiring to construct "middle-income rental housing," rental and cooperative housing for the elderly, and rental housing "in urban renewal areas." Also favored are "special credit risks," who, so long as they receive counseling from "a HUD-approved agency," are eligible to receive federally guaranteed mortgages through their very own program.

HUD's lavish largesse goes on, page after page: Property Improvement Loan Insurance for Improving All Existing Structures and Building of New Nonresidential Structures; Rent Supplements—Rental Housing for Lower Income Families; Supplemental Loan Insurance—Multifamily Rental Housing; Supportive Housing for the Elderly; Mortgage Insurance—Combination and Manufactured Home Lot Loans; Operating Assistance for Troubled Multifamily Housing Projects (also known as the "Flexible Subsidy Fund"); Congregate Housing Services Program, Mortgage Insurance—Growing Equity Mortgages; Multifamily Coinsurance; and Housing Development Grants. There's money for the homeless, the handicapped homeless, and "persons with AIDS." There's money to stop housing discrimination on the basis of race, color, national origin, sex, age, or handicap. There's research money. There's money for public and Indian housing. For the latter, Dumouchel helpfully informs us, one should apply to the Assistant Secretary for Public and Indian Housing. The phone number, if you happen to be interested, is 202-708-0950.

Indeed, if you are an Indian, or have enough Indian blood to be considered an Indian, the Department of Interior, too, is waiting to hear from you. To get your hands on the loot, all you need be is a member "of recognized tribes, bands, or groups of Indians whose residence is on or near an Indian reservation under BIA [Bureau of Indian Affairs] jurisdiction—in need of financial assistance."

But wait: there's more, much more! Civil rights programs. Law enforcement grants. Money to prevent juvenile delinquency. Grants to compensate crime victims. Cash to help handle child abuse cases involving American Indians. And oodles of advice, assistance, and money from the Department of Labor for most anything—employment, training, pensions, trade adjustment, migrant farmworkers, safety, disabled veterans, and homeless veterans.

But don't stop reading yet. There are pages of Transportation Department programs, and scores of environmental grants. Even the Internal Revenue Service has money to give—to volunteers who help counsel elderly taxpayers, for instance. There's the Appalachian Regional Commission, the Equal Employment Opportunity Commission, National Aeronautics and Space Administration. And, of course, the ever-helpful National Endowments for the Arts and Humanities. In 1993 the NEA provided 363 grants under Promotion of the Arts—Expansion Art, which, explains Dumouchel, are intended "for arts projects reflecting the culture of minority, inner-city, rural, or tribal communities. Support is available for activities such as professional training of talented persons, financial assistance to small and emerging art groups; instructional activities for pre-school and school age youth."

Nor is this the end. Dumouchel has done his job well—too well, for those without a strong stomach. Let him count the ways by which Uncle Sam wastes our wealth. There's the National Science Foundation and Small Business Administration. The Department of Veterans Affairs. ACTION. The Department of Energy. The Federal Emergency Management Agency. National Council on Disability. And the wonderful Department of Education. One of the latter's winners: Adult Education for the Homeless, with grants ranging up to $500,000. But the biggest federal trough is the Department of Health and Human Services. Even with his succinct descriptions, Dumouchel requires *125 pages* to cover the HHS' flowing largesse. One of my favorites: Adolescent Family Life Research Grants. Their purpose: "for research and information dissemination activities concerning societal causes and consequences of adolescent premarital sexual relations, contraceptive use, pregnancy and child rearing, adoption decision-making," explains Dumouchel.

Dumouchel follows his program descriptions with summary tables on how much hard-earned taxpayer money is being frittered away on each program, an extensive list of field offices to contact in order to benefit from the frittering process, and a comprehensive index so that you won't miss even one program for which you might, just might, be eligible. The book is obviously well worth its price of $95!

There may be no better exhibit on why the federal deficit is so hard to cut than the *Government Assistance Almanac*. Everyone seems to complain about Uncle Sam's unending tide of red ink, but few want to cut spending. Indeed, everyone seems to have at least one hand in the till—independent businessmen, individualist farmers, iconoclastic artists, and ordinary middle-class, bourgeois home-owners. Until we change this culture of entitlement, the federal government will continue to grow, whoever is president.

So I think it's time to change tactics: if you can't beat them, join them. I'm now checking the *Almanac* for grants for slightly eccentric, chess-playing policy nerds who believe that it would serve the national interest if the taxpayers took over their mortgages, bought their excess articles, subsidized their diet, and generally provided them with a good life. With 850 pages of federal loot to choose from, I must be eligible for a grant or two.

April 1994

# 26

# The Time of the Political Locusts

"This is not just effective lobbying; it's wholesome lobbying," said Rep. John Spratt (D-S.C.), after beneficiaries of federally-subsidized power descended on Capitol Hill to try to protect the Rural Electrification Administration (REA) from President Clinton's proposed cutbacks. Past presidents, too, have suggested closing the REA spigot, but legislators, fearful of the National Rural Electric Cooperative Association (NRECA)—with its more than 1000 member cooperatives and $1.17 million in PAC contributions during the last election—have always run in the opposite direction, genuflecting before NRECA's members when the latter flooded the capital like locusts in Egypt. As a result, the REA, created in 1935 to bring power to poor, rural America, busily makes and guarantees billions of dollars of loans a year to wealthy, suburban America.

When Congress established the REA fewer than 12 percent of American farms had power; by 1953 nine of ten did. Today it's over 99 percent. In 1949 the REA decided to underwrite telephone service to rural America; 95 percent of rural homes now have phones. Thirty years later the REA decided that it had to help "overcome isolation in rural areas through modern communications technology" by providing construction loans for cable television. The Reagan Revolution ended federal subsidies for cable TV, but the REA otherwise remains as busy as ever, handing out some $4 billion in largesse to local electric and telephone cooperatives in 1993 alone.

Having completed its original task, the REA no longer extends service to poor farmers. Rather, the REA underwrites utility rates for middle-class suburbanites and wealthy resort residents. Barely one of ten coop customers today is either a farmer or rancher; one-third, in contrast, are white collar workers or professionals. Among the recent major borrowers from the REA are coops serving the suburbs of Atlanta, Dallas, Denver, and San Antonio. Other beneficiaries represented Aspen, Hilton Head Island, Snowmass, and Vail.

The coops so happily pigging out at the taxpayers' trough were not needy, of course. During the early 1980s their assets jumped more than 50 percent and their profit margins doubled. Yet, as a result of the REA, borrowers paid one-third less in interest than investor-owned utilities, according to the Congressional Research Service.

As interest rates have fallen, however, the coops have been stuck with higher-cost old federal loans, which they now want to refinance with private loans guaranteed by the REA. This proposal—which the Treasury Department says is "under consideration"—is NRECA's prime objective today. In short, the REA's clients want it all: if private loans are expensive, they want federally-subsidized credit; if interest rates fall, they want the REA to help them pay off their old public loans. Too bad the average American can't get the same deal.

How have wealthy recipients of subsidized federal credit gotten away with it? Part of it is a skillful public relations campaign. Ads regularly appear in a range of publications making NRECA's selfish looting appear to be an act of charity. "In literally thousands of communities," states one ad, "America's 1,000 consumer-owned electric systems help young people become well-educated, responsible citizens" through college scholarships and the like. It doesn't even sound like a pitch for a hand-out: "we need rural and community development programs that foster a broader, more constructive federal-local partnership."

On Capitol Hill, however, the approach of the rural cooperatives' lobby, NRECA, with its staff of 440 and annual revenues of $66.4 million, is far less gentle. Put bluntly, seeking political favors is hard work. Observes Robert Bergland, NRECA's head, "it is a tough, head-knocking business NRECA is in." A former legislative affairs director once observed that his organization was "the Avis of narrow-interest groups, number two"—second only to the Social Security lobby—"and trying harder."

And try hard NRECA does. In 1987, for instance, the Reagan administration made a modest proposal to terminate REA assistance to coops in recreational and major metropolitan areas and to big telephone holding companies. Bergland responded by telling his members that it "was warfare." Congress ended up approving a special loan prepayment program that gave the coops *an extra $400 million to $500 million* in interest benefits.

Now President Clinton has proposed ending most subsidized loans to electric cooperatives and telephone companies, which would save the taxpayers some $374 million over the next four years. But the administration is going to have to fight as hard as NRECA on Capitol Hill. Otherwise, the REA's clients are likely to end up with more rather than less taxpayer booty.

May 1993

# 27

# The NEA: They Still Don't Get It

It took a strong showing by Patrick Buchanan in New Hampshire, but
the Bush Administration finally did what conservatives had been pres-
suring it to do for three years ago—fire John Frohnmayer as head of the
National Endowment for the Arts. The decision, announced the day after Buchanan publicly ridiculed the agency, raised predictable hackles
in Washington. Complained the *Washington Post*, "it was a craven performance by the administration."

And craven it was, of course, but not because Bush gave in to the
right. Rather, his cowardice reflected the fact that he did the right thing
because it was expedient, not because it was right. The sorry episode
demonstrates yet again how the Bush administration is governed by polls
rather than principle. Indeed, the lengthy NEA controversy shows that
virtually no one in Washington "gets it," not the president, not
Frohnmayer, not the arts lobby and its congressional allies.

Consider President Bush. A self-identified moral and religious man,
he stood by while moral and religious taxpayers were forced to subsidize immoral and irreligious "art." Yes, the number of grants involved is
only a small proportion of those handed out. But what is at stake here is
an important matter of principle—that people who believe in traditional
morals shouldn't be forced by their government to subsidize attacks on
their beliefs. Alas, it is obvious that the administration just doesn't understand. White House Chief of Staff Sam Skinner was reportedly out-
raged by the latest controversy, the NEA-backed publication *Queer City*,
which ran a poem depicting Jesus Christ as a pedophile. But would he
have minded if there were no primaries upcoming? After all, the president sat mute for three years as NEA grants underwrote an exhibition
with a crucifix submerged in urine, a photo of a man posing with a bull-

whip up his anus, a woman smearing herself with chocolate and putting vegetables up her vagina, a man wandering around stage urinating and simulating masturbation, and so on.

John Frohnmayer, while a decent individual, was even more oblivious to the concerns of decent people across America. He defended the *Queer City* portrayal, explaining that the poem was "emotional, intense and serious." After his forced resignation, he told the NEA staff that "I leave with the belief that this eclipse of the soul will soon pass and with it the lunacy that sees artists as enemies and ideas as demons." He also pledged to work "for quality art, for less hate and for a generosity of spirit that allows us to live with our differences in real community."

But who is the real hater: the Catholic who objects to having his money used to subsidize someone who submerges a crucifix in urine, or the "artist" who does the submerging? Real generosity of spirit would be evident if those who want to offend and shock eschewed public funds. The true "eclipse of the soul" is the belief that one is entitled to force the targets of one's hatred to underwrite attacks on them.

Finally, there are the artists and the legislators who regularly vote to fund the NEA. All naturally cried censorship when the common folk criticized the NEA. But where in the Constitution does it say that artists have a right to federal checks? NEA grants have become the newest entitlement, over which those who pay the bills are supposed to have no influence.

If Congress is going to force taxpayers to pay for art, then it should at least limit grants to activities that are widely accepted. One simple rule of thumb would be that if you can't tell taxpayers in a family newspaper what their money is paying for, the "art" shouldn't be subsidized by the NEA.

Doesn't allowing government officials to pick-and-choose approved activities create the potential for abuse, ask the NEA's backers? Yes it does. The solution is to eliminate the agency. Why should taxpayers in, say, Des Moines pay for a symphony in, say, Buffalo? Let those who like art, whether high-brow, low-brow, or obscene, pay for it. The arts community would probably suffer, but it has no higher claim to tax dollars than do the people who earned the money in the first place. And it's not as if the nation would come to an end; after all, culture didn't start in 1965 when the NEA was created.

The administration undoubtedly assumed that firing Frohnmayer would make the NEA issue go away. But the president's welcome moment of political expediency cannot make up for three years of complicity in the NEA's support for the bizarre and the obscene. Unfortunately, George Bush, along with so many others, probably never will get it.

February 1992

# Index